ALEXANDER WOOLLCOTT: THE MAN WHO CAME TO DINNER

Alexander Woollcott

Alexander Woollcott: The Man Who Came to Dinner

A Biography by Edwin P. Hoyt

ABELARD-SCHUMAN
London New York Toronto

Library of Congress Catalogue Card Number: 67-13458
Standard Book No. 200.71504.6

Acknowledgment is made for permission to quote from the following copyrighted works:

From *Letters of Alexander Woollcott*
Copyright 1944 by The Viking Press, Inc.
Reprinted by permission of The Viking Press, Inc.

From *Harpo Speaks!*
Reprinted by permission of Bernard Geis Associates
Copyright © 1961 Harpo Marx and Rowland Barber

London
Abelard-Schuman
Limited
8 King St. WC2

New York
Abelard-Schuman
Limited
6 West 57th St.

Toronto
Abelard-Schuman
Canada Limited
896 Queen St. W.

Printed in the United States of America

Acknowledgments

The author is indebted to a very large number of people for general personal assistance in the preparation of this biography of Alexander Woollcott, some of them for information, some for steering to source materials, some for the use of materials. They include: Dame Rebecca West, Henry R. Luce, Lucy Drage, Joseph Hennessey, Alfred Lunt, Janet Flanner, DeWitt Wallace, Alan D. Williams, William Eagan, Leo Towers, Merritt C. Chandler, Dr. Frode Jensen, Joseph Calvi, William C. Hart, Arnold Gingrich, Andrew A. Anspach, Tay Hohoff, Stanton Peckham, Charles Lederer, Harpo Marx, Gummo Marx, Professor Robert Rudd, Palmer Hoyt, Florence M. Reil, Edward R. Murrow. These are only a few of those who were of great assistance. Others are mentioned either in the text or in the chapter notes.

The author consulted all of Alexander Woollcott's books from first to last, the Samuel Hopkins Adams biography, published in 1944 by Reynal and Hitchcock, and Woollcott's writings in magazines, at least as far as these could be traced. Woollcott wrote for a large number of magazines catalogued in *The Reader's Guide,* but he also wrote for many magazines not so catalogued. He kept no record of his writings for publications, and so for those magazines that are not indexed the finding of articles came either through some clue in his correspondence or through a word dropped by a source, or quite by accident. Woollcott was an industrious writer for magazines, and so many articles have obviously been missed.

Libraries used in this research include the Castleton, Vermont, Free Library, the Yale University Library, the New York Public Library, the Hotchkiss Library of Sharon, Connecticut, the Scoville Memorial Library of Salisbury, Connecticut, Harvard University's libraries, and Hamilton College's library. The author is indebted to literally dozens of librarians, and especially to W. H. Bond, curator of manuscripts at the Houghton Library of Harvard University for permission to make extensive use of the Woollcott papers (twenty-five library boxes full of them).

Generally speaking, newspapers and magazines consulted will appear in the chapter notes under the specific reference to the article cited. Considerable use was made of the New York *Times,* a vehicle for Woollcott in his early days as drama critic and later as recorder of his public life. The files of the Rutland *Herald* were helpful in tracing some of Woollcott's Vermont period. Photographs are the courtesy of Mrs. Harpo Marx.

Contents

Illustrations

Introduction

WERE AMERICANS EVER NEEDFUL of reminder that fame is fleeting in their fermenting country there could be no better object lesson than the one given in the life of Alexander Woollcott, playwright, biographer, essayist, journalist, and, above all, critic, who at the hour of his death was the most powerful literary figure in the English-speaking world and who, a quarter of a century later, was virtually unknown to the general public.

Unknown? Yes, unknown. In 1943 Aleck Woollcott was loved and hated, despised and revered by thousands of the great and near great, and his opinions were heard by millions who listened to the radio and read popular magazines. Loved or hated, he was known, and he was respected for his power over public taste if for no other reason. In the 1960's few of the youth of his native land had more than heard the name of Alexander Woollcott, nearly none of them knew who he was or what he did, and his work had virtually disappeared from the public cognizance.

The reason for Alexander Woollcott's eclipse is remarkably simple: his most important work was done in the most transitory of media, the newspapers, magazines, and on radio. He left books, but they are long out of print and most of them are heavily dated with the marks of Aleck Woollcott's times. It was sometimes said of Aleck Woollcott that he never really wrote a book, but that bit of misinformation was passed along by those who did not know Woollcott in his youth. He wrote several books as books, including a biography of Irving Berlin. True, most of his books were collections, and he had what his friend Harold Ross of the *New Yorker* termed the "damnedest ability" of making double, triple, and quadruple use of everything he wrote. Woollcott's enemies, and they were many, suggested that there was something slightly dishonorable about this multiple usage of material. Any professional writer would disagree with the critics and sympathize heartily with Woollcott's immense success in the field of the thrice-told tale. Bernard DeVoto once noted that he could not survive in the world of letters did he not make at least dual use of every bit of information that came his way.

His work forgotten for the most part, Alexander Woollcott was best known in the second half of the twentieth century as a character on whom George Kaufman and Moss Hart modeled the central figure of their play *The Man Who Came to Dinner,* a rollicking comedy about an outrageous and marvelous public figure who was the greatest critic in America. In 1967 this figure—and Alexander Woollcott—were reintroduced to the American people with a revival of the Kaufman and Hart play in the form of a musical called *Sherry.* It was *The Man Who Came to Dinner* with bells on. This revival, however, brought back only the public figure of Alexander Woollcott, the figure he invented and played before the American and English people with a vivacity that convinced most of them it was not a pose at all. Nowhere in the Kaufman and Hart play is suggested the brave critic who faced down the Broadway producers in the first major struggle between newspapers and producers about the right of the reviewer to speak as he pleased.

In 1915, as the youthful critic of the New York *Times,* Alexander Woollcott did just this, in battle with the powerful Shubert brothers who banned him from their theaters. In carrying the battle and winning it, Aleck Woollcott and the New York *Times* brought the American theater to maturity. Before Woollcott's battle theater criticism was pap and promotion for the most part, and small beer for the rest. Afterward theater criticism rose to its stature as legitimate journalism. Woollcott's part in this, almost always overlooked, cannot be overemphasized.

Nowhere in Kaufman and Hart's play, either, is suggested the Woollcott to whom George Kaufman owed such a tremendous debt. Aleck Woollcott took Kaufman on as an assistant on the New York *Times* drama desk and trained him in the ways of the theater. Later they collaborated on two plays, neither of them very successful. They were friends for all of Aleck's life.

There is no indication either of the important role Aleck Woollcott played in furthering the careers of many public figures. He helped Rebecca West, when she was a hungry, young journalist. He helped the Marx brothers, and particularly brought Harpo to a peak as a public figure. The Lunts of the theater, the Alsops of the newspaper world, the Roosevelts, Republican and Democratic—all these people were friends of Aleck Woollcott's and he helped his friends over many hurdles large and small. Literally, he had thousands of friends—he needed them much more than they needed him—and that is an important part of the true Woollcott personality which has been so much submerged in time.

There were two Woollcotts, there is no question about it, and not simply two Woollcotts: one the poseur and the other the legitimate figure beneath. Woollcott was not that simple. There was a long-knived critic and a treacly one. There was the praiser of second-rate fiction, and the discoverer and horn blower for such as Ernest Hemingway, John Steinbeck, George Kaufman, Eugene O'Neill, and a score of other figures. It was no treacly critic who spoke out in print and over the air waves in defense of the early William Faulkner; there was an Alexander Woollcott of shrewd discernment. As a literary man Woollcott was most thoroughly condemned for his selection of materials included in the anthologies he presented to the public. To be sure, many of these selections were unusual, and many of them were concentrated on quiet heroism or sweetness and light. Some critics said that few of the selections were literature at all. That is a matter of opinion, and will probably be argued for many years. The fact is that Woollcott dredged up favorites of his own of many years standing and brought them to the attention of the American people, where they were enthusiastically received. His final compilation, a little book called *As You Were,* prepared in 1942 and published in the last year of Woollcott's life, gives quite an opposite view of Woollcott the literary figure. He had set himself the wartime task of preparing an anthology for servicemen abroad, and it was to represent what was to Alexander Woollcott the best of American literature. He had much help in this selection. He called on Stephen

Vincent Benet, Mark Van Doren, Carl Carmer, Booth Tarkington, Thornton Wilder, Carl Sandburg, E. B. White, and many others whose literary reputations have outlasted his own. Yet in the final analysis it was Woollcott's anthology, and Woollcott took full responsibility for it. Here he was doing his best job, because he was doing it for someone else. Alexander Woollcott took a very personal interest in World War II, long before American soldiers and sailors were involved in it. He began beating the drums against Nazism before there was any war. When England became involved, he saw the dangers for what they were, and he was a leader in the fight against isolationism. The job of putting out the wartime anthology was, to him, one of the small contributions he could make to the American war effort, and he turned his best abilities to it.

As You Were, therefore, turned out to be one of the finest anthologies of its kind ever published. Its purpose was to inspire, and show Americans at their best, in greatness and in squalor, in wealth and in poverty, in peace and in war. He chose from Stephen Vincent Benet, from Edgar Allan Poe, Willa Cather, Mark Twain, Bret Harte, O. Henry, Ring Lardner, Walt Whitman, Alan Seeger, Robert Frost, Carl Sandburg. Oh, his own Woollcottian choices showed plainly—there was never any question about that. Ruth Gordon, one of his discoveries, was there. So were Eugene Field and James Whitcomb Riley. Dorothy Parker was included no less than three times. Alice Duer Miller, long known more for her magazine serials than for any other writing, also was included, and, of course, she was one of Aleck Woollcott's very dearest friends. Woollcott was there himself, along with his enthusiasms. He picked *Address Unknown,* a short story about the revenge of Jews on Nazis by Kressman Taylor. He chose three speeches by Oliver Wendell Holmes, Jr., for Holmes the jurist was one of Aleck Woollcott's favorites. He chose the essay of William Allen White written in the *Emporia Gazette* on the death of White's daughter Mary, for that essay never failed to bring tears to Aleck Woollcott's eyes. He chose a letter from Nicola Sacco to his son—Sacco the anarchist, who figured so largely in American history as a symbol of radicalism. This last was natural enough, for Aleck Woollcott was always a political radical. He did not choose to wear his allegiances on his sleeve, but sometimes he indicated grand sympathies with the Soviet Communist design. He was never a communist in the political sense; he was always a sympathizer of equalization of wealth and position and opportunity. It would have been most illogical for him to have held other views, as will be seen by the reader in studying his background, for Aleck Woollcott came from one of the first communist or communalist experiments in America. His family were disciples of Fourierism, an agrarian-based radicalism that had come to America, and to New Jersey, from France. He retained these views until the end of his life and spent most of his own money helping others very quietly in the way he deemed best, which was to educate the young, or the spawn, as he would have called them.

Woollcott in the first two decades of the twentieth century, was regarded with almost equal parts of amazement and amusement by those who knew him. He was a serious young man, a very active one, and a perfectly normal one until the end of his college years when he suffered a severe attack of the mumps and the complications that sometimes affect the male. After that attack the change in Aleck was apparent. He became, in effect, a eunuch, and he began to acquire eunuchoid characteristics. He grew pudgy and his hips broadened. He grew mincing in his ways. He was never totally devoid of sexual interest in women, and he was not a homosexual. Occasionally he conducted brief affairs with women, but he was incapable of sustaining them, perhaps only physically, perhaps also emotionally. That, in its essence, is the reason he never married and there should be no nonsense about it, as there has been in such ill-considered judgments as that of Anita Loos, who in her recollection of days past entitled *A Girl Like I* charged that Aleck was a homosexual. Working in an era in which the psychology of sexuality seemed to dominate all other human studies, I was, of course, conscious of feminism, sometimes waspish spinsterism, in Aleck's character, and I made it a point to question old friends and acquaintances about Aleck's love life. It was not a particularly enjoyable chore. Many of my respondents showed considerable distaste for my questions. In the end, however, I quite satisfied myself as to the facts. Miss

Loos, in her ephemeral acquaintance with the Alexander Woollcott of the Algonquin Round Table, may have concluded that his mincing ways meant he was up to no good as far as her sex was concerned and that he was a potential rival. Others who knew Aleck well, concluded quite to the contrary. Rebecca West, Janet Flanner, Joseph Hennessey, to cite only three, knew Aleck well and intimately over many years, and they all deny the charge.

The charge is important only in the context of the reader of the 1960's, who is supersaturated with concern over such matters. So were some others, including, I suspect, Samuel Hopkins Adams, Aleck's other biographer as of 1967. Sam Adams had known Aleck since Aleck was a pup, quite literally since he was a cub reporter, for Adams was largely responsible for getting Aleck his first newspaper job. They corresponded sporadically over many years, and they visited one another. Immediately on Aleck's death, Sam Adams undertook the preparation of a biography, which was published the following year. To me it has always seemed to be a very odd book, bearing from its first pages an ill-concealed antipathy to the subject of the biography. Throughout, Adams wrote as if he did not like Alexander Woollcott or his ways very much, and he yielded to the view that Aleck had occupied no particularly useful place in American society, that he had best be forgotten with two or three bons mots in Bartlett's *Book of Familiar Quotations,* and the note that he was once one of the "New York Wits" who frequented the Round Table.

Now one of the reasons for this attitude of biographer Adams, I am sure, is that it was a very prevalent attitude in the year following Aleck's death. Aleck had set out at the end of World War I to play the role of public character. He chose the English-speaking world as his stage.

He acquired an opera cape and a stick and went to his first nights so attired, lending himself an absolutely incongruous appearance by the addition of a villainous broad-brimmed black hat. As the years rolled along, he adopted other mannerisms to suit. He became Buddha-like in his fat. He became simpering and publicly endearing to his friends and waspish to them in public. The studied insult, the insulting term of endearment, even the dirty word at the dinner table—all these became Woollcottian hallmarks. It was sometimes said that Woollcott could eat around New York night after night for months on invitations, simply because ardent hostesses wished to be able to call their friends the next day and describe the indignities to which they were subjected by Woollcott.

This was the public pose of Alexander Woollcott. It was so successful a pose that it still threatens to overshadow the Woollcott reputation as writer and critic. Aleck once said that he was the greatest writer of his day, adding that unfortunately he had nothing to write about. Certainly he was a great stylist, and perhaps the most urbane and civilized of his years. Words flowed from his pen capturing mood and precise meaning without apparent effort. *New Yorker* editors said Aleck was fearfully easy to cut—indicating that his writing was ponderous and redundant, or at least thinking that was what they indicated. Actually, Aleck was most difficult to cut if the editor had any sympathy for the writer or his meaning. The trouble was that too often Aleck devoted himself to absolute trivia for the satisfaction of the serious editor.

Trivia was Aleck's declared business. He said exactly that time and again. Yet a study of Aleck's newspaper and magazine articles and radio broadcasts over the years shows that when he said these words he was playing his role as professional shocker and literary ne'er-do-well.

He loved a cause like that of the Seeing Eye—the organization that acquires, trains, and provides guide dogs for the blind. It was exasperating to Aleck's critics that he devoted so much effort to such causes—good causes, yet more or less trivial ones. This attitude was typical of the one side of Woollcott, the professional side. He was also capable, without all this fanfare, of advocating major causes. New York was complaining in the early 1920's that Eugene O'Neill should not have written *All God's Chillun Got Wings* because its theme of racial intermarriage and the moral superiority of a Negro man to a white woman was objectionable. The New York newspapers quite seriously suggested that the play not be staged because of its theme. Aleck came out squarely in favor of the O'Neill drama. He praised *The Emperor Jones* and *The Hairy Ape*, when such were notable largely for the criticisms leveled against them in the United States. He also befriended Paul Robeson, the young Negro who was learning the art of acting in playing the lead in these dramas.

Intellectually and physically Aleck Woollcott was fearless. He showed this fearlessness and independence of spirit first in college, when he chose to fight with members of the football team although they outweighed him by as much as fifty pounds. He showed it in World War I when he pranced up and down the American war front in France as chief war correspondent of *Stars and Stripes.* He showed it innumerable times in the selection of causes between the wars, and when World War II came, and Aleck Woollcott was ailing from the heart disease that finally killed him, he insisted on taking an arduous and dangerous trip to Britain to bolster the morale of his friends there.

Alexander Woollcott was a sweet and sour man, if one can reduce human character to a pungent example of Chinese cookery. The unfortunate matter, as far as his memory is concerned, is that the sourness somehow predominated in the recollections of Woollcott that remained a quarter century after his death, and that the substance of the man threatened to be lost. This biography is the author's attempt to pay to a fine American, and a very important one in the literary scene, the respect he deserves, and to put his life into the context of its time.

Edwin P. Hoyt

I

On the night of October 16, 1939, there came to the Music Box Theater in New York City a new play by George S. Kaufman and Moss Hart, the authors of the Pulitzer Prize winner, *You Can't Take It With You,* which had played on Broadway two years before. This new play promised to be just as hilarious as anything these experts on comedy had ever produced, either together or singly. It was rumored—more, it was known—that the new play, *The Man Who Came to Dinner,* was based on the private and public life of the most eminent critic and public personality in all the land. Along Broadway the secret had been out for months, and two weeks earlier the play had opened in Boston for a tryout session, whereupon the New York *Times* man in Boston had spilled the beans, so to speak.

> Whatever the rest of the season may bring forth it is hardly likely to equal *The Man Who Came to Dinner* in the number of celebrities suggested or named on the stage, or the broadside—with the accent on the first syllable—of polished insults laid down by one Sheridan Whiteside . . . more or less distantly related, so it is whispered, to the distinguished Mr. Alexander Woollcott.

This new Kaufman and Hart play was a great spoof on the acid-tongued, honey-tongued, impossible, enjoyable, infuriating, lovable Alexander Woollcott. Of course, it had not been a secret at all, and no one had intended it to be, or believed it was meant to be secret, with the possible exception of a handful of people who did not like Alexander Woollcott, usually for very personal reasons, and who hoped that producer Sam Harris and the joyful perpetrators of the satire would take Woollcott apart and boil him in oil publicly, beneath the proscenium arch. So, on the night of October 16, 1939, the Music Box was crowded with well-wishers and not so well-wishers who came to see what the two wits of the Great White Way had done to their old pal in the course of taking him out of life and putting him upon the stage.

Everybody who amounted to anything along Broadway or in the world of books and amusement was there, or so it seemed. Harpo Marx was there. In fact he was there twice, once in the audience and once on the stage in the person of David Burns, a red-mopped minstrel who cavorted about as Banjo, a very thin disguise indeed, and Harpo was ready for the portrayal of himself and of his very dear friend and croquet opponent, Aleck Woollcott.

Shortly before nine o'clock the lights dimmed, the curtain opened, and the play began.

The curtain rose on a set that was made to depict a living room of well-to-do people in a small town. The *Playbill* said it was the Ohio home of Mr. and Mrs. Ernest W. Stanley.

As the curtain rose, Mrs. Stanley was standing, waiting near double doors which, it was indicated, led into a library. Through the rear of the stage the audience could catch a glimpse of what was obviously a dining room. On the right were the bottom steps of a circular staircase, and on the other side of the stage were windows and the entrance hall and outside door of the house.

Mrs. Stanley hovered for a moment—the word is the authors' —and then dodged, as a nurse in full white regalia scurried out onto the stage, chased by a rich, full voice filled with anger and loathing, a masculine voice, a voice of power that suggested a man of character and strength who had finally been driven to depths of desperation quite beyond the scope of human resilience.

"Great, dribbling cow!"

To these opening lines, the lucky members of the audience reacted with happy laughter, and settled back in their seats for an evening of amusement.

From this start, the action picked up to whirlwind speed. The nurse rushed across stage and out, ignoring Mrs. Stanley's pitiful request for information about the condition of the owner of the hidden voice. The doorbell rang and the lady's son descended the stairs at the same time. A white-coated servant went to the door, the son went out on an errand, the nurse came charging through the stage again and returned to the presence of the offstage voice, which was heard to be describing a doctor, to his face, as a quack, in the brief moment that the library doors were opened. The servant appeared carrying two large packages and a sheaf of telegrams and cables, the telephone rang, and a very pretty girl about twenty years old, advertised as the daughter of the household, appeared, coming down the stairs. In the course of a very few moments, Kaufman and Hart had succeeded in showing their audience that an entire family had been reduced to panic, confusion, and jellied subordination to something that made a great deal of noise offstage, right. When the presence wanted a rare variety of cigarettes, the scion of the household rushed out, without question, dropping all other tasks, to get them. As he left, a long distance telephone call came in from London. And who should it happen to be? None other than H. G. Wells. When apprised of this memorable fact, the lady of the house suffered bugging of eyes and palpitations of the heart. She was not only buffaloed, it was quite easy to see she was also bamboozled and awed to the point of collapse. The library doors kept opening and closing to admit packages and cables from Alaska, Hawaii, and Timbuctoo, cigarettes, pitchers of orange juice and other goodies, and with each opening of the door came a noisome snarl from the unknown inside, referring to the house as a hellhole, and to the white-clad Florence Nightingale as a "sex-starved cobra" with fishhooks for hands and a brain to shame a large bird.

Then, through the device of one of the ladies reading from a copy of *Time* magazine, Kaufman and Hart let the audience in on the nature of the presence. It was none other than Sheridan Whiteside, tubby critic, lecturer, wit, radio orator and friend of the great nearly everywhere, who had fractured his hip after falling on a piece of ice on the Stanley doorstep, and he might be there even for Christmas. In fact, said the authors in the guise of *Time*, Christmas might be postponed.

The ladies did not understand that remark, but the audience

did: it referred to the self-adulation of the character that was being portrayed—a swollen egotist emerged, an egotist with a razor tongue and the sensitivity of a white rhinocerous.

As the play opened, it was discovered that Mrs. Stanley was laboring under some delusions. She thought that Mr. Whiteside was about to be up and around in a wheel chair and it would be wonderful to have him with the family. He would sit with them in the evening and talk about books and plays and other matters of erudition, drop names and perhaps even read *Goodbye, Mr. Chips!* aloud.

Silly woman! Poor misguided creature!

Within moments the true nature of the disaster which had fallen into the bosom of the Stanley family was revealed. The double door to the library opened slowly. A young woman of about thirty, who was identified as Sheridan Whiteside's secretary, emerged and asked a little anxiously about the cigarettes and was relieved when told they were on the way. All were assembled, for the unveiling of this human monument, the arrival of this magnificent presence. Mr. Stanley, a quiet, conservative businessman, had come downstairs, expressing mild distaste for the complete interruption of his normal household life and the spate of telephone calls and deliveries to the house. Sarah, the cook, was called from the kitchen to bear witness. June, the daughter, was called downstairs.

First came the doctor, breathing false heartiness as he brought his little black bag through the door. Next came the presence, in its wheelchair, a portly bearded figure wearing a velvet smoking jacket and a very colorful figured necktie that clashed most horridly. All were silent, awaiting the first words of beatitude and wisdom from the presence. Coldly, he looked around, drumming his fingers on the wheelchair arm.

"I may vomit," he said.

So, the audience had its first view of Sheridan Whiteside, citizen, character, critic.

In the third act matters began to be resolved—and there were many of them to resolve. Banjo came to town on his way to Nova Scotia. The son ran off to find a freighter, but was captured by his father's agents in Toledo and returned. The daughter tried to run off with the union organizer, but was stopped. Both were brought home, abject, and Mr. Stanley secured a warrant to have Whiteside ejected from the house in fifteen minutes.

Maggie announced that she was quitting, whereupon Whiteside had a change of heart and decided to try to undo the damage he had done. The problem was to get rid of Lorraine Sheldon, and this was not an easy one to solve. But at the opportune moment (five minutes left) a Christmas gift from the Khedive of Egypt was delivered—an Egyptian mummy case, and Lorraine Sheldon was persuaded to try it on for size, whereupon Banjo slammed the lid. The problem then was to get her to the airport in the case in time for Banjo to take her to Nova Scotia.

Stanley came in to announce that he was now having Whiteside thrown out of the house, whereupon Whiteside remembered something important. All through the play a strange faerie-like woman, Harriet Stanley, sister of the owner of the house, had wandered in and out of the scenes. She had given Whiteside a picture of herself as a young girl for Christmas, and all the time he had thought he should place her, but he could not quite come to grips with the image. Suddenly as Stanley came to eject him from the house, Whiteside remembered where he had seen Harriet Stanley before. She was Harriet Sedley, who had used an axe on her father and mother twenty-five years earlier.

Stanley was beaten and he knew it. The mummy case went out, with Banjo, bound for the safety of Nova Scotia. Maggie got her man, with Whiteside's offhand blessings: "Just send me a necktie sometime." Whiteside ended the scene with a warning to Stanley that he would like to hear of the marriage of June to her young labor organizer and Richard's departure to follow his own wishes. OR ELSE, was the way he put it. Then he left, to fall on the ice again, and then to really fracture his hip, it seemed.

He was returned to the living room, screaming for Miss Preen, the nurse, and shouting that he was going to sue Stanley for *three* hundred and fifty thousand dollars.

Had the play not ended at that moment would he have gotten Miss Preen back? It seems highly doubtful. For Miss Preen had walked out in the middle of Act Three, having taken the ultimate insult: Banjo had embraced her and slapped her lewdly on the behind. Whiteside had protested that her conduct in leaving him "helpless" was completely unprofessional, didn't she realize that? Miss Preen said she did. But she was leaving the nursing profession to go to work in a munitions factory. After a month with Whiteside, she wanted to exterminate the human race.

So the play ended, and an audience that had laughed itself hoarse got up from the cramped seats of the Music Box Theater and filed down the aisles, smiling in retrospect and recalling a favorite line or gesture of one of the actors—usually of the bearded, erudite Monty Woolley who had played the part of Sheridan Whiteside (or Alexander Woollcott) to such perfection that later it would be said that he played Woollcott better than Woollcott did.

The Man Who Came to Dinner was reviewed with almost universal approbation, as by Brooks Atkinson in the New York *Times*:

> Whether or not it is the funniest comedy Moss Hart and George S. Kaufman have written is probably a matter of opinion. But it is a fact that *The Man Who Came to Dinner* which opened at the Music Box last evening is the funniest comedy of this season, and is likely to remain so long after the competition has grown stiffer.

As to the characterization:

> None would say that this is a portrait done in the oil of affection. Neither is it etched in acid. It is done out of relish for the bountiful mischief and the sharp tongue of the nation's Town Crier. For a rounded portrait something would have to be done for the good works that Alexander Woollcott squanders lavishly as his old juggernaut goes rolling across the country, knocking down defenseless bores and jostling the celebrities. But this chronicle of a radio publicist, turning testily on his nurse, bombing his startled doctor, match-making and match-unmaking, plotting deviously and always talking with brilliant sardonic wit, is

> one that theater goers are going to relish as much as Mr. Hart and Mr. Kaufman have, and probably Woollcott will also cherish it as one of the fabulous jokes in his Dickensian career.

Burns Mantle, however, saw Sheridan Whiteside as the "irascible, not to say insulting hero" of the play. Heywood Broun, who knew Alexander Woollcott very well, said the play "embellishes a legend rather than presents us with the Town Crier complete and in the flesh." Richard Watts of the *Herald Tribune* said, "What the authors seem to be saying of their pal is that he is a swell fellow and all that and they love him, but in his way he is rather a rat."

Now, was this portrait so broadly drawn a portrait of Alexander Woollcott? His enemies said: not by half, he was much less well-mannered and much more cruel. His friends—some of them—said the play represented cruel and unusual punishment. Vincent Sheean wrote Woollcott, shocked at the "shallow presentation" of Woollcott's character. Edward Sheldon, playwright and later curator of Harvard University Library's theater collection, was more deeply moved, so overcome when he read the script that he could say nothing at all for a time.

"Do you really think you are like that?" he asked Woollcott.

Woollcott did not think so. "Of course this is a libelous caricature," he wrote to one friend. "It is not true that the role of the obnoxious Sheridan Whiteside . . . was patterned after me," he said on another occasion. "Whiteside is merely a composite of the better qualities of the play's two authors, Messrs. Kaufman and Hart."

Some, who called themselves friends of Woollcott said it was exactly like him, that the portrayal of Sheridan Whiteside was Alexander Humphreys Woollcott in the flesh, every two hundred plus pounds of him, that the offhand remark about Kaufman and Hart proved the point.

In the end, after Woollcott was dead, this was the picture of him that remained, the picture of a man of slender talent himself, possessed of some untoward magnetic power over people who heard his voice, who achieved a reputation in his own time that was not deserved by his accomplishments. His first biographer, Samuel Hopkins Adams, lent immeasurably to that portrait, showing Alexander Woollcott as a monster with a good side, an unpleasant man who had his pleasant points, a boor with a thin veneer of social grace, a virtual eunuch who might even be homosexual, and above all, a viper who was to turn against nearly all his friends.

II

The portrait of the viper—high-living, slothful, dripping acid from every breath—the picture of Sheridan Whiteside—was one portrait of Alexander Woollcott, to be sure, and many in America took it to be the picture of the man beneath the greasepaint, especially when Alexander Woollcott himself played the role of Sheridan Whiteside, which he did in a road company in 1940.

There was another portrait, one not known to more than a few thousand of the millions of people in America and abroad who knew Woollcott, his writing or his voice; one that Alexander Woollcott was at some pains to conceal from the world in playing the role of Alexander Woollcott, which he did publicly with such perfection. This was the portrait of the generous giver and lover of mankind, who would do anything within his power to help a friend. This portrait was drawn a hundred times by a hundred different people whom he helped in one way or another; from getting them out of prison to supporting them through college, finding them jobs, and giving them large sums of money that he knew would never be repaid.

One story, which shows as complete a picture of a facet of Alexander Woollcott's character as any that might be drawn on paper, concerned a young man named Frode Jensen, and his relationship to Alexander Woollcott.

Frode Jensen was a Dane. Late in the 1920's he signed up as a cabin boy aboard a Danish vessel and shipped out in search of a career and fortune that his mother could never give him and his stepfather never would. He came to America, making eighteen crossings in all, liked what he saw in New York and jumped ship when promised a job. After some fumbling he found a job with a YMCA and miraculously encountered Howard Kennedy, a divinity student, who had been a passenger aboard the last ship on which he sailed from Copenhagen. Kennedy, whose grandfather was chairman of the board of Green Mountain Academy in Poultney, Vermont, befriended him and arranged for him to enter the academy where young Jensen perfected his English and prepared for a college education. Eventually he was accepted at Hamilton College, where he played on the college football team, and where he was brought to the attention of Alexander Woollcott in 1932 at a football game. The intermediary in this case was Grace Root, wife of Professor Edward W. Root, a good friend of Woollcott's and a strong supporter of Hamilton College, as was he.

Woollcott gave Jensen his private telephone number and issued one of his casual invitations, which were too general really to be invitations at all, to come and see him some time, and promptly forgot about the young man. Woollcott was then well-embarked on his career as a national figure in radio and writing. He had deserted the newspaper business four years earlier, having learned that he could earn far more money as a free-lance writer, besides living a life unbounded by the whims and rules of others. His invitation to young Jensen was made in all honesty; he simply did not envisage any occasion on which it would be taken up.

Having worked his way through college, young Jensen set out to work his way through medical school at the College of Physicians and Surgeons at Columbia University-Presbyterian Hospital in New York City. One day in 1934, Alexander Woollcott came into the hospital for treatment of a minor ailment, and medical student Jensen called on him.

They began talking Hamilton College, which Alexander Woollcott loved to do, and they got around to Jensen's affairs. Woollcott learned that the younger man was earning his way through medical school by translating medical reports from Danish to English for the New York Academy of Medicine, coaching football at Riverdale Academy, and running an elevator part-time. Woollcott asked if that left enough time for studies, and Jensen admitted that it did not, and that he was going to be dropped from the medical school at the end of the year.

Woollcott offered to pay Jensen's expenses through medical

school if Jensen would give up his outside activities and concentrate on his studies. There were no other strings.

For the next four years Alexander Woollcott paid the bills for Frode Jensen's medical education and gave the young man an allowance as any father might his son. This defined the relationship. Alexander Woollcott was in his middle forties when he met the younger man, and had he married and had a son been born to him, he might have been just about Jensen's age.

Jensen did well in medical school, and in the winter of 1936 began looking around the country for the place to take his next step, to intern. He was so far indulged by Alexander Woollcott that he married while in his last year of medical school.

Where was the caustic Sheridan Whiteside in this relationship?

True, there was a hint of him here and there, in Aleck's letters, as that of January 8, 1936, when Frode asked his foster father to be best man at the wedding, to be held in Winnetka, Illinois, the bride's hometown.

> . . . Even if I were to be in or near Chicago on September 12th I would strongly advise against your engaging me as best man. I can tell you right now what poisonous thoughts I would be thinking all during the ceremony. I should be wondering whose love of display and whose servility to fashion had ordained a church wedding with flocks of ushers and bridesmaids for a young couple whose life immediately thereafter such a parade would be a grotesquely inappropriate inaugural. I should be thinking how much better the money thus squandered could have been spent by any young couple upon their immediate necessities. I should be wondering whose interests were being consulted instead of those of the bride and groom, the only people whose interests ought to be consulted. I should be thinking that if you and Deb had slipped over to Middlebury and been married with the legal minimum of witnesses, how much more grace and dignity that wedding would have had. If you have read thus far even your slow Scandinavian mind must have taken in the fact that I think church

weddings are vulgar and stupid. They seem to me as much out of date and as essentially useless as a banquet photograph.

Having thus brightened your day and suspecting that if I am the best man you could think of, your plight must be pretty desperate, I remain,

Yours with deep affection.

Harsh? Yes, but not harsh to the bride and groom. Harsh thoughts for the bride's parents who insisted on the church wedding. And the reference to Frode's "slow Scandinavian mind" was not an insult but a private joke, for Frode was constantly referring to it in his own letters to Aleck.

Yet Frode, the young man in love, was upset, and responded quickly—pointing out that he did not want a church wedding, but that the Leonards did. Woollcott replied immediately.

The wedding was held in Winnetka. Alexander Woollcott came. He brought his secretary who served as an usher, and he brought Thornton Wilder from his faculty post at the University of Chicago to serve as another usher. He served as best man.

At Christmas, 1936, the Jensens went to Winnetka for the dual purpose of visiting the family and seeking a hospital for Frode's further training. Alexander Woollcott had written dozens of letters of recommendation; more, he had persuaded a number of prominent doctors to back Frode, too, so much so that one chief of staff at one hospital suggested that there must be something "fishy" about Frode's recommendations because they were so good and because they came from such awesome sources.

When Frode arrived in Chicago, he decided this was the place for him, and he sought an appointment at Presbyterian Hospital. While there he received a wire from his Rochester hospital, promising him a position if he wanted it. He consulted with Dr. Albert Getman, a prominent Syracuse physician, college friend of Aleck's and now, because of Aleck, sponsor of Frode, but he did not take Getman's advice. He signed a contract to work and train for eighteen months at Chicago's Presbyterian

Hospital. There was no complaint from Aleck, no suggestion that he ought to have followed Dr. Getman's advice.

Woollcott was enormously proud of Frode Jensen, and he devoured the younger man's letters with reports of his victories. By 1939, when Aleck was suffering from various disorders, Frode was prescribing for him, and kept asking about his health, suggesting consultation with experts in various fields. He wrote about some of his triumphs (as when he autopsied a rare case of *polyarteritis nodosa* and declared that only 200 of these cases had been found in the entire world since the disease was discovered in 1852). Aleck read these technical reports with considerable pride, and wrote about Frode's accomplishments to other friends as if they had been his own.

In 1941, Frode Jensen joined a Base Hospital unit that was being organized by the army reserve in Syracuse, and during the following year the unit was called up. Captain Jensen went south to Louisiana, and kept in touch with Aleck while he was in training. He came with his unit to the New York area, and on short notice, in wartime, Aleck found tickets for Frode and three of his fellow officers to see a Broadway play—when tickets were nearly unavailable.

Then came the moment which Frode Jensen had been awaiting with eagerness and dread: the moment of shipping out to go to war. He sat down to write a note to his adoptive father as he waited the last few minutes before moving to the transport that would take him to England. From there he did not know where he would go or when, or if, he would ever be back. It was a sober moment in the soldier's life, and one in which all pretense was put aside. He spoke of his family and how his chances in America had seemed so slender six or seven years earlier, until he met Alexander Woollcott.

> . . . my devotion to you will never change here or elsewhere. My hopes and prayers are that very soon we'll be together again. In the short time which I have left (four minutes to be exact) before we are on the way, I just want to say that you are a wonderful man and I shall always strive to do the things which will make you proud of me.

Many, many thanks, Alex, for all you have done for me and mine—and especially thanks to Grace Root who saw to it that we met. God bless you.

It was Jensen's valedictory to Aleck, and really, although there was one more letter from England via V-mail, his last word with Aleck. For Frode Jensen had scarcely arrived in England before the word came to him that Alexander Woollcott was dead. In his will he left half his possessions to Frode, half to his manager and friend, Joseph A. Hennessey.

Sheridan Whiteside? Hardly.

But if he was not Sheridan Whiteside, and he was certainly not Big Lord Fauntleroy, then just who was Alexander Woollcott, how did he get that way, and why should anyone care? He was dismissed by many, including biographer Adams, as a character of little basic importance on the American scene. It was said he never wrote a book as such. He did. It was said that he made no important contributions to American letters. He did. It was said that his taste was soupy and saccharine, that the books he espoused and touted were almost uniformly so. There were two sides to Aleck in everything, including taste. He could speak highly of William Faulkner in one breath and of *Goodbye, Mr. Chips!* in the next. Other men might die and have their works assessed separately from their personalities. It is often said that it is a crime against literature to confuse the artist and his art. This was not true with Alexander Woollcott. None of the public mourners, the obituary writers, could refrain from discussing Woollcott the wit, Woollcott of the acid tongue, Woollcott the bon vivant and pretender as they discussed Woollcott the man, and few of them discussed Woollcott the artist at all.

The obituary writers were sometimes long-winded. There was little enough to be done with the funeral, because it was not a funeral in the usual sense. A memorial service was held at the McMillin Academy Theater of Columbia University. Five hundred people, nearly all of them good friends of Aleck's attended this simple ceremony at which the only religious note was Paul Robeson's reading of the Twenty-Third Psalm. Aleck's remains were cremated and eventually they found their way t

Colgate University in Hamilton, New York, whence they were sent to Hamilton College in Clinton and were returned with 67 cents postage due. It was a common enough error, one that plagued everyone associated with Hamilton at one time or another, and it was fitting in Aleck's case that it should plague his friends. The Falstaffian joke would have amused him hugely.

There was a quiet ceremony on the grounds at Hamilton when the urn arrived, and it was placed beneath the surface, the dirt was piled on, and Aleck's friends went about their business, feeling sadder and a little older.

The question remained. Who was Alexander Woollcott? Saint or sinner? Man of evil or man of good? Mediocrity or genius? Small talent or great? Egotist or masquerader? Was there one Woollcott or were there two Woollcotts, a private Woollcott and a public one, dwelling beneath the same skin?

III

In a review of Alexander Woollcott's first *Woollcott Reader,* published in the mid-1930's, a British critic adopted the superior position that although Woollcott's writing was delightful as always, one could never expect too much of American writers. Americans, the critic said, had no sense of history. They did not live with history, the characters of history were so many stick figures to them; quite unlike the better English writers, who, the critic hinted, would all know exactly when, how, and why Cromwell cut off the head of Charles I, and could recreate the gory scene at any given moment even unto the color of Cromwell's coat. English writers, unlike American writers, had a sense of being personally involved in the matters of the past.

Perhaps the point was well taken with regard to many American writers, then and later—those who evinced no indications of knowing whence they had come, let alone where they were going—but in choosing Alexander Woollcott as the example for his polemic, this English reviewer was barking up a sapling when the cat was in quite another tree.

Woollcott's writing, all his life, was imbued with an unmistakable sense of history. True, his manifestation of this sense seldom delved back beyond the day of the landing at Plymouth Rock, but that was by choice: he was a scholar in possession of an excellent classical education, more fundamentally, he began life in historic American surroundings which gave him a sense of living with the past. That sense never left him. He could and did talk and write of Washington at Valley Forge in words that recreated the cold nights. When he spoke of the crossing of the Delaware, his radio audiences could feel the lapping of the waves against the sides of the frail boat. When he described Lizzie Borden, the napes of his listeners' necks grew cold and they could see the chubby Liz marching about the stuffy rooms of the Bordens' Victorian house, hatchet in hand. Sense of history? That was Aleck Woollcott's most valuable asset as writer and radio personality. He was a stylist, but beyond style he had a deep sense of personal involvement with what he still considered to be the American experiment; feeling almost unparalleled among non-political American authors; and if his taste in subjects was too saccharine for social critics of his heyday, still his sense of history could not be gainsaid.

This sense of involvement came naturally to Alexander Woollcott because he was born amid the ruins of one of America's most noble social experiments. Horace Greeley of the New York *Tribune* was not just a flat-faced, bespectacled editor to Woollcott, or a man who for some undefinable reason told young people to Go West. No, Horace Greeley was second in command to Aleck's grandfather in this experiment.

The generic name of the experiment was Fourierism. The particular was the North American Phalanx, proud and hopeful beginning of Fourierism on American shores. If one is to understand Alexander Woollcott and his works, one must understand this short-lived attempt to create a Utopia on the newest civilized continent in the first half of the nineteenth century.

Some Americans believed it evidence of a sickly-sweet effeminate character that Woollcott should revere Louisa May Alcott, author of *Little Women.* They quite disregarded the historical fact that Louisa May Alcott was the daughter of dreamer Bronson Alcott, founder of Brook Farm, the most idealistic and shortest-lived Fourier experiment in America, and that she and her brothers and sisters very nearly starved until the family was rescued by Ralph Waldo Emerson. As Stewart Holbrook indicated after he studied those Fourierites in *Dreamers of the American Dream,* saccharine or not, the Alcotts were as tough as iron nails.

Fourierism was the brainchild of François Marie Charles Fourier, a Frenchman born at Besançon in 1772, who grew up to enter a merchant's office in Lyons, then became one of the early advocates of socialism. He believed that competition and individualism were harmful to the world. He proposed a new society, which was to be divided into departments, called *phalanges,* each numbering about 1600 persons. Each *phalange* was to live in a *phalanstère,* or common building, and to work a selected plot of land. Nor was agriculture to be the only means of survival. Inside each *phalanstère* there would be *séries* or *groupes.* They might undertake the curing of tobacco, or the manufacture of woolen cloth, as well as the growing of the product. Private property was not to be abolished, and family life was to be preserved. Each family would have its private apartments. But rich and poor would share the same buildings and social milieu, wiping out, then, social distinction. From the common pool of profit a certain portion would be deducted to give every member of the *phalange* a minimum for subsistence. The rest would be divided in shares to labor, capital, and talent. Religious marriage was abolished but a similar system of license was established.

Fourier's theories came to America where they were propagated by Arthur Brisbane in his column in Greeley's New York *Tribune* and in a monthly magazine called the *Phalanx,* which Brisbane edited.

A number of men in the region around Albany, New York, became interested in trying the experiment and in 1843 they established a stock company and bought a fertile tract of rolling land in New Jersey within the triangle formed by Red Bank, Holmdel, and Freehold. The tract was six hundred acres, and they called it the "domain." There was no religious aspect to the experiment; the 150 original members represented all the major Protestant denominations, with a sprinkling of Jews and agnostics. The leaders of the community were the Bucklin family. John Bucklin became President of the North American Phalanx. The phalanstères divided the work among them, and settled down to grow crops, process them, and sell finished goods in the markets of the east.

For a number of years the North American Phalanx prospered. The most successful project was N.A.P., a hominy, which Woollcott later described as the first "trade-marked breakfast food marketed in this country."

Then, in 1855, a disastrous fire wiped out the mills where the hominy was made from corn. The company the Phalanx had chosen to insure it decided it would be cheaper to go bankrupt than pay the claims, and it promptly went out of business, leaving the Phalanx in some financial difficulty. Even this was not enough to kill the experiment.

The young members of the Phalanx wished to rebuild nearer to New York. The older more conservative members said that it would be more convenient to be closer to the city, but that the whole Phalanx would become corrupted by big city ways. So the Phalanx split, the younger members moved to South Amboy where their organization dwindled away, and the older ones dissolved the stock company and relapsed into competitive life. The Bucklin family took over the food processing business under the firm of J. & S. Bucklin, Choice Canned Goods.

By this time the colony was much reduced, but the people of the Phalanx had grown used to living communally and they continued, although a few of the younger generation moved away each year.

Frances Bucklin, one of John S. Bucklin's daughters, met an English immigrant named Walter Woollcott. They fell in love, much against the family's wishes and better judgment. They were married, and began wandering about the nation, Walter Woollcott practicing his specialties of bookkeeping and business management, but never successfully enough to grow roots of his own, and Frances coming back to the Phalanx to bear her succession of five children, then return to the latest roost of her husband to try to make a home for the family. The fifth of these children, whose arrival was much frowned upon within the bosom of the family, was Alexander Humphreys Woollcott, named for Alexander Humphreys, a public utilities man who was later to be president of Stevens Institute in New Jersey because Humphreys' wife, Eva Gallaudet, was Frances Bucklin Woollcott's dearest friend.

When the boy was born on January 19, 1887, Frances sent word from the natal chamber that "a young gentleman has arrived whose name is Mr. Guppy." This Dickensian quotation was lost on the family, so deep was the disapproval of Frances' gravidity, but the love for Dickens which inspired it was transmitted to that son, and all his life long he maintained a fondness for that particular author and his works.

By 1887 the 85-room house of the Phalanx was going to

seed. What paint was left after thirty years of downward fortunes was rapidly peeling in the annual convulsions of the climate of America's northeastern shore. The family was poor but not too poor, considering all the fifty or sixty people the big house sheltered, to manage to meet any specific need or purpose.

With the exception of a few brief years in Kansas City, Alexander Woollcott grew up in this environment, in this huge old house which he later described as "bleak as a skull in winter" but quite changed in the spring "when the vines that encase it and hold it up against the sun break into myriad blossoms . . . making the old house seem gay and important." He grew up in the moral and intellectual atmosphere of this place, filled with Dickens in his early years, immersed in the works of other classical authors, taught by women within the group as any boy is taught by women in the family.

It was a large family in every way, large and imposing and broad of view, if not totally worldly. Grandfather Bucklin was a stern old man who wandered at the age of eighty-eight in his bathrobe giving lectures to the household. William Bucklin, his son, had the happy eye of an artist and a bad case of wanderlust. He went off painting the scenes of the wild west while the canned goods business languished.

Aunt Anne, his wife, was the matriarch of the family in Aleck's day, and she made or superintended every important family decision. Aunt Julie was the nursemaid and governess, and she was responsible for much of Aleck's early education. Aunt Mary was a slender, weak woman, who finally died of a "decline" leaving behind another bit of history: her doctor for a time had been a young Frenchman who visited at the Phalanx, named Georges Clemenceau.

Altogether it was a radical but thoroughly stimulating community, where the young learned French and read what they would, where they were exposed to socialism in theory and practice, and where they also felt the stigma of "being different" when they went into regions other than their own. They were called queer or cranks and the newspapers hinted that they practiced free love at the Phalanx, which was not true. But the charges made others look askance at the community, and gave each member a feeling of loneliness when outside the friendly portals.

Spending many of his formative years in the Phalanx strongly influenced the career and character of Alexander Woollcott, even though he spent time outside it because of his mother's frequent trips.

"One feature of their economics always interested me," Aleck wrote later, "as a contribution to that problem which is the most besetting one in a democracy. Who is going to do the dirty work? This country, though nominally a democracy, has neatly evaded that question—first, by having a slave population, second, by successive waves of hunky immigration. Of late, the question has grown more acute. [This was written in 1928.] The army solved it by making the dirty work a part of its scheme of punishment. At the Phalanx there was this general scheme. Let us say all kinds of work were paid a dollar a day. To this, there would be two exceptions: if work required special training or if it was peculiarly unpleasant, it was paid double. Thus, my grandmother would get a dollar a day for shelling beans, but the doctor got two dollars a day and so did the man who cleaned the drains."

In this atmosphere there were no formal exhibitions of religion. When Aleck was born, he was not christened, for such observances were not in the Phalanx scheme. Half a century later, the adult Aleck's abhorrence of a wasteful, expensive church wedding for his adoptive daughter-in-law might easily be connected to this atmosphere and this training. It was radical training and it imbued in Aleck a calm acceptance of radicalism which stood him all the rest of his life. He never became a communalist, but he had thorough understanding of the factors which brought men to these extremes, and he had none of the fear of strange social or economic systems that other Americans shared so widely in their hatred of anarchy, syndicalism, socialism, and finally, communism.

When Aleck was three, his mother took the family off to Kansas City where Walter Woollcott had become secretary of the Kansas City Light and Coke Company.

In later years, Aleck Woollcott's memories of Kansas City were of a time when money was short. This need not have been:

his father was earning $250 a month. Older brother Harry and Sister Julie had jobs with the company, too. Harry received $125 a month and Julie received $75 a month. The family took in a lodger who paid $25 a month. If Walter Woollcott could not manage on $475 a month even with seven mouths to feed, there was a hidden reason for it; quite probably it had something to do with his personal habits and the Kansas City Club's card rooms.

The Woollcotts lived in Kansas City for six years, until Aleck reached the age of eight. Only in the last three years, at most, could any real memories be attributed to these years.

Aleck did remember Roswell M. Field, known as Rose in the neighborhood, who lived across the street and wrote a column for the Kansas City *Star*. Aleck became thoroughly awed by "Rose" Field, when he learned that the newspaperman received free tickets to various theatrical performances. Field, in fact, was instrumental in getting Aleck into his first stage performance, or his niece was. Field's niece, daughter of the poet and newspaperman Eugene Field, came to visit her uncle one summer. Aleck remembered her as a tall, slender, beautiful girl with a wealth of golden hair, and also that in the *tableaux vivants*, living representations of still pictures, he was cast as Puck.

Through the Fields he gained two ambitions, to become a newspaperman (so he could have free theater tickets for the rest of his life) and to go on the stage. From his father he learned to play cribbage and a further appreciation of literature, and perhaps because he did not like his father, he gained a healthy disrespect for expensive or showy clothing. He much preferred going out with Rose Field, and one day that kindly newspaperman offered to take him on a shopping tour, where he could buy anything he wanted. Aleck scorned chocolates and tops and hoops. He went into a clothing store and picked out a warm winter coat.

In 1895 Walter Woollcott lost his job when the Kansas City Light and Coke Company went into the hands of new owners. The family packed up and returned to the haven of the Phalanx, and there Aleck spent much of the rest of his boyhood years. This year also marked the breakup of the family. For a time the Woollcotts lived in Germantown, Pennsylvania, but Frances returned to the Phalanx often. Aleck went to school from there, walking two miles each way. Walter Woollcott had a job with the United Gas Improvement Company of Philadelphia, but his habits were so uncertain, and the family ties to the Phalanx were so close that the call of the community was greater than the call of matrimony. From time to time Aleck boarded with the Agnew family of Germantown, whose son George Smyser Agnew was just Aleck's age and was to be his lifelong friend. It was school and summer at the Phalanx, and then the friendship was carried on by letter. Aleck wrote, when he was twelve, of doing all the things that boys do. One day he and his brother Phil and his cousin Tod began printing old plates they had found in some disused storeroom of the Phalanx, and selling the prints to members of the group who could recall these heroic figures. Another day he led a party of three boys on a bicycle trip fifteen miles away to Highland Beach. And in a letter to Agnew he talked about girls in that mysterious, furiously uninterested way of twelve-year-old boys.

The next year, Aleck was sent to Philadelphia to attend the Central Public High School, but he was back in the big building of the Phalanx for the summer, playing croquet on the lawn. (In the first three weeks of July he boasted of having played more than 300 games of croquet.) He went swimming with other boys and crabbing at the beach. He claimed to be suffering from malaria that summer, and he may have known whereof he spoke, because malaria was not uncommon in the United States at the turn of the century, and at the Phalanx the residents slept nightly under mosquito nets during the summer.

He was a bright boy, a bookish boy, whose flair for the use of the language became apparent even at the age of thirteen, when he wrote young Agnew that "the thermometer has been singing the tune of 100° and I have been so cooked, boiled, broiled, baked, fryed and poached since the weather that I know all the microbes must be dead." He also had already acquired an intimate habit of addressing his friends and equals by odd titles or pet names. He would call Agnew "my dear child," or when they were both reading *The Casting Away of Mrs. Lecks and Mrs. Aleshine,* he would refer to his friend as My Dear Mrs. Aleshine and sign himself Mrs. Lecks.

In these years of elder childhood or approaching puberty Aleck already carried on a voluminous correspondence. One day he said he had been writing to his mother and three others, even though he was receiving no answers.

But as for the rest, he read, and he played croquet furiously, and did whatever he could to amuse himself in a huge house on a big, rundown estate. When Smyser, as he was called, came to visit the Phalanx, Aleck warned him not to expect too much, but promised croquet and swimming in Hop Brook and opportunity to rummage through the old factory. He was a little bit ashamed of the Phalanx, because now that he was going to school in Philadelphia he was very conscious that his people were "different" from others, and he pleaded with his friend not to "gossip about any peculiarities" he might notice.

In the winters, Aleck studied at the high school. He also began to write book reviews and other essays for the *Evening Telegraph* and the *Record*. Here as in Kansas City he was very much drawn to the theater, and he saved his money so that he could buy a gallery ticket as often as possible. He had no particular friends at Central High School, and recalled the period as more unpleasant than any other in his life. He had developed the ability to mimic others and he did so when he disliked someone. Sometimes this caused argument and sometimes it caused a fight. He was never unwilling to fight, although because of his poor vision he seldom won and often lost. But more than that, at Central High School, Aleck was an alien. There was one brief period in which his father had struck it rich on the stock market and moved the family into a large house on West Walnut Lane, but within a year this temporary prosperity vanished in more gambling, and the family returned to the Phalanx, while Aleck returned to still another boarding session with strangers. Most of the boys who attended Central High were living at home, and immediately this put a barrier between Aleck and all but Smyser Agnew, whom he had known earlier. He acquired the nickname Cream Puff. He wrote a parody of *Romeo and Juliet* in which he played the role of Juliet with gusto. He was skinny and not very strong, but his lack of physical strength never kept him from saying what was on his mind, and even in high school he was known to be quick with a verbal thrust. This was also the period of his greatest formative reading. Since he had much spare time after school hours and on weekends, Aleck frequented the Friends Free Library where he had a card. He could only take out a few books each week so at the boarding house he canvassed everyone, soliciting cards from the other boarders, the owners, and the cooks and maids. Then he would go to the library on Saturday morning, trudging to Market Square, pulling a wagon load of books behind him.

Through high school, he nurtured his two interests, newspapering and the drama, and he once told an acquaintance that he firmly intended to become a drama critic when he had finished college.

In the spring of 1904, his last year in high school, Aleck's cousin introduced him to the world of newspapering in a truly professional fashion. She was Helen Sears, and at that time in charge of the book review page of the Philadelphia *Telegraph*. He wrote reviews for her regularly, taking the books as his payment. On one occasion, when she found it necessary to be away from Philadelphia for three weeks, he put out the book page for her with such success that there was no complaint or any public notice that there had been a change in editors.

That summer, Ivy Ashton, a successful playwright, came to visit the Phalanx because she had relatives there, and during the visit she brought her husband, Edwin B. Root, member of a family with a long history of attendance and service at Hamilton College in Clinton, New York. Ivy Ashton and her husband took considerable interest in the lively and yet bookish young man. Although he was eager to go on to college, and his excellent showing at Central High School indicated that he would do well, the family could not afford to support Aleck through college. The Roots arranged for a scholarship which paid tuition. Aleck borrowed money from Alexander Humphreys, then president of Stevens Institute, who was pleasant enough about lending it to his namesake for so useful a purpose. That summer Aleck worked in the family cannery at the Phalanx, and in the autumn he was ready to go away again—not for the first time, but so far away from friends and family that it was almost like going to a foreign country.

IV

THERE WERE NOT MANY POOR BOYS at Hamilton in the Class of 1909, and in that sense Aleck stuck out like a crow in an apple tree in January. He wore his poverty as a badge; there was nothing else he could do and he saw no point in sniveling about it. For the first week he stayed with the Roots in their house on "the hill" as the Hamilton campus is aptly named. It is located atop a steep flat hill, above the Oriskany River valley, some two miles from the little village that serves the college, and which in 1905 had little other reason for existence, except to supply the farmers in the region. The buildings were laid out in a quadrangle atop the hill and professors' homes, the dormitories and the fraternity houses straggled down the hill below the college. Everything was separated from the village below in distance and even further in intellectual interests.

During that first week Aleck managed to fall in love with Laura Root, the youngest daughter, who was just a little older than he. She taught him to dance and she later accompanied him to a number of college parties, because he could never afford the luxury of an outside weekend guest for these affairs—the cost was at least $50.

At the Root house Aleck was given an introduction to style. The house was one of the oldest on the hill, having been built in 1790 as an inn. Every room was on a different level. What appealed to Aleck most was the furniture; for the first time he saw a complete collection of period furniture—every piece an authentic colonial piece, from paintings to china and the silver on the table.

In that first week, Aleck matriculated and decided on his courses. Immediately, it became apparent that he would have to settle for the lesser Bachelor of Philosophy or Bachelor of Science degree, because he lacked sufficient background in the classics. The other, wealthy boys, who had come from the private academies, offered Greek and Latin. Aleck had no Greek. He might have conquered this deficiency and worked for the higher degree, but he saw in the curriculum too many other subjects he wished to attack, and he settled for Latin, without the Greek or the chance of achieving an A.B. degree. This was to be a source of ragging from his friends, and put him on his mettle from the beginning.

College fraternities played an important part in the life of Hamilton, although the school contained only about two hundred students. The first few days, before the opening of classes, were devoted to "rushing" for the fraternities. Sponsored by the Roots, Aleck was invited by the fraternities to box luncheons, dinner parties, and card parties. He went to the fraternity houses and looked over the members while they did the same. The Roots were closely affiliated with the Sigma Phis but Aleck was not to their liking nor they apparently to his, for he was one of that year's four freshmen to pledge Theta Delta Chi. Sixteen boys lived in the fraternity house, four from each class, with two women who served as cooks and housekeepers. From the beginning Aleck loved the routine of college and fraternity life, perhaps because it offered him a greater stability and feeling of belonging than he had enjoyed in those hectic years of boardinghouse life mixed up with seasons at the Phalanx. Now, he knew that for four years he would be living as he was in the autumn of 1905. He wrote Smyser Agnew:

> We all go to chapel every morning at 8:30 and have a short opening service. Then every Sunday we have a regular service that is supposed to be non-denominational but the leanings are decidedly Presbyterian. One of the seniors plays the organ, a big beauty that covers the entire front wall of the chapel. For voluntaries he always gives some good music instead of hymns. For instance, last Sunday we had the Warmarch of Tannhaüser overture afterwards. There is a choir of the eight best voices in the college and we all open by singing a chant. Then there is

the responsive reading which is followed by singing the Doxology, and the Lord's Prayer is given and then the sermon. I don't think much of Dr. Stryker as a teacher but he certainly is the most eloquent preacher I ever heard and he gets his ten thousand year for that very reason.

Aleck made friends, quickly and more easily than one might have believed for a rather lonely boy who was an outsider to the way of life most of these young men had enjoyed. He spoke of his friend Selden Talcott Kinney of the senior class. He got on well with the football players of his fraternity, although he showed absolutely no proclivity for athletics. He and a small group of young men of more intellectual bent came together to form various organizations on the campus. Among these were Hawley Truax, Robert Rudd, C. Mossman McLean and Harry Dounce.

Aleck, of course, did not fit everyman's ideal as a college boy. He continued to be lank and owlish in appearance and much too inclined to a bright, cutting remark for the comfort of certain acquaintances. He was never the most-loved man on the campus, but neither was he the worst-hated. And as in later life, he was content that this should be so; he was capable of lavishing the greatest of affection on those who appealed to him; he did not bother hating those whom he disliked, he simply ignored them.

When winter came in 1905, Aleck had his troubles. He did not have enough clothing, and what he had was mostly summer weight. In Clinton the temperatures tend to go well below the zero mark and remain there. In Aleck's day it was boasted that there was good sleighing for three months of the year without interruption. Aleck had no long underwear, and he shivered through that first winter because of it. But his enthusiasm continued. He wrote Smyser Agnew about his life, telling how he and the other young men each brought a sled up the hill from the fraternity house about three-quarters of a mile below the chapel when they came up for classes in the morning. Then, on their way back to the fraternity house for lunch, they picked up their sleds and made it down the hill in one minute flat.

"I continue to love it here with all my heart and everything is just ideal," he wrote. "I have several very close friends in my own and the upper classes and there is always so much to do. We gave a small informal dance here to about fifty people and I was so tired when I crept into bed at five in the morning that I slept until three the next day. The boys invite their damsels from all over the state and girls pack up and come all the way from New York just to attend the Theta Delta opening dance. In February is dance week when the whole week is used in gayety, and our crowd gives a house party, each boy bringing a girl for the week and sleeping in the dormitory to leave the house clear for the girls and their chaperones. There are dances every night and sleighing parties in the daytime."

But because it cost money, on these occasions Aleck said he either escorted Laura Root, another faculty girl, a town girl, or he went stag.

Having examined what he had just written, Aleck made haste to assure Smyser that life was not all play. The "shirks," he said, never got past the first term of the freshman year.

Aleck was anything but a shirk. He carried a heavy load of classical courses this year, including Latin, French, English Grammar, Elocution and Bible, and he was doing honors work from the beginning. Besides, he had his hand in the Hamilton literary magazine, apparently from the moment he arrived on the campus. His first effort, which appeared in the October, 1905, issue of the magazine, was a review of two novels: *Sir Richard Calmady,* by Lucas Malet, Charles Kingsley's daughter, and *Pam,* by Bettina, the Baroness von Hutten. The novels were of a new school, wherein such matters as the seduction of women was openly discussed. Aleck found the book by Miss Malet had been called improper and disgusting "and no doubt," he said, "the expression of such sentiments also had its effect on the demand for the work on the market, for it must be admitted that a notorious book often has the commercial advantage over one that is merely noted." The major claim to fame of *Sir Richard Calmady* was that it had been banned by many censorship bodies in many communities in the English-speaking world.

In the other novel, where there was no seduction, but a simple question of a couple living in outright sin, and where the author had tacitly approved the sinful relationship, there had been no banning, no sensationalism, no charges. Aleck said the real problem here was taste over ethics, because in *Sir Richard Calmady*, bad as the taste of the author might be in discussing the dissolution of certain characters, at least the author was on the side of conventional morality. That book was criticized and banned. The book of the baroness, advocating, as it did, a life of sin, was not banned. Aleck's point was that it was a strange world in which these confusions arose.

A month later Aleck was writing about the "passing" of the historical novel, such as those of Winston Churchill (the American) in favor of the nature novel, and he specifically commented on the new book by the young writer Jack London, *Call of the Wild*:

> . . . we have every right to expect great things from Mr London. He is a young man but he has already produced a book gemlike in its simplicity and classic in its splendid strength.

The next month, December, Aleck appeared again in print, this time with a story, an uninspiring piece of fiction, based freshmanically (he was not yet a sophomore) on what he imagined from his readings to be English drawing room manners, and set in England. It need not be reproduced here, for it added nothing to Aleck's stature as a budding writer nor to the sum of human taste or knowledge. It was exactly the kind of writing which belonged in a college literary magazine, where the young intellectuals might experiment.

Aleck's first year at college was not an unqualified success, for he was having some difficulty in adjustment, and he was much misunderstood by some of his more fortunate fellows, who attributed his strange dress during the winter to being a "queer one" or a "putrid" not realizing that Aleck was making the best of his poverty. He acquired the nickname "putrid" during his freshman year, and on several occasions because of his sharp tongue or his appearance, he was hazed by the sophomores in the cruel fashion of the day, by being thrown into the fountain in mid-campus.

Yet long after Aleck's career was ended, the myth of his unhappiness at Hamilton persisted, as did the myth that he was a misfit who gloried in being different. The facts indicate that Aleck was a distinguished student and distinguished member of the Hamilton student body and that he enjoyed himself thoroughly in college. Why else would Hamilton always thereafter be so dear to his heart that he gave of money, time and emotion to it freely, and in the end asked that his remains be taken there for burial?

V

As a literary cub, Alex was indefatigable. The simpering story of December was followed by one of considerably more ingenuity in January, 1906, called *An Old Dodge* or the *Wisdom of Solomon.* The next month came the story *The Precipice, A Story of Bohemia,* another comedy of manners, but of a much higher calibre than *The Hearth and the Cloister.* Yet *The Precipice* did have a certain collegiate rakishness about it, as might be ascertained from this description of one passionate scene. Just after Nana, the heroine, who is not much better than she ought to be, has been kissed by her lover:

> For some time she did not move, and when at last she did, it was to reach out for the Benedictine which stood temptingly near on the *tabouret.* She loved this cordial—it seemed a part of her new world, and was full of the sparkle and warmth of Bohemia.

That scene comes near the beginning. Later the story moves into a living, squirming pit of passion, cigarette ashes, lovers' reproaches, accusations, revulsions, illusions and stuttering, desolation, loneliness, and unrequited love—all within a half-dozen printed pages.

This particular story was notable because it won the Ninety One Manuscript Prize of $25, which was donated by George M. Weaver, Jr., and Samuel Hopkins Adams, two "old grads" of the Class of 1891 who had moved on into the literary world.

Weaver and Adams were loyal Hamilton alumni, and when commencement came and prizes were being handed out, they were on hand for the ceremonies. Weaver talked with Adams just after he had visited with the prize committee and learned the name and nature of the literary gem which had won the prize that year.

"My God," he said. "Look what we've done."

The Precipice, luckily for all, represented nearly the end of Aleck's creative literary efforts for the year. He sold it to the *Bohemian,* a pulp magazine, for $12. In the spring he tried out for the glee club. As a singer he was not a notable success, but he did manage to secure a place in the Glee Club as monologist. The Glee Club traveled considerably and it was thought best to have a program as varied as could be arranged without going into heavy sets of properties and expenses. Aleck possessed considerable histrionic talent, and he particularly liked to dress up as a girl and perform. There was nothing sinister or unusual in this: it was quite common among college youths, and in the middle of the 1960's chorus lines featuring hairy legs and football ankles never failed to bring down the house. Female impersonation was one of the young Woollcott's specialties and he was so expert at this art form that in Philadelphia he had once attended a party as a young maiden from Ohio, and had carried off the masquerade successfully during an entire evening. His character for the Glee Club impersonations was *Mabel, the Beautiful Shopgirl.*

Aleck spent the summer of 1906 working in the Roycroft Colony, a cultural spa at East Aurora, New York, the creation of Elbert Hubbard in the 1890's. The Roycrofters devised and printed many books and pamphlets of a headily cultural nature, hand-illuminated and hand-bound. An art school was established there offering courses in painting, clay moulding, and terra cotta workmanship. Initially Roycroft must have attracted Aleck because of the communal nature of the colony and the work, but the attraction did not survive the summer. He came back to Hamilton talking about the pretensions of Hubbard and his crowd. He did not return to East Aurora.

In Aleck's sophomore year at Hamilton he became one of the editors of the literary magazine. In the November issue he was responsible for the editorial, a discussion of the Hill Walk, and its importance to the campus. He suffered through the pangs of love off and on during the year, with a succession of young ladies. Smyser Agnew said that Aleck had been introduced to sex during the Philadelphia days when he was staying at a boardinghouse, where also lived a handsome twenty-two-year-old young woman and her husband, a traveling salesman. During the husband's long absences the young matron became strongly attracted to Aleck, and invited him to share her bed. These moments of dalliance continued until one day when the husband arrived at home at the wrong moment, finding Aleck, if not in his bed, at least in his wife's arms. That particular tale had the ring of Mack Sennett comedy about it, rather than truth, and this was not unusual for the young Aleck Woollcott, who was an inveterate spinner of adventurous yarns, most of the time with himself cast in what he considered to be the hero's role. He spoke sometimes of the days of his college youth when he was an absinthe addict. (How he found absinthe in Clinton, New York, or even in Utica, is anyone's guess.) He talked of being "something of a drunk," which no one who knew him could confirm. Mostly, of course, these were examples of the heroic exaggerations practiced by many young men.

Once in a while Aleck let himself go in verse in the literary magazine:

> Betty, your hair was of the gold
> That filtered from the sun-lit skies . . .

It was not bad poetry of the greeting card school, and certainly not worse than the other contributions from the literary group of the two hundred fortunate fellows of Hamilton College.

That same issue of "The Lit," as it was called on campus, contained Aleck's story, *The Pearl,* which was a romance of college days. The distinction of this tale was to be found in one line. The hero, Billy, asked the heroine, Pearl, why she was named.

Retorted Pearl, "It's because I'm cast before swine."

Which predated the similar remark by Aleck's friend, Dorothy Parker, by some dozen years.

There were other stories. He wrote *The Swan Song,* a theatrical tragedy of a heroine with a heart condition of some unstated variety who realized that the play must go on and sacrificed her life to it.

Then came *Out of the Clouds,* another sophomoric story, and in the spring of 1907 two more stories, one called *The Rushing of Timothy Starr,* which had the virtue of being written in dialogue that just might have been possible, on a subject with which, for a change, the author was totally familiar. The next month, May, Aleck reverted to style and wrote another story called *Anniversary*, a tale of English manners which ended in death, as any sophomore's literary efforts ought.

Aleck's first permanent cultural contribution to the welfare of his beloved Hamilton came in the spring of 1907. He was joined by his particular group of friends, Robert Rudd, A. F. Osborn, Hawley Truax, Horace Griffith Getman, Roosh Wilson and Harry Esty Dounce. The plan was to re-form a dramatic club that had died out through neglect. Many years later, Aleck recalled the events:

> . . . The organization did not come into being in response to any popular demand for the revival of the long languishing dramatic club. To the best of my recollection, there was no such demand whatever. Nor did its organizers feel earnestly that Hamilton should have dramatics. No, indeed. They simply felt earnestly that they would like to act. Certainly, there was no notion that there was need for a further undergraduate interest, for, as matters stood, there was one major college activity to every 7¼ students, or thereabouts. . . .
>
> The first Charlatans hadn't the faintest idea of inviting the class or the college to compete for positions in the cast. Such a method might have left the organizers with only thinking parts and the thoughts would have been very bitter. Besides, the new club was a private, personal, self-selected enterprise, dedicated not to the drama but to the amusement of its members.
>
> But in the background, there loomed ominous the classes of 1908 and 1910, two hulking groups of Philistines with strongly developed powers of derision: they existed solely as a corrective in 1909. They may have been created for some other function, but that is the only one they served. We had visions of their going callously to Utica on the night of our performance at the Scollard Opera House, Clinton's own Covent Garden. There occurred to some of the prophetic souls among the pioneers—in their night-

mares—that if they did attend, we might wish they hadn't. So as a sop to these ruffians, as a bald corruption of the press and public, the gate receipts were pledged to the exchequer of the track team, in the financial condition of which we really had no interest at all . . .

I have never since had so much fun as I had at those rehearsals nor ever since seen a performance I considered so altogether brilliant—particularly in one role. There is no room to mention all the talent. I am afraid Rudd was the star: he alone looked so ravishing that Gibbon grew rich selling his pictures. I am certain Bryant was the comic relief. Only he could so twist his lines that it was impossible to disentangle them without injury (generally to the director). Only he could fall flat on his back at the dress rehearsal, and, at the first performance, sneeze with such vehemence that his already strained corsets simply disintegrated while he waited in the wings for his cue. Only he would kick over a table laden with bon-bons and cigarettes at the gala party given afterwards in honor of the Charlatans. And Roosh Wilson—he was a triumph after we had abandoned the struggle to have him acquire an English accent and, by the simple expedient of giving his part a Yankee instead of a Piccadilly past, made him a superb "Down East" comedian.

But it was none of these, nor any member of the original organization, nor any member of 1909, who saved the bacon of Charlatans. That dubious, though then highly admired service, was rendered by Harry Esty Dounce, '10. Four days before the first performance—I keep speaking of the first performance when there really was only one—Truax, who had spent six weeks patiently perfecting the longest role in the play, retired to a bed of pain, his suffering assuaged only by the pleasant consciousness of how much trouble he was causing. We were desolate. Dounce was the only hope. Would he take the part? Could he learn it in time? He replied coldly that he would and could and, after chapel, he retired to his room and locked the door. At five that afternoon, we found him bouncing heavily on the tennis court and reviled him for a slacker.

> "H---," said Dounce, "I know the part already."
>
> Whether he really did know it then, we can only guess. Certainly he walked on letter perfect at that aforesaid first performance. He had had two rehearsals and did not falter once, despite the natural agitation caused by his whiskers, which betrayed a tendency to fall into his lap at moments of emotional outburst.
>
> By all means, Dounce—or someone who shall be nameless—should have been elected president of the Charlatans next season, but by some undetected subterranean intrigue, Truax walked off with that honor. I was so incensed at the time, that I was on the point of handing in my resignation but I withheld it because of a horrid suspicion that it might be accepted.

In the spring of his sophomore year Aleck moved out more into campus and town society, which included the society of Utica which was just a few miles away from the college. He wrote Smyser Agnew toward the end of June that he had recently attended four large dances, three teas, and a wedding —and all this a few days before examination week. "It is hard to shine both in your studies and in gay society," he said. Yet, shine he did. Again he was on the list of high honor students, now taking German and Latin and French and other far from easy subjects, such as trigonometry, biology, and Middle English.

After examination week, on Monday night there were three dances, on Tuesday night there were three dances, on Wednesday night was the alumni banquet and on Thursday, commencement day; the ball began early in the evening and lasted until six o'clock in the morning.

Altogether, Aleck had enjoyed a most satisfactory year. He had formed many close friendships, and he had overcome his original shyness about his poverty. "I am the only poor guy in the crowd so they take me motoring, to dinners and theaters, and I roll around as if my pockets were bulging." He would never forget these favors, and in time, in his own way, he would repay nearly all of them a dozenfold.

Then, in the spring of his sophomore year, Aleck went back to work to earn enough money to keep himself through the following scholastic year. He still had the support of Alexander

Humphreys, who guaranteed him $750 a year, and his grades allowed him to continue his scholarship support, but this was not enough to live and clothe himself. He left Hamilton before the ball on Thursday, partly to save money, but also because he was to start work on Friday at Chautauqua, the big cultural summer school on Chautauqua Lake, near Erie. He would be a waiter at the hotel and receive board and room. Three other young men and three congenial young women worked with him, and Aleck enjoyed it thoroughly. He had his tips, and he had another job, as janitor, and one as ticket taker in the main hall. He had time to himself, and read what he called "a whole library." He also wrote many letters (twenty-two in one week), went swimming and rowing when the weather was warm, and enjoyed the music, speeches and other entertainments. On one Sunday he listened delightedly to a performance of Haydn's *Creation* in the amphitheater with a choir of four hundred and orchestra, and he reveled all summer long in the six or eight entertainments that were available to him every day. He did not cover himself with much intellectual glory that summer—he wrote Agnew that in July, when the Chautauqua held a spelling match, he entered for New Jersey, and missed the first word they gave him—but intellectual matters could wait. Aleck Woollcott was enjoying himself as a young man might, and he was quite at peace with his world.

VI

In his first two years of college Aleck had been given to theatrical exaggerations. When he returned to campus for sophomore classes he brought with him an old .45 calibre revolver which he had picked up in a secondhand store. He sometimes indicated to his intimates that he was considering doing away with himself with this lethal instrument. Some believed him, some did not. It seems likely that this was as much a part of a public performance as his celebrated pugnaciousness on campus. He gained a reputation for picking fights with football players who outweighed him by some fifty pounds. It is unlikely that this happened more than once or twice, and it is most likely that this, too, was part of Aleck's love of theatricals. For in the fall of 1907, when he was safely busy with the farcical performances of the Charlatans all year long, his public theatricals diminished. Alec was always playing roles in public; there was no question about it; he began it as a child and he was never to abandon the practice. The difference was that in later years the roles changed until finally there was only one major role, which he wrote, directed, and performed—the role of the celebrated Alexander Woollcott.

In the later college years there were hints of the coming public character. Aleck continued to be a brilliant student. He became editor in chief of "The Lit" this year, and he was by far the most accomplished editor the magazine had ever boasted, or would have for many, many years. Before Woollcott's time the *Hamilton Literary Monthly* was suffered by the faculty as necessary evil and was read lethargically, if at all, by the student body. Under Woollcott, the magazine took on life, related itself to Hamilton and its world, and became "must" reading.

Aleck took the magazine and his role seriously. He was so busy in the fall that he did not have time to produce fiction for "The Lit." His was the job of prodding others, of writing editorials, of criticizing and editing. He did write a critique of the American Theater which appeared in November that year, noting that on the death of Richard Mansfield the place of the heroic lead was left vacant, and despite suggestions that E. H. Sothern might fill it, it was his belief that Mansfield's position in the theater threatened to remain vacant for a considerable period of time.

This year Aleck spent much time at the theater in Utica, particularly on Saturday afternoons, when he and Bob Rudd would cajole a ride to the city.

He was, he wrote later, "the eternal sophomore at Hamilton College, who, as soon as his midwinter math exam is over, gets himself into something pretty doggy in the way of a coonskin coat and hies himself straightaway from the immemorial Busy Corner in Utica."

After enjoying the amenities of the Busy Corner, he and Rudd would move on to one of the town's legitimate theaters. Utica was on the New York, Albany, Schenectady, Utica, Syracuse, Buffalo circuit. Someone—usually Rudd, according to Aleck—would plunk down the $1.50 price for his orchestra seat and they would go in to enjoy the show.

Christmas time Aleck went home to the Phalanx for his annual visit. It was the only time of the year he felt he could afford to make the trip. He had nearly three weeks vacation then, and he used it to visit New York, see his mother, sisters, aunts, and other relatives in the big communal house in Red Bank, and go to Philadelphia to visit the Agnews, who invariably invited him to stay some time with them. Then it was back to the grind of college. The penultimate year was a difficult psychological period when he was not quite sure what he might make of himself, and when, in the gloom of winter his studies hung very heavy on his hands. He alternated between living in the fraternity house and the dormitory, as was quite customary among Hamilton students. Life in the fraternity was intimate and secluded. Life in the dormitory enabled the young men to find friends outside their immediate fraternal associations, and in later life Aleck's friends were very much divided between friends of the fraternity, and those he made in his college activities.

He spent much time at the homes of professors. Two of his professors, in particular, were fond of him and encouraged him in one way or another. One was Professor Shepherd, the French professor. Aleck began with French, and because of his life at the Phalanx where everybody learned French as a matter of course in early childhood, he was by far the professor's most talented student. Before he was graduated, Professor Shepherd said that Aleck Woollcott had a better command of the French language than he had. Aleck's other faculty mentor was Professor Herman Carl George Brandt who lived halfway up the hill in a big square house decorated with an unlikely but welcoming Bavarian sign above the top doorsill: *Das liebste Haus, das beste Haus.* Aleck, who studed German with interest and considerable skill, too, spent many happy evenings in his junior year at dinners at Professor Brandt's.

The junior year was the heaviest of all scholastically and in this year Aleck worked his hardest. His reward would come in the following year when it was the Hamilton policy to give the seniors more time for reflection and polishing of their acquired skills. By the spring of 1908, Aleck was thoroughly sick of studying, and he nearly yielded to the blandishments of one of his wealthy friends who suggested that the two of them set out on a trek to Europe. The lure was great, but whereas for his wealthy friend it would be strictly a lark, for Aleck such escapism would mean the end of his college career and he was wise enough to know that if he showed such irresponsibility he could not ask Alexander Humphreys for more help. Without the Humphreys stipend he could not finish his education.

He contributed to "The Lit" again. In February, 1908, his story *The Hand of the Potter* appeared, another comedy of manners. In June he published *Paradise Lost,* yet another comedy, and a humorous poem, *To Laura,* which was addressed to Laura Root, who still occupied a corner of his affections although she kept him similingly at arm's length. Aleck, by now, had accepted the fate of becoming "good friends."

In the summer of 1908 it was again work, and then back to Clinton for senior year. Aleck became serious for the first time about a girl in the autumn of 1908. Her name was Katherine and she was the daughter of the rector of Grace Church in Utica. He had spent many Sundays and evenings at the rectory, although he called himself a "rank heathen." He liked the rector, who told "most unrectorish stories" when the ladies were not at the table, and the rector liked him. In the spring of 1907 Katherine had sailed for Europe for a finishing tour and an indefinite stay. This was obviously one reason that Aleck's thoughts in the spring of 1908 had turned toward Europe, and they turned again in the fall of 1908. Katherine was still abroad, but Aleck visited the rectory often and continued to pay his respects to her mother. He spent election night there in November, and to while away the time Katherine's mother played the piano for him. "Hearts and Flowers" was the piece he remembered. He went home in a satisfactorily nostalgic mood, his heart repledged to Katherine, "whom I hope to marry some day," he wrote to Smyser Agnew. The next night nostalgia had vanished in the face of an attack of the collegiate vapors.

"I have a great fireplace in my room," he wrote Agnew in November, "with woodboxes which the Freshmen are supposed to keep full, only they don't. Last night the snow was so thick and the wind so noisy that we darkened the room and lay all evening in two Morris chairs in front of the fire. It is a harmless way to spend a few hours. About ten we sent a Freshman over to Commons for some eggs on toast, candy and cigarettes, with the result that I have a rather sour stomach this morning. It is still snowing and the sleds are out in full force, which will give you a hint as to the climate here."

The "we" referred to his special pal of the senior year, Phil Welch, another well-to-do young man, and a football star. They were likely to be together most of the time when not in class, he said, which meant "Utica and the theaters when his pockets are full and my room in the dormitory when they are empty."

Aleck was still slender and owlish in his twenty-second year. He was also the most accomplished man on the campus, and one of the busiest. He was president of Theta Delta Chi's local chapter, which was called Psi Charge. He was still editor of

"The Lit." He had been taken into the local chapter of Phi Beta Kappa during his junior year, and he was heading for a degree with high honors. He was the organizing force behind the Charlatans. He was also a character playing a part gain, although the part was much misunderstood by such men as Samuel Hopkins Adams, then one of the principle muckrakers of the magazine world, and a man of a very conservative turn of mind.

In the spring of 1909, when Aleck won the Ninety One Manuscript Prize for the second time, he met Samuel Hopkins Adams on the steps of the Hamilton library one day by appointment. Here is Adams' description of the young Woollcott:

> . . . an odd figure came into view, crossing the campus with an undulant prance. The youth was clad in excessively wrinkled and baggy trousers, a misshapen corduroy coat, grimy sneakers, and a red fez with a gilt tassel. . . . I was struck with the owlish gravity of the eyes behind the large lenses, and an air not so much cocky as confident, suggesting the trustfulness of a tenderly reared baby.

Aleck, of course, was that day playing Literary Aleck. The red fez was the tipoff. Aleck had earlier written to Adams and made an appointment. He introduced himself to Adams, thanked him for the prize that had been donated to the college, and asked if Adams would help him secure a job on a newspaper. Adams' innate conservatism was appalled by the Woollcott getup, but when he went into the library and looked over several issues of the literary magazine, he saw, with a professional eye, that Aleck had made something of what he recalled as a moribund publication dedicated to the reprinting of dull chapel talks and the President's messages. He saw that Aleck had introduced an interesting technique to pep up the magazine that year. Beginning in October there had begun a serial romance entitled *Even As You and I,* which dealt with the adventures of a beautiful young actress named Edith St. Clair. Aleck, of course, had invented the basic plot, which was melodramatic, to say the least. The serial had soon become the wonder of the campus because it was written by six different authors (Aleck wrote the first installment) and no author was given a tip or a peek at the previous author's work. He must read it in the magazine, and then produce the next installment for the following issue—which gave him about a week for writing.

Adams was impressed enough that he promised to write to friends in the newspaper business in New York, and he did write Carr Van Anda, managing editor of the New York *Times,* who was engaged then in making the *Times* into a much better newspaper than it had ever been before and on the lookout for bright young talents.

Adams did not approve completely of the young man he recommended and he shuddered at his appearance, not realizing then, or ever, that Aleck was simply making the best of his bad situation and adding a fillip or two to create a new role. Rather than be simply poor boy, he chose to be public character. So the recommendation to Van Anda was at best lukewarm, but it was better than nothing. Aleck was a member of the senior honorary society—elected by the students, he was popular on the campus—but he was also editor of the magazine, and Phi Beta Kappa. He just did not look right to Adams. Had he been less flamboyant he would have been a more understandable character to Adams and most of his contemporaries.

Adams sent Aleck a letter to take to Van Anda, suggesting that he had best see him during Easter vacation, any time after 3:30 in the afternoon. In writing this letter, Adams was considerably more friendly to Aleck than he had been in private to Van Anda, doing his best, apparently, to help the young man without engaging himself too specifically as sponsor of so strange a character.

Aleck did go to see Van Anda in the spring and was disappointed to learn that there would be no opening on the day after commencement. Phil Welch had found such a job, as a cub reporter for the New York *Sun.* Aleck did not know quite what to do, but he was helped again by Alexander Humphreys, who secured a job for him with the Chemical Bank of New York. He would start at the bottom of course, as a messenger. If he worked diligently and did not wear his red fez to the office he might hope in a year or two to become a clerk, and someday he might become a vice-president.

Such a career held no appeal at all for Aleck, but New

York did and New York alone. Where else was the capital of the theatrical world? Where else could he become a drama critic? Oh, there were other cities and other newspapers in those cities had drama critics, but there was no theater but Broadway; everything else was an offshoot, and for Aleck there was no place to start but a New York City newspaper. If he could not get the newspaper job on the *Times* he would come to New York and work in the bank and wait until opportunity came to him.

The ninety-seventh commencement of Hamilton College was held on Thursday, June 24, 1909, in the college chapel. At ten o'clock in the morning the trustees, the faculty, and the classes assembled, all by seniority, and marched in caps and gowns and stoles signifying their honors from Root Hall to Commons Hall and then to the chapel. Four orations were to be heard. Lloyd Paul Stryker would make one of them. Ravaud Hawley Truax would make another. (Both men were close friends of Aleck's.) Aleck had no interest in orations, and he had made no attempt to win one of the honors in this field. He had started packing several days before, and after the alumni banquet and the ball that lasted until dawn he made ready to leave the campus where he had spent four happy and triumphant years. Considering what he had to start with in physical assets, Aleck had come a very long way on brains and courage.

VII

In New York City Aleck took lodgings in a rooming house at 34 West Twelfth Street in what was the most respectable sector of Greenwich Village, a few feet off Fifth Avenue. In the same lodging house lived his sister, Julie, who worked for a Jersey City utility company, and Phil Welch, Aleck's college friend, who began his job on the *Sun* at the same time Aleck began at the bank.

Less than three weeks after he started work at the Chemical Bank, Aleck awoke one morning to discover that he had a swelling below his ears. He knew what that meant, for he had never contracted mumps, and now that he had come to young manhood his fear of this particular disease was acute. "It took me about two minutes to fly into my clothes and start for the Phalanx," he said. His instant diagnosis was correct. It *was* mumps. His head swelled up like a pomegranate, and in a few days he could not move at all and had to be lifted from the bed. As he feared there were complications, and his groin swelled until the pain was almost unbearable. The doctor came and gave him injections and morphine to ease the pain, and in two weeks he was almost recovered. Then he returned to West Twelfth Street and the ménage where elder sister Julie managed the finances for the three of them. Aleck was earning fifteen dollars a week at the bank, Phil Welch was earning about the same amount at the *Sun,* and Julie was earning considerably more at her utility company because she had experience that dated back to Kansas City days when she earned $75 a month. She supported the other two, but she also indulged her own expensive habits, which included a liking for good food and the joys of the theater. None of them, it seemed, ever had very much money but Julie always had enough to lend the others a dollar or so toward the end of the week to tide them over for cigarettes until payday.

All summer Aleck slaved in the bank—for that is how he considered the job—and marched up to the *Times* when he could to see Carr Van Anda and renew his requests for a reporter's position. In the fall a reporter's job did open up, and Carr Van Anda hired Aleck.

For two years Aleck worked in the city room of the *Times* as a cub reporter, rewriting handouts from press agents, taking the routine police news from the police reporters, covering fires and interviewing people who walked into the offices of the *Times* bearing stories for the newspaper. He received regular small raises, but quickly realized that he would never make any money in the newspaper business. "But I love it," he wrote, and that was enough for the moment. He spent much time at the theater, sometimes managing to obtain free passes from the drama department, and one week, in the fall of 1909, he went to four plays.

After serving over a year of apprenticeship under the close eye of city editor Arthur Greaves he was sent down to the old criminal courts building down town and assigned to cover various crimes and trials.

On a Saturday morning in the spring of 1911, while browsing around among the records of happenings in the previous few hours, Aleck came across an affidavit signed by a young man who was to be tried on Monday morning on charges of grand larceny, stemming from the theft of a diamond crescent pin from the wife of a prominent New York builder. The young man had been tracked down and arrested with the pawn ticket for the crescent in his pocket and had been positively identified by the pawnbroker. To the district attorney's office it was an open and shut case, and Aleck would have paid no attention at all except that in reading the affidavit he came across what was obviously a very good story, and since the affidavit was a part of the court record he was protected from a libel suit, although the material involved was most racy.

The young man swore that he had not stolen the diamond crescent. Not at all. He had met the lady in question quite properly and she invited him to her house. They had become friendly and in a short time when her husband had gone out of town, they had embarked on a round of entertainments, including dinners at the fashionable Rector's restaurant and nights in discreet hotels. Too soon, however, the young man's money had run out and he had been forced to tell his paramour that their gaiety must come to an end. The lady was loath to give up her fun, and so she gave him the diamond crescent with orders to pawn it and use the proceeds to continue. He had done so.

All was well until the husband returned to the city and for some reason asked his wife what had happened to her diamond crescent pin. She was vague. She must have lost it, she said, or it must have been stolen by some sneak thief from the apartment while she was out.

The husband grew angry and righteous and telephoned the police, who began searching the pawnshops. The pin was found, the young man identified, and thrown into jail.

He kept silent for several weeks, hoping that his ladylove would confess the true state of affairs to her husband, but she did not seem to be in any mood to do so, and now the trial was to come up the next week. So on Saturday morning the young man had told his story to an assistant district attorney.

Aleck went to the telephone book and looked up the name of the man who had made the charges, Hartwell L. K. Drayne. Yes, the name was in the book, and so was the telephone number. He called the number. There was no answer. He called for several hours, intermittently, and then came to the conclusion that the Draynes were out of the city for the weekend. He wrote the story, and it appeared in all editions of the Sunday newspaper, on the front page.

On Sunday morning, arising at his rooming house and reading the *Times,* Aleck suddenly had a sinking feeling in the pit of his stomach. Where had he gotten those initials? He started to go out to the criminal courts building, then remembered that it was Sunday and the offices would be locked up. He rushed down to a Sixth Avenue drug store, and there looked at the telephone book. Holy of Holies—there were two Hartwell Draynes in the book, a Hartwell Drayne and a Hartwell L. K. Drayne. He panicked. Then he reasoned with himself. His

Drayne was a prominent builder. He looked in the yellow pages. Both Draynes were builders.

So it was Sunday and nothing could be done until Monday, when much might happen. If he had mistaken those initials he was in for a reprimand, and he might be out of a job, and the *Times* might be sued for a large sum of money.

In this situation, Aleck said, there was only one thing to do. He went back to the rooming house, took out a bottle of whiskey and drank as much of it as he could as quickly as he could. Then he lay down and went to sleep, hoping that he would not awaken until eight o'clock the next morning. At nine o'clock the next morning he had his answer, as his trembling fingers picked up the original affidavit in the criminal courts building. The name *was* Hartwell L. K. Drayne, just as he had written. He had just suffered and recovered from the newspaper reporter's nightmare.

Soon Aleck was released from the bondage of the court beat and sent out on general assignments that the city desk considered to be important stories. One day in August he was sent to Coatesville, Chester County, Pennsylvania, where a singularly vicious and brutal crime had been committed.

In Coatesville there lived a Negro named Zach Walker, who was not very bright and who lurked on the fringes of the law. The police were forever dragging him into jail and beating him up, and on several occasions he had been convicted of crimes that he claimed he did not commit. He was, it was generally conceded, the town police force's whipping boy. One day in the summer of 1911 Zach Walker had taken more than he could stand, and when a policeman named Rice decided to drag him into jail and charge him with another crime, he said he would not go, and punctuated his remark with a revolver shot. Policeman Rice fired, too, and the battle was on. When the smoke cleared, Policeman Rice was lying dead and Zach Walker, with a gunshot wound in his leg, was unable to flee before other police and citizens arrived to cart him off to the hospital.

There was very little question about this crime, since there were witnesses to the shootings. Policeman Rice suddenly became the martyr to the cause of law and order, and thousands of sensitive people in Coatesville came to the funeral and followed his coffin to the graveyard, weeping copiously. Then, some five hundred of these citizens repaired to the Coatesville Hospital, where Zach Walker lay on an iron cot, manacled by his ankles to the bed. The representatives of the five hundred could not find the keys to the manacles, so they took Zach and the footboard of his iron cot through the window, down a long hill, and into a field, where in the presence of two thousand white citizens they built a fire under him and roasted him to death.

Soon the New York and Philadelphia newspapers knew of the burning. Aleck was sent by the *Times* to get the story. He went to Coatesville and began milling around with the other reporters. He went to the house of Mayor Shallcross to see what action the municipal authorities intended to take in this shocking case of murder. Mayor Shallcross was at that moment interviewing a youthful reporter from the Philadelphia *Public Ledger* named Walter Davenport, who had become discouraged by the failure of the authorities to take the matter seriously and was making ready to leave without a story.

Suddenly Davenport was aware of Aleck, now grown a little chubby, but not without his light, flowing step. Aleck came into the room, notebook in one hand and a pencil in the other.

"Mr. Shallcross," Aleck said calmly, "I represent the New York *Times*, which must insist that you take immediate measures to fetch the perpetrators of this wholly unnecessary outrage to book or justice or whatever your quaint custom may be here in Coatesville."

The mayor dropped his jaw. If he understood Aleck, which was questionable, he did not know quite what to say. He waved ineffectually toward the door, indicating that he would prefer it if the reporters would go outside.

Aleck bored in.

"My personal feelings and opinions aside, Mr. Shallcross," he said, "it becomes necessary for me to warn you that the New York *Times* will not overlook reticence on your part. Personally I knew neither of the victims of this untoward incident. . . ."

Mr. Shallcross interrupted with a strangled gasp and the reporters were soon outside.

Walter Davenport, the cub from Philadelphia, looked at his temerarious companion in awe.

"Jesus, kid," said he.

"Sh-h-h-h," said Aleck.

And the next day in the New York *Times,* Aleck's story began thus:

> COATESVILLE, PENN., CHESTER COUNTY, August 14 —After a night in which thousands of the people of this borough moved quietly to a field a stone's throw from its borderline, there to stand guard and watch while a dozen or more of its members burned a Negro to death Coatesville went about its business today with every external evidence of peaceful intentions. . . .

Aleck then told the details of the crime in all their horror, including the sight he saw of men rummaging among the charred bits of the bones of Zach Walker with what he described as "pleasure." He gave Coatesville both barrels, and when he was done the reader had a picture of a town of savages who masqueraded sometimes, but only sometimes, as civilized men. The Chamber of Commerce of Coatesville could count the dollars of outside business flying out the window. To anyone who read the *Times* in 1911, Coatesville was a town best skirted by fifty miles.

In April, 1912, when the White Star Liner, *Titanic,* collided with an iceberg and sank, Aleck was sent to Halifax, Nova Scotia, to meet the survivors and cover the story. For several days he filled column after column of the *Times* with his reports. When gambler Herman Rosenthal was shot down in a Broadway restaurant and a police lieutenant was tried and sentenced to the electric chair for the crime, Aleck was chosen among all the *Times* staff, to cover the story. He was, then, the *Times*' star local reporter.

For the next two years Aleck was reporter and feature writer. He continued to live with his sister Julie in the 12th Street rooms for most of this period, until she became engaged and married a printer named Charles Taber. Then he took rooms on West 15th Street and invited various graduates of Hamilton to share them with him. For a time, Al Getman lived with him while training to become a doctor. Other Hamiltonians, old and new, slipped in and out of the premises, given bed and board without thought of payment if they happened to be short of cash at the moment. Aleck kept open house. The one difficulty about his open house was that he worked from late afternoon until two or three o'clock in the morning—even later if one considered the post-final edition poker game in which he was usually a player. When he returned to the apartment sometime in the small hours before dawn, he was quite likely to awaken any and all who were on the premises and engage them in extended conversation about the events of the day. After an hour or so of this he would drift off to his room to bed, and the household would again be serene until around noon.

Between 1912 and 1914, the Phalanx crowd fell on evil days and it took the combined efforts of all relatives of all Phalanxers to bail out the old homestead, for the sheriff was called in to foreclose and portion out the property. The matter was finally resolved, however. For a time Walter Woollcott moved to New York where he prospered, but none of the Woollcott family received any support. Then one night he dropped dead in the street. Aleck left the *Times* offices long enough to make arrangements for burial of the body, and that was that. Aleck never wasted any affection on his father and in letters to his friends he almost never referred to Walter Woollcott. In later years when he mentioned his father it was only in the most disparaging of terms.

As for his mother, he was sorry for her and he maintained a reservoir of affection and a strong sense of family responsibility. As his affairs prospered on the *Times* he took on the greater burden of her support; by 1914 it was settled that she would never again leave the Phalanx except for an occasional visit, perhaps. This was her life, it had been so for twenty years, and she was content with it.

Aleck worked hard at his newspaper job. He was brought in from the general assignments desk to become a rewrite man, which was the most important assignment on the city desk side of the newspaper. He was offered an opportunity to go to Paris as the bureau chief of the *Times*. He turned down the job and it went, instead, to Walter Duranty, Woollcott's close friend, poker companion, and chief conversational companion in those long nights on the death watch when the newspaper was ready for its final edition, and in the saloon and coffee sessions afterward.

Aleck kept up his interest in the theatrical world quite unbeknown to the staff of the New York *Times,* or at least to the management. He went to the theater two or three times each week. He read every book and every newspaper and every magazine article written about the theater. He studied plays and players, and continued to yearn to become a drama critic.

In later years the New York *Times'* method of choosing a drama critic would be to bring him up from within the ranks in the newspaper drama section or to go outside and hire another critic. In 1913, however, the drama department of the *Times* consisted of one man, critic Adolph Klauber. The reason for this was simple enough. The *Times* was far from the most profitable or best newspaper in New York. The *Sun,* the *World,* the *American,* were all far more powerful. There was no money to be wasted on the theater, and so Klauber did the job alone.

Sometimes, of course, there were multiple openings on Broadway, and then some reporter must be deputized to help Klauber cover the drama. But Aleck never did this, at least as far as Carr Van Anda knew; he was totally unaware of Aleck's interest in the theater. He was much more aware of Aleck's interest in becoming either a full time feature writer or an editorial writer, a purpose Aleck pursued by enrolling in courses at Columbia University, ostensibly in search of a master's degree. But the Columbia courses put too great a strain on him. It was a long way uptown and he found himself not nearly so interested in resuming his former education as he had thought he might be. He lasted through one semester and dropped out.

Aleck had been with the *Times* about three years when he saw a play at the Fulton Theater which increased his love for the drama, but also appealed to him greatly for its own sake. This was *The Yellow Jacket,* which translated into English and into American stage ways some of the techniques of the Chinese drama, including the use of a chorus, or interlocutor to tell the audience what the action on stage represented in terms of the total story, and a properties man, who acted as curtain, among other services, and changed the props while the actors were on stage — both common factors in the traditional Chinese drama. Aleck remembered this play; it was quite the hit of the fall season of 1912 but it was far more than that for him, it was an entirely new experience, and one he would not forget.

Aleck was a most valuable man to the *Times* and he was appreciated by Carr Van Anda. One day Adolph Klauber, the *Times* critic, announced that he was going to marry actress Jane Cowl and become a theatrical producer. Van Anda had no particular interest in the theater; the drama section was one that he regarded as something of a necessary nuisance. He did believe it would be helpful to have someone with a very good sense of newspaper judgment in the job, and so he asked Alexander Woollcott if he would like to take on the task. Aleck had wanted the job so much and had considered it to be so far above his station at that moment, that he had not even joined the list of applicants for the post, but when Van Anda offered it, Aleck accepted with the feeling that his every prayer had been answered. At twenty-seven, he was handed on a silver platter exactly the job to which he aspired.

VIII

ALECK WAS NOT LONG IN SETTLING into the shoes of his predecessor and making them his own. His first main assignment as drama critic—a most welcome one—was to take a trip to Europe to learn what he could about the season in London and to acquire a veneer for cultured discussion of the theater, which the authorities at the *Times* thought he needed, aware that they had hired an excellent reporter as drama critic, but not aware that this reporter's first love was the theater and that his store of knowledge about the theater was already impressive.

He went to Europe in June, to France, to England, to Germany. His manners, Hamiltonian classical education, his care in choosing the words of the English, German and French languages, his bearing and his open-handed friendliness were such that he was readily recognized, particularly in London, as one of the acceptable Americans. The other kind had been charging back and forth across the Atlantic for several years, collecting castles and trading bags of gold for coronets. (The British with their delicate sense of bookkeeping, were glad for the commerce, but they had no more use for American business types than for their own—and they would not even allow Sir Thomas Lipton, the millionaire yachtsman whose hands were soiled only with his tea, to come inside the premises of the Royal Yacht Squadron.)

Aleck was in Europe as war clouds gathered on the horizon, in that last genteel summer before the world changed. He was traveling on June 28 when the Archduke Franz Ferdinand was assassinated at Sarajevo. He was home, however, by July 28, when Austria declared war on Serbia and the powers of Europe were unleashed to dash for each other's throats.

The New York critic's lot in 1914 was a busy one. Not only were thirty legitimate theaters in operation, but the critic was also in charge of reportage about the world of vaudeville and the growing cinema. Aleck leaped into the stream of the amusement world with the flick of a trout released from a hatchery and immediately he was swimming strong.

The world of dramatic criticism in the second decade of the twentieth century was a smaller world, in a sense, than it would be a half century later when there were fewer theaters, fewer plays, and fewer critics. In the fashion of the *Times,* Aleck was unknown to the public. The management believed that the newspaper and not any of its employees was the important entity, and its articles were unsigned. In show business Aleck was known as the critic, but not to the general newspaper reader.

Aleck Woollcott brought much to the American theater besides a solid background in its history and an excellent sense of taste. He brought a total independence of spirit, and this was rare in the theatrical world where the newspaper relationship to the theater was very much like the present day newspaper relationship to the motion picture industry. The producers did not want reviews of the plays, they wanted puff notices. They were willing to pay well for such puffs, in advertising and in bribes to the theater critics, and they had been doing so with great success for a number of years. Good critics existed: Percy Hammond, Burns Mantle and George Jean Nathan might speak out, but the lesser critics of the lesser newspapers were inclined to write simple reports of what they saw on the stage without regard to the quality of offering or of performance. There was no open criticism in most New York newspapers as there was, for example, in the sports pages of the Dodgers, Giants, and Yankees. A sports writer of the period who wrote with the fear and trembling of the theatrical writers would have been hooted off the page in a week, but the theater-going public, by and large, did not look for its criticism of the drama in the newspaper columns. Aleck's independence of spirit, coupled with the search for excellence of Carr Van Anda and the free hand given him by Adolph Ochs, the proprietor of the Chattanooga *Times* who had bought the half-dead New York *Times* just before the turn of the century, were to bring about an incandescent uprising and a basic change in the American theater in not too long a time.

Aleck began slowly, as befitted the youngest critic in the theater circle of New York. He did not like the flaccid writing of his peers, particularly that of William Winter, the dean of the theater critics, whose almost daily dullities appeared in the New York *Tribune,* but before making an outright attack he established himself as a man who knew whereof he spoke.

One of Aleck's first moves was to ask that Brock Pemberton, a junior member of the *World's* drama staff, be hired away by the *Times,* so that the newspaper could cover more than one play on one day with an informed review. Carr Van Anda agreed. That autumn of 1914, while Aleck was reviewing the first nights of the most important dramas, Pemberton was either on the road, looking over the tryouts of coming plays, or reviewing summer stock. It was possible, then, for the New York *Times* to be simultaneously at Northampton, Massachusetts, checking on the latest offering of the third season of the Northampton Players, and at the opening of G. Bernard Shaw's *Pygmalion* at the Park.

"All that was essential," Aleck wrote on the night of October 12, "in cast and production for its hearty success in London is most happily reproduced in its preparation for the enjoyment of New York. In chief it presents Mrs. Patrick Campbell, who is delightful in the delightful role of Eliza Doolittle, and, in the part of Professor Higgins, Philip Merivale rather more than reconciles one to the fact that Sir Herbert Tree did not elect to come over with the rest of the company. And the play itself is as simply entertaining a piece as the author has ever deigned to write."

Soon, the *Times* theater page was the talk of New York for Aleck offered a new kind of reviewing. On November 3 he reviewed *Outcast* with Elsie Ferguson. He told its history, and in the first sentence praised Elsie Ferguson's "able and sincere" performance. The second paragraph of the review discussed author Hubert Henry Davies' intent, which Aleck found laudable. The third paragraph contained a time bomb: "His play is sincere, straightforward, intelligent, unaffected. That is why it is interesting from first to last. Also, that is why it is cheerless."

Later, having told the plot—a man's difficulty with his mistress—Aleck returned to his critique:

> It is Mr. Davies's disposition to study and picture moods that, while it provides him with interesting material, heightens the impression that *Outcast* is indeterminate.
>
> *Outcast* is also curiously and troublesomely lacking in what may be called filling. In his intellectual absorption in his main study it seems as though Mr. Davies had forgotten to add those little touches of the atmospheric, the incidentally amusing, the casual, the irrelevant, which may do nothing to push a story on its way, but which often serve to give succeeding scenes the light and shade patchwork quality of life.
>
> Miss Ferguson apparently does not seek to have the play seen in her shadow, but she meets to the full the demands of a varied and by no means easy role. Here is a discreet, intelligent and artistic performance. It is apace with her marked progress in the theatre. Mr. Cherry is fully satisfactory in a part immeasurably better suited to him than the one in which he appeared at the same theatre two months ago.
>
> Mr. Davies has not tried to make Geoffrey a hero and Mr. Cherry makes no furtive attempt to defeat the playwright's intentions. Miss Lestle is not blessed with a comfortable role. She is asked to present a portrait which Mr. Davies himself never finished.
>
> But the play is essentially Miss Ferguson's. She is one of the reasons why it is interesting, for *Outcast* is decidedly that. It is also unpleasant. It could not honestly be anything else.

In terms of a critique Aleck's study was balanced and he quite leaned over in his attempt to be fair and decent to the players. It was only the play he did not like, and he said so. Yet, by no stretch of the imagination could this be called a "selling review" and selling reviews were the demands of the shopkeepers along the rialto.

Aleck was softhearted about players. He knew what went into the portrayal of a role, for he had played enough himself. He admired the people of the theater. While he was in Paris in the summer of 1914, Burns Mantle had attempted to give the neophyte playgoer a bit of sound, paternal advice. He must never consort with the people of the theater, said Mantle. He must stand off and regard them at all times with a cold and fishy eye. Only thus could he achieve the proper perspective, and not be swayed by his involvement with the people and productions they represented.

This was one approach to drama criticism. It was much like the approach of some political writers to politics. They never engaged in politics, they never thought seriously about the political factors involved in government decisions; they refused to become involved with politicians on a personal basis lest these involvements color their views.

Aleck could not accept such a view of the responsibilities of criticism. He felt he must know all about his people, all about what they were doing, and all about the theater in order to do his best job. He was stagestruck, there was no question about it. He was not a spectator, in the sense that he stood off and watched the activity from afar. He was very definitely a part of the theater, just as the audience was a part of the theater. He was actor. He had been prop man. He would be playwright, and he would always bend over backward in order to be kind to the players. His answer to Mantle on the day that they had their friendly talk in Paris was to announce that he was going off to call on the immortal Sarah Bernhardt, which he did. And in a very short time Aleck achieved a reputation as one of the most soft-hearted critics on Broadway.

Yet that was not all of Aleck as critic.

He also achieved a reputation for running the most spirited theater section among all the New York newspapers. Aleck was twenty-seven years old and he was fast becoming the most prominent critic in the city. Burns Mantle wrote of his place among others in the winter of 1915, saying Aleck "became the most talked-of and the widest-read dramatic critic in town."

Aleck petitioned Carr Van Anda to give him a place in the Sunday paper, too, and soon turned the space into a reflective weekly essay called "Second Thoughts on First Nights," which was a compendium of critical afterthought, historical information about the theater, and juicy but kindly gossip about the people of the theatrical world.

Aleck was a friendly soul, and he was well-liked and well-respected in the theater by actors, directors, fellow-critics, and everyone except the jealous and the producers. These malcontents soon began to grumble about the intractability of young Woollcott, although they were forced to admit that his praise, when it came, was worthy enough to use in the one-inch advertisements boxed together like so many little squares of chocolate in the daily *Times* theater pages. When he praised a performance or a play he did not stint. Then and all his life he was more inclined to overenthusiasm than to any cutting remarks, although he was quite capable of slashing a performance.

Loudest of the grumblers were the Shubert Brothers, former haberdashers of Syracuse who had acquired control of a string of theaters across the nation and now considered that their claim to Broadway extended from 14th Street as far north as the last marquee. In March, 1915, Aleck fell afoul of the haberdashers of Broadway, who took the eminently sane merchandising position that a play was just like a silk shirt and ought to be properly advertised, not examined.

The play that set off the fight—for it was that—was *Taking Chances*, an adaptation of a French comedy. It opened on March 17 at the 39th Street Theater. Fifteen critics, the representatives of the daily and weekly newspapers of New York, attended the opening. Eight found the play hardly worth the effort, six said nothing at all except to give the plot and name the players, and one said he liked the show.

Aleck wrote that it was not a very amusing farce, describing parts of it as "quite absurd" and said there were "moments when a puzzled audience wonders what it is all about." This, in Aleck's fashion, was restrained criticism of a very bad play.

The Shuberts were lying in wait for Aleck and the New York *Times* that night. In *the same issue* that his review appeared, the Shuberts caused to be published in all the newspapers, the following advertisement:

TO THE PUBLIC

Do not believe everything you see in the notices today.
And though some of th... ng in humor, may
...ere there is some-
... *Taking Chances,*
...ances in extend-
...ression is decid-
...*nces* just as the
... the play scored
...its ever known

...e Management

...e *Times.*
... one of the more

...s *not* one of the
... *Times* was young
... eager to pick a
...*merican* and the
...ng and evening
... the entire indus-
...ewspaper to its
... relatively small

... a duel to the
... that Alexander
... to review the
... sensible thing,
...w York *Times*
... Mr. Woollcott
...ered from the

The first move of the Shuberts was to request through their press agent that another staff member be assigned to the next Shubert opening at the Maxine Elliott Theater. Carr Van Anda replied that the play was an important one and deserved the attentions of its drama critic, Mr. Alexander Woollcott. Then

Charles Dillingham, manager of the Shuberts' Hippodrome sent tickets for his next opening to Van Anda, but said reluctantly that if they were presented by Alexander Woollcott they would not be honored. Van Anda sent the tickets back.

Aleck went to the box office of the Maxine Elliott Theater and bought tickets for the opening of the next play there, acting on instructions from Van Anda. On opening night when he presented the tickets, he was turned away from the door by Jake Shubert. So he went back to the *Times.* (This occurred twenty-two times.)

Now a decision had to be made. Either the Shuberts would dictate who would review plays in their theaters or the *Times* would make that decision. From Carr Van Anda's point of view, that was all there was to it. From Aleck's point of view there was a good deal more because if he was not backed by his newspaper his writing career might well be ended. He was coming along, but he was not nearly well-enough established to take a stand against society and survive. Never before had a newspaper elected to stand up and fight when threatened by the theater men. Would the *Times* fight now?

The issue was decided by the owner of the *Times,* Adolph Ochs. It had to be decided on that level in 1915 because there were no precedents, and if Van Anda fought it was bound to cost the *Times* money.

Van Anda explained the position to Ochs, who elected to fight. Aleck could now be sure of being backed.

Accompanied by the *Times'* lawyers Aleck went to Judge Nathan Bijur's court and secured an injunction against discrimination by the Shuberts under the Civil Rights Law of the state of New York. The injunction was granted on Saturday, April 3, and on that same night, presenting it, Aleck appeared at the Shubert theater to review a revival of *Trilby,* a four-act play by Paul M. Potter, adapted from a best-selling du Maurier novel of twenty years earlier.

Aleck presented his usual balanced and sensible review of the play. He knew whereof he wrote because *Trilby* had thrilled him as a boy and he had seen the Potter play before. His review was gentle and it praised most members of the cast for their performance, but it was not a rave.

He permitted himself a single puckish comment on his difficulties with the Shuberts.

> However the big audience that picked its way through the snow to the Shubert theater last evening seemed largely made up of those who did know their *Trilby* well and the reception accorded to the revival was a notably hearty one. Indeed, *Trilby* in its present performance has much to please, and is well worth going to see—even if you have to get in by the use of an injunction.

The Shuberts, however, were determined to destroy Aleck or make him crawl back into their theaters bearing a tray of puffs before him, and they went to court to plead that they had the right to exclude anyone they wished from the theater. They cited Aleck's extreme youth, and they noted that he had only been a drama critic for a year. Shubert lawyer Max D. Steuer presented the producers' case in court on April 7, when it was to be decided whether to make the injunction permanent or to vacate it.

> The case of Mr. Woollcott could very well be disposed of by calling attention to the fact that this court has no power to grant an injunction restraining a theatrical manager or owner from excluding any person from his theater. Messrs. Shubert do not desire the impression to go forth that they have arbitrarily or as a result of some whim or caprice, excluded the critic of the New York *Times* from their theatres. They have therefore directed their counsel not to stand solely upon legal propositions, but to call your attention to the facts in the matter and to show that they would have been fully justified in thrusting Mr. Woollcott from their premises.
>
> The Messrs. Shubert have no quarrel with the New York *Times*. They have no grievance against the publication. They recognize in it a great instrument for good; they realize that it is an important and influential paper with a large circulation. They feel it justifiably has a splendid reputation and is entitled to the respect of the public. Their grievance is entirely with Mr. Woollcott, the plaintiff

> in this action. He has, according to their view of it, solely as the result of prejudice, malice, and bias against them as individuals, made use of his opportunity, afforded him by his position with the New York *Times,* to injure their enterprises, to adversely affect their interests, to impair the respect to which they are entitled from the public by reason of their position in their vocation and to hold them up to ridicule and contempt.

The Shuberts cited twenty cases in which Aleck had reviewed their plays unfavorably. (One could feel the blood dripping from every pore of Jake and Lee Shubert as they read the reviews and quivered with rage in anticipation of the evil effects of these reviews at the box office.)

The facts, however, were that the Shuberts were citing anything and everything negative that had appeared in the *Times* in a number of months. Five of the plays they mentioned were not reviewed by Aleck at all, and two of those were reviewed before he became the *Times* drama critic. So it was apparent that the Shuberts were simply trying to stifle independent drama criticism. They were particularly incensed against the *Times.* Why? Because they regarded the *Times* as an adder they clutched to their open breast, an adder they had fed so well for so long.

Said Lee Shubert, indignantly:

> During all this period that this man has been writing these things about our plays . . . the New York *Times* received on an average of from $600 to $700 a week for advertising the very plays which this man condemned. We paid the paper on an average of $35,000 a year. If the *Times* believed that this man's criticisms were accurate, that they were fair and honest reports, then the *Times* should not have advertised these plays to the public so that the public would attend them and take $35,000 a year for so doing.
>
> I have said that I have been a theatrical manager and producer for upwards of twenty years. During that time, for the purpose of enabling me to judge plays, their

desirability, their quality of attracting the public and pleasing and amusing it, I have visited theatres all over the world. I have made it my business to see and read plays and have become thoroughly familiar with plays, with those qualities which go to make up a play. In the choice of plays for production purposes, I have exercised the best judgment of which I am capable. The court will readily understand that we do not select plays for the purpose of losing our money or wasting it, and that we make an honest endeavor to select such as will please. I have a competent staff of play readers and use every amount of best judgment upon the plays that we produce. We, of course, have had our share of failures, but also our share of successes, but from no other writer have we received the universal condemnation which this man accords, not only to our productions, but to such as are produced in our theatres.

In other words, since the Shuberts were experts, what right did this pipsqueak have to come along and gainsay them?

The injunction was upheld in the New York court but the Shuberts were now thoroughly aroused—the more so because the *Times* on April 1 had cut off their advertising. The Shuberts said that if they could not advertise in the *Times* then why should the *Times* critic be allowed to enter the Shubert theaters? They took the case to a higher court, and there they won a reversal of the lower decision. A man could be turned away from a theater in New York because the owners objected to his opinions about the plays, the court said.

So Aleck was again barred from Shubert theaters, but the Shuberts soon learned that their victory was no victory at all. In Albany, Senator Ogden Mills of New York City introduced a bill to make it a crime for a theater owner to discriminate against a reviewer, or any other person, without a very good reason—and the reason would not include unfavorable reviewing.

Most unkindly of all, the other citizens of Broadway refused to follow the Shubert lead. Instead of ignoring Aleck Woollcott they began courting him. His was the most widely read column in the city, his "Second Thoughts on First Nights" was given four columns instead of three half columns, and his salary was increased from $60 a week to $100 a week. Instead of losing money because of the vanished Shubert advertising, the *Times* was making more money than before because of the increased advertising from others and the increased circulation and attention to its drama section. The Shuberts made of Aleck, overnight, a celebrity and an unqualified success.

The battle lasted for a year. It was not usual for pure, unalloyed justice to triumph in a business society, but here the cause of justice was tempered with gold; it became very bad business for the Shubert advertising to be absent from the *Times* and there was only one way it could be returned.

Following the same aggressive, determined, independent policies in other departments that it was following in the drama department, the *Times* picked up steam and circulation. Toward the end of 1915, Oliver Morosco, the California theatrical manager, who had for many years given the Shuberts exclusive rights to the staging of all his productions, looked at the circulation figures of New York newspapers and discovered that the *Times* was selling 300,000 copies daily. His enthusiasm for the Shubert cause was negligible and now it became undiscernible. He announced that in the future it was going to be more convenient for him to parcel out the rights to his plays to theatrical producers who had no hampering and harmful rules attached to their houses. The Shuberts heard and understood.

A flunkie was sent to the *Times* to see if Shubert advertising would be accepted, and was told that it would be as soon as it was clear that any person designated by the *Times* management to review the plays would be seated in the Shubert theaters. Aleck attended the next Shubert opening night. He was undisturbed, and the advertising began to reappear. The battle was over.

Aleck was a good winner. He never took unfair advantage of his victory and he did not rub it in. He reviewed the plays of the Shuberts in 1916 with exactly the same eye he cast on the plays of others. He was not jaundiced. He allowed himself to become enthusiastic whenever there was anything to be enthusiastic about. He was still the youngest drama critic on

Broadway, and the most aggressive of them all, in seeking new formulas for the interest of his readers and new ways of approaching the delights of the theater.

In January, 1916, Aleck decided to send an interviewer from the *Times* city staff to Portland, Maine, where old William Winter was living in retirement after leaving the *Tribune*. Ada Rehan, one of the grand ladies of the American theater, had just died, and Aleck was trying to secure something new for his Sunday theater page. Winter responded promptly to Aleck's request, and equally negatively.

> If you were to send an interviewer in quest of me, his quest would be in vain, even if he happened to get to me, which, probably, he would *not*. I do not like interviews nor interviewers; and I do not consider it proper that men of letters who earn a living—such as it is—by writing should be asked to give away their only means of livelihood.

Having delivered that rebuke, Winter then invited Aleck to use whatever he wished from Winter's many writings about Ada Rehan, and guided him to the pertinent books by chapter and by page.

Aleck saved that letter (although he saved few other letters in 1916) and cherished the idea propounded by William Winter. He was to follow Winter's advice in later years; never would an interview appear in the drama section of the *Times* as long as he was editor; only on one or two occasions would he ever grant interviews and then only under the most severe pressures. He came to prize and value the writer's time and privacy so that he demanded fees for all that he did—even if much of the time he gave away the money.

In the spring of 1916, Aleck scored a major triumph when he created a special Shakespearian supplement for the New York *Times* of March 12. The major article was his own, a discussion of the great odds against Will Shakespeare amounting to anything if he had tried to sell his wares in the theatrical marketplace of 1916. By autumn he was branching out in the Sunday column. One day he wrote an article about "how to go on the stage" with tips for young hopefuls. A few weeks later he produced an article on "The Promising Actor":

> . . . There are precious few producers who give any heed whatever to the artistic nurture of the youngsters who pass in and out of their employ. Mr. Belasco has taken a few actresses and brought them up systematically in the way they should go, but he has done no more than that, and he is almost alone. Since the palmy days of Palmer and Daly, precious few producers have had enough stability of program and continuity of policy to look beyond the immediate needs of the production in hand . . .
>
> The actor-in-the-making is allowed to shift for himself and develop as best he can, in the roles which chance throws his way.
>
> . . . It sometimes happens when we on the other side of the footlights have caught the glow of the real fire and applauded wildly with hand and typewriter, that the young actor, bearing his blushing honors thick upon him, hunts up the manager next day, pokes him in the eye, demands a larger dressing room, asks to have his salary trebled, and is never heard of again.

A true professional, he was concerned about the theater in all its aspects. Could he have developed such concern by following Burns Mantle's sage advice to spurn association with the people of the theater?

IX

THE 1916 VICTORY over the Shuberts established Alexander Woollcott as more than the youngest critic on Broadway; it made of him a celebrity who was pointed out on the street and in restaurants as the fellow who had beaten the most powerful producers in the United States. New doors were opened to Aleck; the magazines asked him to write for them, and book publishers began to believe that even though the young critic was *very* young, still he might have a book in him. He did not, at that time, but soon one was to be created, a combination of magazine articles of a type that would later be known as the "as-told-to" school, although these really were *as told to* and took the form of conversations. The subject was Minnie Maddern Fiske, the grand lady of the American stage in 1917.

Mrs. Fiske was then in her middle fifties. She had been in command of the American theater for several years, and she and her husband, Harrison Grey Fiske, prince of American playwrights, had taken one play after another to Broadway, where, after a successful run, they would take the play on the road themselves. Consequently Mrs. Fiske was known from San Diego to Sauk City by Americans of almost every age and fiscal condition.

For years publishers had been trying to get Minnie Maddern Fiske to write her memoirs, or to write a book of How To Do It for the theater, or to write anything at all. Always Mrs. Fiske had refused. She also refused to have much to do with the many reporters and writers the editors and publishers sent around to call on her, until Alexander Woollcott came along. Then there was an electric spark and from it was kindled the idea of a series of articles for the *Century* magazine and a book for The Century Publishing Company. There was something in Aleck that appealed to ladies who had passed the threshold of the wandering eye, and there was something in them that appealed to Aleck. Years later Janet Flanner was to call this the theme "dominant of his social emotional existence" and to say "that he liked intelligent ripe ladies and their company and they liked his."

Even when it was agreed that Aleck and Mrs. Fiske would collaborate on what she came to call "our book," it was not an easy task for the writing member of the team. Mrs. Fiske was a busy woman. She had played Hester Crewe in Mr. Fiske's play of the same name; Marie Deloche in his *The Queen of Liars;* Nora in Henrik Ibsen's *A Doll's House;* Gilberte in Mr. Fiske's *Frou-frou;* Hedda in Ibsen's *Hedda Gabler;* Nell Sanders in Edward Sheldon's *Salvation Nell;* Mary Page in Sheldon's *The High Road,* and in a score of other notable plays written by her husband, herself or the growing coterie of American playwrights.

In 1914 she played Lady Betty in *Lady Betty Martingale, or The Adventures of a Lively Hussy,* by John Luther Long, and after a very successful New York run, she and Mr. Fiske took the show on the road. They returned in 1915 and there was a bit of time for relaxation at the Fiske country house near Waterbury, Connecticut, before work began on *Erstwhile Susan* by Marian de Forest, which Mr. Fiske would produce and in which Mrs. Fiske would star. It was agreed that if Aleck would come out to the country, or make himself available when he could match his free time with hers, they could cooperate on the articles and book, and that is how it was done.

First it was at supper after the play, in a tryout of *Erstwhile Susan,* and there Mrs. Fiske told Aleck why she did not think repertory theater would ever be—or should ever be—popular in the United States. They ate an omelet and Mrs. Fiske said she did not like repertory because it taught young actors to play six parts badly each year rather than one part well.

Second, while at a house the Fiskes had taken in New Jersey with a mongrel that was largely Great Dane at their feet, Mrs.

Fiske talked about Henrik Ibsen's popularity in the United States, and lamented the failure of any American critic to appreciate him. They talked of Tyrone Power (the elder) and George Arliss, with whom she had played in Ibsen's works. And so the meetings continued.

Aleck stayed up late at night, after his work at the theater and worked on his articles, and he got up early in the mornings and worked on them again. They were simple and unpretentious and the author was subordinated to the subject in every one. They ran in the *Century* for five straight months beginning in January, 1917, and as soon as they were finished the book publishing side of The Century Company took the material, plus some additional notes Aleck had prepared, and made a book of them. Even at the end of it, Aleck brought out Mrs. Fiske as the heroine and himself only as the foil.

> I told her once that her performance as Lona in *The Pillars of Society* was the finest acting I had ever seen. She smiled her thanks, but eyed me critically. Had I seen her play *Hedda Gabler*? No, I had not.
>
> "Ah," she replied, "then you do not know how well I *can* act. And did you ever see Duse?" (Eleanora Duse, Mrs. Fiske's ideal of the greatest American actress).
>
> "No," I made answer, somewhat crestfallen.
>
> "Ho! Ho! Then what do *you* know about acting?" said Mrs. Fiske.

Just prior to doing the articles with Mrs. Fiske, Aleck's romantic interest was centered on a young lady named Amelie Randall, who was a pretty twenty-year-old whom he had known for three years. He took her to the theater and to dinner and to parties, but the romance was hampered by her youth and by his awkward hours for courtship of a gentle young girl, who, after all, could scarcely be seen about after midnight, and who did not much appreciate going to the theater with an escort and then being sent home alone in a taxi just before the end of the play, missing the climax, so her escort could rush to a rented room in the theatrical district and begin typing out his criticism.

Aleck's romance with Amelie was a stormy one and it ended just about at the time he was doing the articles with Mrs. Fiske; Amelie either tired of waiting for Aleck to ask her to marry him or she tired of the idea of living as a hostage to first nights. She married a successful surgeon who might be expected to get up early in the mornings but who at least would be at home for dinner once in a while.

But it wasn't the desertion of Amelie that caught Aleck's interest in the spring of 1917; it was the surge of patriotic fervor which swept across the land after April when the United States Congress declared war on Germany.

Aleck decided he wanted to go to war. It would have been very easy for him to have stayed out of it, had he been so inclined, much easier than it was to get in. The life he led had added several apparent years to Aleck's age, he was as portly as a forty-year-old because he ate well and drank well and stayed up very late and got no exercise, but this was not a problem. The army was making a specialty of taking the fat off other young men. Aleck was extremely myopic, which destroyed any hopes of securing a commission, although his education fitted him for one, nor could he expect to join an infantry unit. He might be given a job as a clerk, but the chances were that he would never get overseas to fight, and Aleck wanted to go overseas. So he found his way into a unit of the medical service in the spring of 1917, enlisting in May along with a group of some 150 youths whom he characterized as "bouncing undergraduates from Princeton and Rutgers who had enlisted early in May in order to escape the June exams," and officers who were staff doctors from New York hospitals, hastily uniformed and commissioned.

For two months the unit sweltered on Governor's Island, waiting for transportation to France and practicing close order drill on the hotter days—or so it seemed. Hospital No. 8 it was called.

Aleck spent the time brushing up on his spoken French,

which was already very good, or had been when he left Hamilton seven years earlier. He also caught up on his correspondence, mending a few fences he had left untended during the busy weeks just past.

Finally, the army had everything assembled for Base Hospital No. 8 and it was time to sail.

The troops were moved aboard an old ship called the *Saratoga,* in the dark of night, and they waited for the morning, which was sailing day. Aleck told the story later in a broadcast:

> On that day a foul old craft called the *Saratoga,* one of the first transports of the AEF, had started at dawn from its pier in Hoboken with all the troops hidden below decks lest the good German citizens, pausing with steins of beer in mid-air, should be so shrewd as to suspect that this country was shipping soldiers to France. We got no further than the lee of Staten Island, where we cast anchor and waited for the signal from the other transports in the convoy. At high noon we were still there with no cloud in the sky and nary a breeze to ripple the sea. From the promenade deck, a group of us idly watched the liner *Panama* just in from Colon, bearing down on us on her way across the harbor. It fascinated me to see how little room so big a ship seemed to need in which to manoeuvre. "Now look," I said, "wouldn't you swear that boat was going to run into us?" Just then she rammed us, she did, and sank us with all our equipment. She rammed us so hard, in fact, that for a while we stuck on her bow like a hunk of cheese on the point of a knife—a merciful interlude during which all of those who had not been killed by the actual collision could be taken off, dry and whole, by one or another of the lighters which emerged from nowhere and swarmed around us like water-bugs. It was sundown by the time these scattered detachments were reassembled on Governor's Island, which we had left only the day before—dauntless crusaders who had marched off to fight the Hun

but who, in our first attempt, had got no further than Staten Island . . .

In spite of this disappointing beginning, Aleck did get to France, whole and healthy, aboard another transport, the *Finland,* after a short delay while the army reoutfitted Base Hospital No. 8.

Theoretically, Private Woollcott was supposed to spend the voyage in the hold, which had been fitted out with bunks for the enlisted men, but he did not care much for that idea, so he offered his talents as a French tutor to the officers of the unit. Major Edmund Devol, a New York City internist who had known Aleck in civil life, was the point of contact. Through Eddie Devol, as Private Woollcott knew his superior officer, the lessons were arranged and it seemed that so many officers wished to perfect their knowledge of medical French that Private Woollcott was constrained to take his meals with them to save time and so late was he occupied in the evenings with this useful education that it would have been unseemly for him to have crawled back down between decks, turning on lights and awakening the troops, so he slept on cots in various cabins.

On the last morning, off the coast of France, there was a sudden alert, and the soldiers donned their lifevests. Aleck had his patented rubber diving suit, which probably would have taken him straight to the bottom. When he appeared on deck in this contraption some uncouth companion remarked that he looked like a pregnant mermaid.

Fortunately there was no need to test his lifesaving device, since the submarines disappeared and the transport headed in to dock safely at St. Nazaire and unload its cargo of warriors.

Toward the end of the voyage he wrote his sister Julie, telling her how it was "rather fun" to roll up in army blankets and poncho and sleep on the forecastle deck under the stars, and how it was "not half bad" to come up at four o'clock in the morning and stand in front of a hose and get a bath. Of course, he did not actually say that he, Alexander Woollcott, did these things; he simply commented on them as being available. He did sing in the choir at the morning services one

Sunday, to the great amusement of everyone who knew him. Then, suddenly, it was time to polish shoes and side-arms and get ready for the landing.

Altogether, as far as Aleck was concerned, it had been a very decent voyage.

X

ALECK'S WAR BEGAN a little less auspiciously.

To save transport and create an impression on the jaded infantry that the medical corps could hold its own, on the day that the troops of Base Hospital No. 8 landed at St. Nazaire, the commanding officer marched the men thirty-five kilometers under an August sun to the old Breton village of Savenay. Thirty-five kilometers was twenty-one miles, a good clip for a bulging drama critic who had spent most of the past month lying on his back on a cot, smoking cigarettes and telling stories about the ladies and gentlemen of the theater to an eager crew of officers. But Aleck did not whimper. He had come to be a soldier and if this was what it meant, he would accept it. He was very serious in his approach to soldiering, or to its essentials, or to what he considered to be its essentials.

There was some difference between Aleck's definition of military essentials and that of General Pershing. He was content enough to arise at 5:15 and do what needed to be done, whether driving the ambulance, or running the operating room, or working on kitchen police peeling potatoes or working as a hospital orderly, holding down spinal meningitis patients or doctoring syphilitics. He did all these things. He kept records for a very short while—and that he hated. He was put to work unloading boxcars, and that he liked. He was employed in the morgue, measuring corpses for coffins, and this did not upset him. He was sent out on temporary duty to do jobs such as finding a harmonium for the chaplain. He was happy to go out on foraging expeditions, to buy supplies from the farmers in the countryside, and he spent part of one afternoon importuning, with no success at all, an old woman into organizing a berry pickers league to harvest the wild raspberries that lined the road, which the French had always scorned.

Heywood and Ruth Hale Broun tracked Aleck down in September and came to see him in the cubicle where Aleck held forth during working hours, presiding over a bottle of port wine. Aleck told them of the little excitement of the day before, which represented his basic difference with the army. It was customary at the hospital for an officer to be assigned each day to take the enlisted men out for a short bit of close order drill, just to remind them that although this was a hospital, they were still soldiers.

On the day before, the officer in charge had found Aleck in his cubicle, and had insisted that he come out to drill. The officer was a famous oral surgeon from New York.

"I refuse to be drilled by a dentist," said Aleck—or that was how Broun reported it. And he got away with it.

Broun also saw with his own eyes another of Aleck's small objections to the military order. While they were drinking port and talking, into the room marched Major Edmund Devol. Aleck was sitting in the only comfortable chair in the room and the Brouns were sitting in what was left. The only other perch was the top of a footlocker.

"I think," said the officer, "that just as a matter of form you ought to stand up and salute. What if Pershing were to pop in suddenly?"

"Eddie is suffering from delusions of grandeur," Aleck explained to the Brouns, without moving.

As army billets went, the old girls' seminary into which they had thrown Base Hospital No. 8 was not bad at all, said Private Alexander Woollcott. Along with the other enlisted men he objected to the rank system which prevented the army nurses from fraternizing socially with the enlisted men, but there were the French girls, and Aleck was constantly being visited by various friends who held every rank from YMCA civilian to colonel. On his first night in Savenay, Aleck had stumbled onto a tiny *buvette* or bar, run by a Mère Cocaud, and here he made his headquarters, when off duty. He went there for dinners of sausage, omelette, French pancakes, and honey and wine. The price for a dinner was perhaps three francs, or about 70 cents, and it was worth going a mile to eat. One day in September, five Hamilton graduates got together for dinner, enjoyed themselves immensely, and sent a postcard, signed unsteadily, to Dr. Stryker, president of the college. Aleck kept in touch with the Brouns, who were spending most of their time in Paris, and they invited him to spend Christmas in Paris when he had a five day pass. They said he would see Wythe Williams and Walter Duranty, old friends from New York. They drew a cross on the sketch of his room in their apartment on the Boulevard Raspail. That, they said, was where he would fall when he collapsed from overeating of Christmas dinner.

On Halloween the hospital planned a party and celebration for patients and personnel. Aleck wrote a one-act play entitled *And Ye Took Me In* which was rehearsed for several nights in the X-ray laboratory. The lead was played by an actor in the hospital unit, Schuyler Ladd, who had appeared in *Yellow Jacket*. It was a huge success—depending almost entirely on local jokes and army humor and starring three of the most attractive of Base Hospital No. 8's nurses—so how could it be otherwise?

Just the day before the show was to be put on, the stage crew brought the scenery into the mess hall, which was to be the theater, and discovered that it would not fit. They were moaning about the need to cut out some of the scenery, when the engineers came to their assistance by giving them a new barracks as a theater. The barracks was not quite complete, so the engineers said it would not be too hard to knock out one end, build a stage, roof it over, put in scenery, knock out a stage entrance, put in headlights and footlights and a curtain. They did it, too, in time for the play. After the war, when an American magazine printed a symposium about America's greatest achievements during World War I, Aleck said in his opinion one was the engineers' construction of the Savenay theater in twenty-four hours.

The performance was a rousing success, so much so that it was repeated by command at the main camp of the YMCA eighteen miles away, and there a thousand soldiers were in the audience. Correspondent Heywood Broun saw the show, and wrote it up for the New York *Tribune,* whereupon Aleck had an offer from Broadway producer Arthur Hopkins to do a full length play—at the end of the war.

Christmas, 1917, came and Aleck went to the Brouns' on Boulevard Raspail for one of the memorable celebrations of his life.

Aleck had dozens of callers. When he came back from Paris and fell ill, he was clapped into a ward himself and Dr. Devol wrote Ruth Hale Broun that there was a constant line of people waiting to see Aleck.

He kept up a prodigious correspondence, with Mrs. Truax, sister Julie, his aunt Julie, Lucy Drage of Kansas City, the Strykers, the Rudds, and many other friends from the Hamilton days, and with Mrs. Fiske and others of the theater. He wrote to comfort his sister on the first anniversary of the death of their mother.

". . . It is well that she left the world last winter," he wrote, "well she has been spared a time so full of heartache for so many people and sure to be full of woe before the business is through. I find life indescribably poorer because she is not living but I am glad she is out of a troubled world which would have saddened her last years . . ."

In January, Aleck was promoted to sergeant, a promotion he thought he had enjoyed some weeks before when the colonel in charge of the hospital had recommended it to Paris. But at that time, in the autumn, the AEF headquarters was undergoing one of its frequent upheavals, and all field promotions were suspended. January in western France was as wicked as always, cold and damp and thoroughly miserable, and Aleck's spirits were very low. During the visit with the Brouns he had suffered a holiday attack of conscience and homesickness and had bared his soul to them, under the influence of wine. He spoke in a letter to Ruth Broun about dissecting himself and showing "the progressive corruption" of his soul. It made no difference, he said, "what happens to my dirty little soul." It was not the first critical self-analysis Aleck had indulged in, and it was far from the last. No matter how powerful he became, no matter how arrogant he seemed to others, Aleck was constantly measuring himself against the yardstick of his ideals, and never in his life did he give himself the benefit of the doubt or find that he measured up.

He was gloomy, too, because he had had few answers to the letters he had been writing; somehow the answers had gone astray and like other soldiers he was beginning to believe that he was forgotten at home. Then in January came the Christmas packages that had been delayed, and he found packages from the Phalanx, packages from Van Anda and the people at the *Times,* from Professor Shepard at Hamilton, and from many other near and dear friends. He was not forgotten at all, and immediately, he began to perk up. Still he was eager to get out of the inactivity in which he found himself, and to have something more personal to do with the war.

"The first weeks at Savenay were stimulating enough," he wrote later, "but by February the outfit was stale. A good portion of the men were born for the activities of the front line and fairly ached to escape to it."

So many were the applications for transfer, Aleck said, that the colonel in charge of the hospital automatically turned every one of them down, and if any man argued about the refusal of his request for transfer, he was immediately cast into the guardhouse.

The colonel was away attending a court martial at Neufchateau one Sunday night in February, 1918, when a wire came from the office of the Surgeon General at Tours, saying that Sergeant Alexander Woollcott had been requisitioned for the *Stars and Stripes* and asking if the colonel had any objections.

"I was just coming from an evening of pancakes and honey at Madame Cocaud's buvette," Aleck wrote, "when the adjutant, a genial and lawless soul, called me stealthily into his office, showed me the telegram, and explained that he would have to answer it in the colonel's absence."

So the two of them composed an answer which was sent out that night, before the colonel could return from his contemplation of the sins of soldiers at Neufchateau and automatically refuse Aleck the privilege of going to *Stars and Stripes.* The reply, sent in the colonel's name said this:

Sergeant Alexander Woollcott has done magnificent work here, but can be spared.

Stars and Stripes? What was that? At the moment Aleck knew only that it was some kind of soldier-run newspaper which had been started a few days before. He was not at all sure that he wanted anything to do with it, but he knew one thing—he wanted to get away from the bedpan brigade, and this promised him an opportunity to do that much if nothing else. So he held an auction of all the goods he could not carry, and as soon as the travel orders came through he set out for Paris.

XI

Aleck arrived in Paris on the night of the most devastating air raid the French capital suffered during the entire war, which was perhaps a symbol of things to come. He stayed in splendor at the Hotel Continental that first night, then, the next day reported as ordered to the Hotel St. Anne, which was the headquarters for the new army weekly *Stars and Stripes.* There he encountered the three first members of the staff of the newspaper, hard at work on bits of copy paper, sitting before three little cast iron tables of the type the French used at sidewalk cafes. The three were: first, Hudson Hawley, once of Yale and then of the Hartford *Courant* and the New York *Sun,* who had been a machine gunner with the Twenty-sixth Division and had been, as Aleck put it, "dug out of the mud at Neufchateau"; second, was John T. Winterich, of Brown University and the Springfield *Republican,* who had come over in the air service; third was Harold W. Ross, who at twenty-four had been a reporter on many newspapers, last the San Francisco *Call;* Ross had come overseas with the engineers, and had left an officers' training school at Langres when he heard that a newspaper was being started for the enlisted men of the army *by* the enlisted men; he had, as Aleck observed, "run all the way from there to Paris."

Woollcott put his barracks bag down on the floor and handed over his orders. Private Ross, who was the leader of the gang, inspected them darkly, casting disapproving sidelong glances at Woollcott's sergeant's stripes. He asked Aleck what work he had done and on what newspaper, and when Aleck informed him that he had been a drama critic Ross "howled with maniacal laughter."

Aleck then met the more genial Private Abian A. Wallgren of the Marines, who drew a comic strip that was the sensation of the newspaper. Later he met C. LeRoy Baldridge, another marine, who was to tour the front lines drawing sketches and pictures of the American soldiers in action. He also met Seth T. Bailey, who was to write a column devoted to letters from "Henry's Pal," back in the States, to "Henry" who was in France. This column was, for many, to become the brightest star in *Stars and Stripes*. The others connected with the newspaper were Captain Guy T. Viskniskki, officer in charge, Captain Richard H. Waldo, business manager, Captain Grantland Rice, Captain Franklin P. Adams and a handful of other officers.

The idea for a soldier's newspaper had been Viskniskki's. The staff was assembled around the Hotel St. Anne, and the printing was to be done in the offices of the *Continental Daily Mail*, opposite *Le Matin* on the Rue du Sentier.

In the beginning, the newspaper suffered somewhat from the fetters of military discipline. Captain Viskniskki, a syndicate salesman himself, was a man of high purpose and strong character, while the three privates who ran the paper were also of strong character but had a slightly different purpose in mind. Private Ross sensed from the beginning that *Stars and Stripes* could succeed only if it was the soldiers' newspaper, and that did not include officers. Thus it could not become, in any way, a propaganda sheet for official use.

Several harsh and lengthy battles were fought over editorial policy, and on several occasions Private Ross was placed under arrest by Captain Viskniskki. (Aleck was once arrested for being "beaten" on a story by the *Continental Daily Mail.*)

Now, Aleck, Sergeant or whatever, sat down to write handouts and do what he was told by his superiors, including managing editor Ross.

As did all the others, Aleck ran afoul of publisher Viskniskki in short order. His encounter came when Ross and the rest of the editorial entente decided that they ought to appeal to the troops to write more letters to the folks back home. Mother's Day was the occasion.

We got up a drawing of an aproned, wrinkled old

woman, standing beside a picket fence and staring incredulously while the postman passed her by. To go under it I wrote a broadside which began:

YOUR MOTHER IS WORRYING ABOUT YOU!

"Sergeant," the chief said, "we cannot afford to tell those doughboys that their mothers are worrying."

I replied that "worrying" was what I had meant, but that of course it was among his privileges to substitute any other word out of the dictionary.

"What about *think?*" he suggested.

I said that it did not strike me as particularly forcible.

"Sergeant," he said severely, and the listening Franklin P. Adams' face was lamed for life by the strain of his efforts at keeping it straight, " 'think' is a good word. Christ used it."

This was the officer, not editor Ross. Ross was a harsh taskmaster, but Aleck and the others were all professional newspapermen, and this fact kept matters from getting out of hand. Also, as professional newspapermen of the old school, they felt it incumbent on them to celebrate when they were not working. On the first day the non-officerial staff took off after it began functioning, Aleck and the others repaired to a restaurant where they filled themselves with good French food and good red wine, and then moved on to a cemetery in Montmartre, filled also with the joy of life and feeling the need to emulate their heroic commander in chief, Black Jack Pershing, who had visited the Comte de Lafayette's tomb to announce to the shade of Lafayette that the Americans had landed to repay their debt of the Revolutionary War.

The rag-tag *Stars and Stripes* soldiers marched up to the grave of Heinrich Heine, genius of German literature, and an enemy alien in Paris in 1918. Private Hawley bared his bald pate, whipped a wreath from beneath his coat, and laid it on the grave, whispering "in the ear of History" as Aleck put it,

"Heinrich, hier sind wir."

The original half dozen enlisted men of the *Stars and Stripes* lived a pleasant life for soldiers, although it was still the soldier's life and from time to time they were reminded of this by outsiders. In 1914, when the Germans were reducing the French fortresses at Liege and Namur, the enemy used a 42.0 centimeter gun which the French called *Big Bertha,* naming it laughingly for Frau Bertha von Bohlen, wife of the head of the Krupp arms works. A few weeks after Aleck arrived in Paris, the Germans unleashed another monster gun against the city. This gun measured 8.26 inches in calibre, it was 110 feet long, weighed 142 tons, and fired a shell that weighed 264 pounds, from a distance of 76 miles, into the streets of Paris.

One Sunday morning in March, Aleck, Ross, and the others closed up the newspaper shop and went off to lunch in what Aleck described as "some chauffeur's bistro."

> It was the second day of the Big Bertha, the still puzzling phenomenon of shells bursting every fourteen minutes from some fabulously distant gun. One shell passed Private Ross like a breeze and laid out four men on the sidewalk in front of him, thus considerably impairing his morale. With true German precision, the firing ceased from twelve to one.
>
> "Heinie is having his lunch," we all said, as we devoured our own confiture and cream cheese in comparative silence.

Promptly at one o'clock, Big Bertha opened up again. She was to fire about every third day over a period of 140 days, to add to the tensions of the people of Paris, and a few days after Ross's narrow escape 156 people were killed or wounded in the church of St. Gervais when a shell struck during Good Friday services.

Needless to say, not one member of the staff of *Stars and Stripes* was in the church.

One of the problems of the army newspaper was to maintain a certain order and transmit information about the American war effort in France, and yet keep the respect of the soldiers. As the number of Americans began to increase, so did the problems between Americans and the French population, and American Expeditionary Force headquarters grew quite concerned about the damages done to French property by American soldiers. The men of *Stars and Stripes* figured out an answer: they persuaded headquarters to put out an order stating that soldiers who went absent without leave—A.W.O.L.—would be rounded up by motorcycle squads and would be put into a special division, whose job it would be to repair French roads and other property. Naturally, this division would be the last to sail for home. When this was put into soldier talk: "Skids Greased For AWOL's," in *Stars and Stripes,* the number of AWOL's decreased and so did the amount of damage.

This was the work, but work was hardly all of Aleck's life in Paris. He lived in the top floor of an old hotel on the Rue d'Antin and he ate in the little French restaurants of the area. He and F.P.A. (Franklin P. Adams) had known each other well in New York, and now they held mammoth parties in Paris. Old friends kept looking him up—people such as Walter Wanger, later the motion picture producer, who was an aviation cadet, and that meant more parties. From time to time, Aleck was assigned to keep Private Wallgren in condition to draw his cartoons. This was a detail that fell to every man on the staff, for Wallgren had to uphold a reputation for drinking, and he did his best to uphold it all over Paris. The MP's were forever picking him up and putting him in the brig, and it was said that he had a special room there, the most comfortable jail cell in Christendom. Aleck and Wallgren wandered about Paris, and one day they went to the tomb of Oscar Wilde, where Wallgren placed an onion with reverence. Sometimes they wandered to the left bank, where Aleck liked to sit in the Café des Deux Magots or across the street at the Café Flore, or to eat at the restaurant on the third corner, across from the church of St. Germain des Prés.

In the spring, after such an excursion he sat down to write about it to Mrs. Truax. When his letter was written, Aleck took it to F.P.A., one of whose official duties was to censor the letters of the enlisted men on the staff of *Stars and Stripes*. F.P.A.'s method of censorship was to cross out certain words, but so gently that they were perfectly legible—and the words he censored had absolutely nothing to do with military secrecy. In this letter, for example, he censored out the name of Oscar Wilde, and when Aleck recalled how he thought fondly of the days in the Truax apartment in New York, F.P.A. censored out the words "West Fifty-Seventh Street." He also made sidelong comments on the edges of the letters, and on this particular letter Wallgren drew a picture of Aleck with a huge stein of beer sitting at a table in a boulevard café.

Wallgren made of Aleck a cartoon character who was to become famous all along the western front, a fey chubby soldier in uniform and a raincoat, his gas mask worn correctly across his chest, and a small musette bag at his side, tin hat placed correctly, straight across his head, puttees rolled beautifully, prancing with that almost effeminate rolling gait of Aleck's—in the strangest places. One picture showed Aleck standing in the mud with a ruined town in the background. "Oh, Mercy," he was saying, one hand clasped to his mouth, the other outstretched in a limp gesture with a pencil in it, "it must be a terrible battle! Why you can actually hear the cannon shots." And the caption below said "Our Intrepid Hero, Med. Sgt. Alexander H. Woollcott—A War Correspondent For Whom The Front Never Had No Terrors."

War correspondent?

Exactly.

In the late spring, all this idleness came to an end. Aleck, having covered drama, was dispatched to cover the only drama in sight, which was occurring at the front lines. Thus this tubby, genial, myopic, military reject found himself in the thick of nearly every important engagement which involved Americans.

The ground was laid late in March, when the Germans under General Ludendorff launched their great Spring Offensive in the hope that they might decide the issue before the Americans could arrive in force, while the Germans still enjoyed a numerical superiority in the field. The German assault was begun on March 21 on the Somme battlefield. Within the next few weeks the training of the American troops was rushed through, and they were committed to action as a unit, an American army. Some American troops were assigned to serve with the British and some with the French, but the vast majority went into the line under American command, as General Pershing had insisted all along that they should. The American commitment to the front came to its head at the end of May, 1918, when the Germans began a drive along the Chemin des Dames, north of Aisne, to reach the Marne on a forty mile front about fifty miles from Paris. When this occurred, all the petty problems that had separated the Allied commanders seemed less significant, and the American Second Division and elements of the Third and Twenty-eighth Divisions were thrown into the line. On June 3 this developed into the battle that was to be known as the Battle of Château-Thierry, where the Americans and the French stopped the German drive.

Aleck had been dispatched from Paris in May with an order in his pocket signed by the highest American military command, to proceed wherever he saw fit in order to cover the war activities of the Americans in France. Now Aleck headed directly for Château-Thierry, the little town that lies on both banks of the Marne. By the time Aleck got there, the German advance had driven the Americans and French back to the south bank of the river, but there the allies were holding.

Hitching rides and walking when he must, Aleck made his way to the front, to write the story for the *Stars and Stripes.* He went everywhere, this large, lumpy civilian-in-uniform whose puttees bagged and whose blouse and trousers seemed made for two other soldiers. He became dirty and unkempt—because he was spending day after day in the front lines and just behind them, at first aid stations and with the artillery. He told many stories of the battle of Château-Thierry, but probably the most famous of them was the tale he wrote of Verdun Belle on June 14, 1918.

Belle was a shabby, brown-and-white, undersized setter bitch who attached herself to one of the privates of one of the marine regiments stationed near Verdun. She was trench broken and an old hand at gas attacks who had her own gas mask made from a cut-down French mask. She had come to the regiment months before, but soon enough to be able to present the regiment with nine puppies. Two died but seven were alive when the regiment was ordered into battle. Belle's private took the seven pups along, carrying them first in a basket and then, having had to kill four of them, carrying the other three inside his shirt. Belle trudged behind. Then one of the pups died, and

Belle was lost in the confusion of movement to the front. The Marine tried to feed the puppies. He found an eyedropper. But he could not do a good job, and besides, now the sound of battle came grumbling with the wind up from the valley, and he knew there would be no time for anything but fighting. So he turned the puppies over to a lieutenant attached to a field hospital and went on. The next morning, when a new contingent of marines passed the field hospital, there was Verdun Belle, looking for her marine and her puppies. She found the puppies, smelled their scent and rushed to them. Aleck told the story:

> So, with renewed faith in her heart and only one worry left in her mind, Verdun Belle and her puppies settled down on detached service with this field hospital. When, next day, the reach of the artillery made it advisable that it should move down the valley to the shelter of a fine hillside château, you may be sure that room was made in the first ambulance for the three casuals.
>
> This was the Château of the Guardian Angel, which stands on the right of the Paris-Metz road, just north of La Ferte as you hike towards Château-Thierry.
>
> In a grove of trees beside the house the tents of the personnel were pitched, and the cots of the expected patients ranged side by side. The wounded came—came hour after hour in steady streams, and the boys of the hospital worked on them night and day. They could not possibly keep track of all the cases, but there was one who did. Always a mistress of the art of keeping out from under foot, very quietly Belle hung around and investigated each ambulance that turned in from the main road and backed up with its load of pain to the door of the receiving room.
>
> Then one evening they lifted out a young Marine, listless in the half stupor of shellshock. To the busy workers he was just Case Number Such and Such but there was no need to tell any one who saw the wild jubilance of the dog that Belle had found her own again at last.
>
> The first consciousness he had of his new surroundings

> was the feel of her rough pink tongue licking the dust from his face. And those who passed that way on Sunday last found two cots shoved together in the kindly shade of a spreading tree. On one the mother dog lay contented with her puppies. Fast asleep on the other, his arm thrown out so that one grimy hand could clutch one silken ear, lay the young Marine.
>
> Before long they would have to ship him on to the evacuation hospital, on from there to the base hospital, and on and on and on. It was not very clear to anyone how another separation could be prevented. It was a perplexing question, but they knew in their hearts that they could leave the answer to someone else. They could leave it to Verdun Belle.

This was one of Aleck's stories about the Battle of Belleau Wood, the first major American engagement of the war. It lasted from early June until July, when the Second United States Division recaptured Vaux and Belleau Wood, in the company of the Fourth United States Marine Brigade.

Aleck reported on the matters that interested the soldiers: the cooks, for example, and the bravery they showed in bringing food to the men under fire. He told a tale of one cook who was bringing "hot slum" to his men when he was stopped by an M.P. officer who told him noncombatants could go no further. The cook drew a gun on the M.P. and said he was going ahead and that not even Black Jack Pershing could stop him from getting his food to "them poor bastards up in the line."

This was a soldier reporting to soldiers, and although Aleck was the most unmilitary man in the United States Army, he became one of the most celebrated. Wherever he went, thanks to Wallgren's cartoons that had been appearing for months, he was recognized and beloved.

Almost immediately, Aleck had to call for reinforcements to cover the American war because even a good reporter can only be in one place at one time. His first few dispatches were taken back to Paris by a courier who met him in Nancy, and with them went his plea for help, for now other Americans were engaged in the Third Battle of the Aisne.

So back in Paris, Private Ross looked about the newsroom of *Stars and Stripes* and spotted Lieutenant Grantland Rice, who did not seem to be doing anything at the moment. He ordered the lieutenant to Nancy, to place himself under Sergeant Woollcott's orders. (Later a brass hat was to ask the whereabouts of Lieutenant Rice and Captain Franklin P. Adams, and be told that Private Ross had ordered them into the field, whereupon the brass hat blenched visibly and disappeared from the offices.)

Private Ross came up to the front himself to help cover the story, and went with Aleck into action. On this occasion, Ross said, Aleck met an officer who had been with Base Hospital No. 8 at Savenay. He was so excited that he ignored the 155 shells that were coming over every three or four minutes as he and the officer talked.

"He would try to get down on his belly when he actually heard the whistle of the shell," Ross said. "I would dive flat on the ground like a base runner sliding for second and then look back at Aleck and his major. Aleck and the major would be getting to the ground, a knee at a time, like a descending camel. They never got further than their knees by the time the shell burst. . . ."

These two months brought a basic change in Aleck's approach to life, as he wrote Mrs. Truax.

> . . . I am becoming week by week, a passionate enthusiast on the subject of America, something I never was before. I was ever so much more interested in the total cause, and not so very deep in my heart, there were doubts about the record America would make. I used to listen to the boys on the boat and in camp prattling away their easy optimism to the effect that the American would make the best soldier in the world, that an American could beat the life out of any German, that there was something essentially strong and brave about an American, etc. etc. And I used to shudder because it seemed provincial, because I thought it would sound offensive in the ears of the French and the English, etc. Well, I have been living at the front with the infantry, getting to know the American under fire, getting to know whole rafts of men from all corners of

America as I never knew them before, and I do believe with all my heart, there never were braver, gentler, finer, more chivalrous soldiers since the world began. I think I first came to know mine own people in the woods near Château-Thierry.

Aleck's problem was not to find stories to be written but to pick and choose from all the stories he learned in his restless wandering along the front, to find the ones that would describe best the war to the men who were fighting it, and would give honor where honor was due. Sometimes, as in the issue of *Stars and Stripes* of September 20, he would have two stories in the newspaper, both unsigned, both telling of some battle or incident at the front. That was the issue in which he described the St. Mihiel advance. He also described what he called the "battle of dreadful roads" in a separate article about the roads over which that battle of St. Mihiel was fought. "For parts of these roads," he wrote, "never perfect in their prime, had not known the turn of a wheel in four long years. All through those years they had been scraped and torn and upheaved by exploding shells. From the early months of the war they had been broken and sliced by the network of French and German trenches."

He wrote of the traffic jams, in which litter bearers took the litters from their stalled ambulances and hiked to the front lest they be too late, in which majors and privates shared cigarettes from the same pack as they waited, looking along an endless line of vehicles in which not a wheel was turning, in which the sounds of a crap game could be heard from the inside of a big stalled truck and one cook confided to the world that he had lost 400 francs in one kilometer.

He wrote of the storming of Montsec, northwest of Toul (a hill so thoroughly tunneled and entrenched by the enemy that he called it "disembowelled"), only to find the gun pits deserted, and no living creature save a setter known forthwith as Fritz and four red-eyed rabbits which had been penned up by the Germans for future eating. In that same issue of *Stars and Stripes,* Aleck wrote character sketches, without names, of two of the most daring officers of the AEF—Brigadier General

Douglas MacArthur and Lieutenant Colonel William F. Donovan who would come to be known as Wild Bill. His story did much to embellish the reputation (a deserved one) of MacArthur's bravery and even foolhardiness.

Of MacArthur:

> As the sun came up on September 12, he might have been seen by his fellow officers (and he certainly was seen by the Germans) standing erect, adventurous and oblivious on a painfully exposed parapet. One hand held his field glasses to his eyes, the other was clenched in excitement as the infantry just ahead charged through a wood. His adjutant—call him Smith, for the purpose of this story—stood at his elbow. Machine gun bullets were hissing and hitting all around. A captain jumped up out of the trench and touched the general on the arm.
>
> "If I might suggest, sir," he said, "your position is dangerous. The machine guns are reaching here."
>
> "Eh, eh, what's that? Oh, yes, quite right, quite right. Thank you. Smith—" this with a glare at his adjutant, "get down in that trench at once."

And of Donovan: Aleck described the crossing of the Rupt de Mad, a trickling stream which winds past Mazerais but which the storms of early September had swollen into a river. At a bridge leading up to the town enemy machine guns were in control and the brigade led by Donovan came to a halt. Donovan grabbed an engineer officer, put a rifle in his hand and put him in charge of fifteen men who were to approach the town below the bridge. The fifteen were down there already without an officer, halted by a steady fire of machine guns.

"We've got to get them boys," shouted the colonel. "Open fire every man of you, and then swim for it."

So he did, and swam to the other shore himself. The soldiers followed him, and in a moment they were ashore, dashing forward firing as they ran, and a German officer and forty men surrendered the bridge and the town to the twelve of the fifteen that were left. . . .

"When the excitement was all over," Aleck concluded, "the

chaplain (who is worth a chapter all to himself) came chuckling to the colonel."

"Well," he said, "they tell me they've written your epitaph."

"Who have?"

"The Boys in your old battalion."

The colonel fidgeted uneasily. He remembered the hikes he had set them, the drill and the drudgery, the ceaseless work.

"Let's have it," he said, resigned to the worst.

The Chaplain quoted the epitaph. It read:

"Wild Bill was a son of a ——, but a game one."

These tales from *Stars and Stripes* later found their way into the legends of both men.

When he could, Aleck went back to Paris for a few days. Then, he relaxed. He stopped to see one of his god-children—he had a number of French god-children and this one was Marcel Benoit Dick, the eldest twin son of the owner of a restaurant he liked. On one trip he presented his god-son with a gold and silver spoon. He went to see the Sacristan of St. Germain L'Auxerrois, who took him into the old Norman tower and showed him his twelfth century psalters and seventh century chests. He went to a nightclub called Freddie's one night, where a long-haired poet sang Musette's song and an opium-soaked female recited from Baudelaire and Freddie announced that a young American would sing something in French and American. Aleck clapped and hooted loudly with the rest until he learned that he was the American. Then he sang—a bawdy song. Seeing the poet and the opiumed one dividing the gate, he demanded his third, but settled for a drink.

Aleck took everyone he knew to Montmartre, having been introduced there himself by Wythe Williams. One night he and Walter Duranty went to dinner, and on the way home they were accosted by a prostitute. Duranty told the girl Aleck was as passionate as a lion, and Aleck told her Duranty was as passionate as a rabbit, which he said was more to the point. The girl left them in disgust, remarking that the two of them were as passionate as two plates of wet noodles.

Sometimes he wrote about civilians in the war. At St. Mihiel he wrote the story of the *curé-doyen* of St. Mihiel, a haggard priest when Aleck knew him. Through the tale of the priest, Aleck told the story of the suffering of St. Mihiel, which for four long years was a slave of the Germans, with its 2,200 people warned not to communicate with their countrymen. When Aleck arrived in St. Mihiel, he saw this sign, erected by the Germans a day or so before they evacuated the village:

> Whoever is convicted of communication with the French, by whatever means, will be immediately shot. Yesterday an inhabitant fired on a German officer. If this action occurs again, the house from which the shot comes will be immediately burned and a hostage shot.

He told how, on September 12, at 4:30 in the afternoon, the Germans had taken sixty-seven men and boys as hostages and had then evacuated the village, and when he wrote the story a day or so after the Americans arrived, he ended it on a note that would show the Americans how the French were faring in this war:

> The news came with the abruptness of a thunderclap. The memory of that parting is seared forever into the mind of St. Mihiel. The German officers snapped out their orders. The men and boys were huddled desolate in the rain. Their mothers, wives, children, wept around them. Erect in the heart of the group, the gaunt priest stood, his eyes alight with compassion and something more than that, his hands outstretched in blessing on each one of his petits, thus driven into slavery on the eve of the city's redemption.
>
> There were sixty-seven of them. One was the vicar. The memory of their going fell like a shadow across the jubilation of Deliverance Day. For many hours all nerves were taut with the vain hope that before the sixty-seven had plodded as far as Vigneulles, the American troops would have blockaded the path to Germany. But it was not to be.

The hope, however, that the sixty-seven will soon be back runs high today in St. Mihiel where once more mass is said for the French soldiers in the old church, and where as never before, the base of Joan of Arc's lovely statue is a mound of fragrant, rain-drenched, newcut flowers, laid at her feet in love and thankfulness and hope.

Once St. Mihiel had been won, and the victory consolidated, the Americans were ready to move on elsewhere and the next target would be the Meuse-Argonne. Aleck was there, as he was everywhere when action popped. Heywood Broun, who had gone back to New York after covering the arrival of American troops in Paris, wrote of Aleck's adventures after hearing a report from one who was there, in the company of Aleck and Arthur Ruhl, war correspondent of *Collier's*.

"All hell had broken loose in a valley just below us," said the narrator of the tale, "and I was taking cover in a ditch as Alec and Arthur Ruhl ambled briskly past me on their way into action. Alec had a frying pan strapped around his waist, and an old gray shawl was flung across his shoulders. Whenever it was necessary to duck from a burst of shellfire Alec would place the shawl carefully in the middle of the road and sit on it. In another quarter of a mile we would be in the thick of it. I saw that Ruhl and Alec were having a terrific argument, and so I managed to catch up to find out what men would quarrel about at such a moment. Suddenly we all had to fall flat, but while still reclining on his belly Woollcott turned and said, 'I never heard anything so preposterous. To me Maud Adams as Peter Pan was gay and spirited and altogether charming as the silver star on top of the tree on Christmas morning.' "

The argument continued, and Aleck was so aroused by Ruhl's negative attitude about actress Maud Adams that he stopped that night, wherever he found a place to lay his head during the battle, and wrote Miss Adams a long letter by hand, there being no typewriter handy at the front line.

When, as all of us do sometimes, I get very tired of shells and shell-holes, tired of an endless wilderness of crumbled homes, tired of mud, mud, mud, I like to shut my eyes and listen to the music that used to usher Peter in through the high nursery window, to see Nibs dancing the pillow-dance in the firelight, to wait while Miss Thing comes down the silver stairway to that absurdly perky strain. All that dear music has been with me through more than a year of exile. I can hear the Bobbie waltz in Caddence Wood. If I must, I listen to "Mrs. 'Awkins" and think of the tragedy beside that big laundry table. But, there, I hear a lot of voices proclaiming the plans and specifications for Wendy's house and cheer up immediately. . . .

But what I want you to know is that . . . the fiercest of them is a good deal like Michael slaying a pirate or two. I knew that, the other day, as I stumbled at dawn over an exhausted doughboy who had come out of the line and gone to sleep in his tracks with his face, that has yet to meet a razor, pillowed on his gas-mask. I wished, then, that you were near and that I could introduce you to him. I know him so well. I know that his first-aid kit is gone because he has used it to staunch some other fellow's "wounds in the rain"—a rain, lady, of shrapnel. I know that, for his buddie, as he calls his pal, he would gladly lay down his life. I know that the last time he fought for three days and nights with nothing to eat, he didn't complain. I know that, when his leave comes and he draws a great handful of back-pay, he will be burdened with its responsibility and that suddenly it will all disappear. Only those who watch him closely will ever find out that he has sent it all in to the army newspaper as a gift for some French war waif. You, yourself, at the first glance, would see that he can't be much more than seventeen. And you would see for yourself, what I'm rambling along in an effort to tell you, that the American soldier—I mean the plain, unadorned infantryman—would make his strongest appeal of all to Wendy. . . .

> Anyway, it is the first and only love letter I have written from France and may the lightning smite you if you feel under the faintest obligation to answer it.

The struggle that was to be known as the battle of the Meuse-Argonne began on September 26, and Aleck covered it, as usual, from the front. Everyone knew him, but he was most proud when he encountered someone who had known him before Wallgren made him famous as the fat mincing correspondent of the AEF. One of his fond memories was of a cook who stood guard over the last cup of coffee in a company kitchen.

"I am saving it for that fat medical sergeant with the specs," he said. "He took care of me at Base last fall."

But as time went on the soldiers came to know who was writing these tales of their exploits, and Aleck's reputation could never then be tarnished by the libelous cartoon character over which Wally labored.

Aleck wrote two stories about the famous Lost Battalion which was surrounded during the Argonne battle and refused to capitulate although badly shot up, but waited until other Americans fought their way to save them. When this reached Paris he had a message from his chiefs at *Stars and Stripes*—"Battalion story superb. Have you plenty of winter underwear?" They cared about him in Paris, too, it seemed. He wrote an article titled "In Memoriam," about Father Flaherty, chaplain of the Twenty-Eighth Infantry, who was killed in action at Very, ending on the epitaph composed by his soldiers: "he was too damned brave." He wrote about the tank corps and the observers who rode in airplanes, and the photographic corps and finally he wrote about the big offensive of November, 1918, a long dispatch that was a combination of the "big picture" and intimate detail.

> November 8, 1918. It was on last Friday morning, when the eastern skyline was tinged with the first faint promise of day, that the infantry moved forward for the third great assault of the Argonne drive—moved forward after the most stupendous artillery preparation in American history. It is not enough to say that behind them the guns were wheel to wheel. The cannon used in some areas could not

all have been crowded in had they been placed wheel to wheel. . . .

That was the big picture. He gave the background, told how the observation planes had been out for a week. Then he told of the moving out of the men, and the fighting, naming the places as they fell—by the fourth day they had moved ahead 20 kilometers. He also wrote of the brigade commander behind who complained that he had orders to leap-frog the other, "but my God, how can I, when I can't catch up." He called the action now the spirit of pursuit, and he gave the flavor of it in anecdote, as when a messenger came to a Marine command post:

> Now, with night coming on, he would push on afoot, wriggling through stalled traffic that even a motorcycle could not penetrate, slipping in the mud, taking the wrong turning, using his last match to consult his map once more, getting back to the right road, groping his way forward and finally stumbling through the dark to where a crack of candle light, gleaming under the flap of a gunnysack curtain, told him he had reached his goal.
>
> "Here's a message for the brigade commander."
>
> "Well, he ain't here. This is an engineer headquarters now. The Brigade P.C. is up six kilometers ahead. Or at least it was late this afternoon. There was some talk of its moving on."

Now, Aleck's reports were not just news dispatches, but stories, and even dealing with so heroic a subject as the big push, he was able to bring it into perspective:

> Once, in the middle of the night, stalled traffic on the roads was soothed by the strains echoing from a nearby roadside house invisible in the darkness. The burden of the refrain, played over and over again, caught up and hummed up and down the line, was "There's a long, long trail a-winding."
>
> There is indeed, but not so long as it seemed last spring.

Three days later the war was over.

XII

One does not turn off an army newspaper the way one can turn off the war news in a civilian newspaper at home, and so although the Armistice came on November 11, 1918, and thereafter the flow of war correspondents began to turn back toward Paris and homeward, the job of the men of *Stars and Stripes* went on. It became less heroic, but it was even more important that the newspaper keep up its quality and the interest of the soldiers in behalf of American army morale.

Aleck wrote:

> On the eleventh hour on the eleventh day of the eleventh month hostilities came to an end from Switzerland to the sea. Early that morning, from the wireless station on the Eiffel Tower in Paris, there had gone forth through the air to the wondering, half-incredulous line that the Americans held from near Sedan to the Moselle, the order from Marshal Foch to cease firing on the stroke of eleven.
>
> On the stroke of eleven the cannon stopped, the rifles dropped from the shoulders, the machine guns grew still. There followed, then, a strange, unbelievable silence as though the world had died. It lasted but a moment, lasted for the space that a breath is held. Then came such an uproar of relief and jubilance, such a tooting of horns, shrieking of whistles, such an overture from the bands and trains and church bells, such a shouting of voices, as the earth is not likely to hear again in our generation.

Aleck went back to Paris, but was soon with the troops again. He went into Luxembourg. He spent Thanksgiving with the Third American Army, a hundred kilometers from the Rhine. He traveled into Rhenish Prussia, along the Moselle from the frontier to the Rhine, from Trier to Coblenz, and he settled down with the army of occupation in Coblenz.

For several years Aleck had coveted a print of a certain picture painted by the artist Böcklin, which hung in the museum at Basel. It was called the "Sacred Grove" or *"Der heilige Hain,"* and it showed a group of Druid priests emerging from a dark corridor to kneel before a Druid altar. This was 1918 and such painting had been out of style for at least a quarter of a century, but Aleck's artistic sense was never very highly developed. He had once tried to buy one such print in New York without success, and he had seen a print in Paris, only to discover when he found the money (which he said he won in a crap game from F.P.A. and others) that the art shop in the Rue Drouot where he had seen the print had been demolished by a bomb.

Now, in Coblenz, Aleck spotted a print in an art shop window and was gazing at it one December day, nose pressed to glass, when who should come by but Damon Runyon, war correspondent of the New York *American* and the Hearst news services, and an old acquaintance from the New York newspapering days. Aleck suddenly remembered that he did not have any money or even a cake of soap, which was at that moment more highly prized in Germany than money. Runyon was wryly amused by Aleck's interest, and when Aleck said he wanted the print, Runyon went in and bought it for him.

Aleck remained with the occupation for a few days, writing about the "softships of the Third American Army" and then sought an excuse to return to Paris.

He was "waiting in line for some bread and coffee on an evening of drizzle," Aleck wrote, "when a major from G.H.Q. came over and asked me whether I had heard of any trouble back at the *Stars and Stripes* office." There had been a serious row of some kind, the major said.

What the major characterized as "a row" had been, in fact, a revolution. The dispute had arisen over the refunding of *Stars and Stripes* subscription money to homeward bound troops, but that was only the last of many struggles between the staff and the officers over it. Lieutenant Adolph S. Ochs, a nephew of the publisher of the Chattanooga *Times,* had been serving as treasurer of the newspaper, which now had a considerable amount of money in its treasury. Ochs had received an order from his commanding officer which he flatly refused to obey, and he so told the high command, indicating that they could come and get him and court martial him.

This might have happened had not the fourteen enlisted men on the staff, led by Private Harold Ross, signed a petition demanding an investigation. The revolution was against Captain Guy Viskniskki, and it had been boiling for months. Viskniskki had demanded that the newspaper be run along some sort of official standards. Ross and the others had met at a bistro every morning and figured out the best methods of defying him and keeping it a soldier's newspaper. The trouble came to a head now, and members of the highest commands of the AEF were immediately involved, because *Stars and Stripes* was big business. It had grown to a circulation of 500,000 copies at ten cents a copy, which was larger than the daily circulation of the New York *Times* when Aleck had left it.

At first the brass hats seemed inclined to throw Private Harold Ross and the others of the staff into the brig, kit and kaboodle. But if they did so (and the editorial staff of *Stars and Stripes* indicated that they would not mind the rest time), there would be no newspaper and army morale would go to pieces. Further, scanning the horizon, the brass hats could see no conceivable replacements to be pulled in on short notice.

So the enlisted men won that war without firing a shot. Major Mark S. Watson, a graduate of the Chicago *Tribune,* was detached from more important duties and assigned as overseer of the newspaper, but it was understood that the enlisted men of the editorial staff were in charge, and in overall command was Private Harold Ross, editor-in-chief. From that day on, the staff of *Stars and Stripes* was referred to moodily at G.H.Q. as The Soldiers and Workmen's Council—which was a distinct hint that Ross and his associates had been behaving along the lines of Nicolai Lenin and those other Bolsheviks.

And so *Stars and Stripes* continued on its merry way, only more so. There would be no pretense that the chocolate in the YMCA messes was hot, or that what the boys called "monkey meat" was edible, or that the pay system of the army was adequately administered or that the boys did not want to go home even after the Armistice until "the job was done."

With this prospect in view, Aleck left Coblenz just before Christmas for a trip to Paris. He heard that the profits had been so great and the paper so successful that sumptuous new quarters would be opened on the Rue Taitbout. He was also sick of Coblenz and wanted a change. He drove to Nancy and stayed at an inn in Alsace-Lorraine that first night. The next day he went to Metz, and was in Paris by midnight. Then it was arranged, with editorial conferences of the Soldiers and Workmen's Council, that his presence would be required through Christmas.

For Christmas Aleck wrote a letter home which appeared on the front page of *Stars and Stripes*:

> Dear America:
>
> Your sons are coming home. The task you set before them is nearly done, and now, day by day, week by week, month by month, your ships are bringing them home.
>
> If we have done well, it was for love of you. Dimly we understood that we had been sent forth to slay something which, if it throve unchecked, would one day reach out across the seas and destroy you. Very clearly we understood that by ourselves would you be judged among the free peoples; that the hour had struck for us to show mankind the mettle of our pasture. And believe this—there was not one of us who did not walk a little straighter, live a little cleaner, work a little better, fight a little harder, on that account. "Mammy," a stevedore wrote in his Mother's Day Letter last spring, "I want folks to see your raising in me."
>
> America. It was so with every one of us. We wanted all the world to see your raising in us.
>
> And this is written just to tell you that those ships will bring back more than 2,000,000 men, every one a better citizen than when we sailed away.
>
> Better citizens, because we know each other better. Rich and poor, high and low, rough and polished, East and West, North and South—the war has mixed us all together.

Alabama and Iowa have joined to form a single brigade, and what a brigade! Oregon has fought shoulder to shoulder with New York and means more to New York than ever she meant—than ever she could have meant—before.

Better citizens because many of us—almost a million of us—have, for a time, dwelt in that community spirit which nowhere in this workaday world is quite so animate as it was in that strange simple country which was called the front.

Above all, better citizens because you, America, mean more to us than ever before. For one thing, we have had to learn what it is to do without you. Some for a little while, others for interminable months, we have been obliged to do without you. Of course, the whole A.E.F.—though we have tried to hide it in our letters—has been as abysmally homesick as the most jealous mother could have wished. But surely that was no bad thing.

Then too, we have seen such shining things done in your name. We who were at Château-Thierry and northwest of Verdun have seen men in olive drab and forest green beside us show themselves made of such stuff as taught us a new wonder for the land that could breed them. There were some of us who had to set forth from our own front gate and journey all the way to the Marne to discover America.

We of this generation had come to take our country for granted. We had come to take our liberty as a matter of course, like the air we breathed and the unfailing sun. It was not so with the generation that fought the civil war to prove whether that nation, or any nation, so conceived and so dedicated, could long endure. But we—we of the easy spring of 1917—were like the idle sons of some rich men, inheritors of a fortune which only he could value who had by toil and sacrifice amassed it. Now we have done more than inherit the treasure. We have earned it. We were children of a great estate. We have added to it.

And so, dear America, we write you from the Rhine. In the name of those who cannot return, in the name of the best of all, those who lie beside the Marne and the Ourcq and the Vesle and the Aire and the Meuse, we wish you a Merry Christmas and a Happy New Year. The American soldier sends you his love.

A.E.F.

For the cynical correspondent of the cynical soldier's paper that poked fun at officers and defied the brass hat corps, this was quite a mouthful, and for Aleck, it was the full statement of a creed he very carefully concealed most of the time, but which had been building in him since those first days when he ducked in the trenches, eating corned willy out of a frying pan without bothering to take off his tin hat. Quite a change from the Aleck who had quarreled with Captain Viskniskki over whether or not the boys should be told that Mother was worrying at home.

Like the others, Aleck, at heart, was serious and proud of his soldier's newspaper. He wrote Major Devol asking if he did not think *Stars and Stripes* was "darned good." The staff had slaved to make it so, he said.

There was a Christmas celebration by nine members of the old staff at Nini's restaurant in Montmartre, at which suitable gifts were exchanged: Winterich gave Ross a pair of second lieutenant's bars. The printers gave Aleck 30 commas to make up for those he never used. On Christmas Aleck's friend, M. Jacques, gave a dinner for these special patrons.

Life was gay and pleasant, but not all Aleck's thoughts were for wine and conversation. He wrote his sister Julie to tell her how relieved he was that Christmastime to know that President Wilson was in Paris. He said he could feel the undercurrents of European intrigue blowing away before Wilson's tread, and that he believed Wilson would really be able to assure the world a decent peace.

That was the serious side of Aleck, one he did not often exhibit because he was determinedly non-political in his approach to his career. He was the *Stars and Stripes'* number one feature writer, and that is the way it would remain.

The romantic side of Aleck's character blossomed this year, but in fierce competition with the romantic side of lanky, moody Private Ross. Miss Jane Grant, who had once been a society reporter on the New York *Times,* arrived in Paris with the Y.M.C.A. Motion Picture Bureau. Aleck wangled her a transfer to the Y.M.C.A. Entertainment Corps as a singer, in a unit in which Schuyler Ladd, an actor friend of Aleck's who had been at Savenay, was also playing. Aleck made it a point to see much of them and he was, at least for a time, romantically interested in Jane Grant. Alas, she preferred Private Ross and eventually married him. Aleck found solace with his scores of other friends in Paris and everywhere else in France and the occupation zone.

When in Paris, if he had any money, Aleck liked to live grandly. At first, when he had come to France, he had arranged for the transfer of funds from his New York account to a Paris bank, but this had long since run out in the purchase of lavish gifts, and adoption of French orphans. So when Aleck wanted money he wrote extra articles for such publications as the Red Cross Magazine, just as Ross and others organized an impromptu publishing company to put out a booklet called *Yank Talk.* For Christmas, 1918, for example, Aleck bought and sent our hundreds of copies of *Yanks,* a paper-backed book of poetry reprinted from the pages of *Stars and Stripes.*

Immediately after Christmas Aleck returned to Coblenz to write his article for the Christmas week issue of *Stars and Stripes.* Aleck was now developing the mature style that would mark his human interest stories of the future, and perhaps it could be said that this style was tempered in the trenches of France, where Aleck achieved a feeling and respect for the tastes of the average American to whom he would direct his writings in the future. The touch was visible in this Christmas story:

> And more than all else, one thing made the Army of Occupation homesick the week before Christmas. It was not the comfortable modern houses. The very sight of the eminently American plumbing gave the men a certain nostalgia, but it was not that. It was not the orchards, though they are eloquent of home. It was not even the shop windows all bright with Christmas favors and tinsels.
>
> It was none of these. It was the rows upon rows of

Christmas trees for sale in public squares. Their high fir points, where one might easily conjure up the topmost, wobbly candle—Mother would be in such a panic for fear it would set the tree afire—these points it was that pierced the Yankee to the heart.

In another issue of *Stars and Stripes,* Aleck had an additional soldier's article: the echo of a loud complaint that could be heard from Ste. Menehould to Sedan and from Grandpré to Sun-sur-Meuse. It was the cry of the doughboy that he wanted to go home. These were the soldiers left to shift the graves of the dead, to mend the roads, to build the bridges, and guard the prisoners who worked on the roads. Looking at a detachment of German prisoners on the road one day, a sergeant spoke his mind to Aleck. "Well," he said, reflectively, "it seems we won the war and they lost it, but here we are together, both working on French roads. I don't know but what they've got the edge on us slightly. They don't have so far to get home."

Aleck wrote:

> There is at least one part of the Argonne, however, that is utterly deserted. Not a prisoner toils. Not an engineer works, in the Forest of Argonne itself. No form of human life can be found on those extraordinary ravines of which the slopes have been so completely fitted out with dugouts by the Germans during their long tenancy that an entire Yankee regiment could take its repose in a single ravine.
>
> Some American hustler will make a million dollars out of one of those ravines. He will rent it for several seasons from the French government, which will think he is crazy. Then he will shore up the dugouts and shacks that have given way under the winter rains. He will pick up the litter of tin cans and pretend that he has fumigated all the cooties out of the ravine. Then he will run a bus line to Ste. Menehould and plaster the Paris hotels with signs inviting all American tourists to come and camp out overnight in the Forest of the Argonne.

BED AND BOARD ON THE BATTLE FIELD
TASTE LIFE AS OUR SOLDIERS LIVED IT
SPEND A NIGHT IN THE ARGONNE
FIFTY FRANCS A NIGHT

After writing this article, and illustrating it, Aleck and Baldridge went back to Paris, where they organized the Lafayette Publishing Company, hired a printer, and put out "Château-Thierry; A Friendly Guide for American Pilgrims Between The Marne and The Vesle."

XIII

JUST BEFORE ALECK'S DISCHARGE he, Private Ross, Private Winterich, and Private Baldridge decided that there must be a farewell party, and it was held, with a banquet and play to celebrate the end of something—it was hard to name it—for *Stars and Stripes* would go on after they left. For the occasion Aleck and Baldridge composed a playlet, in which they appropriated the leading roles. Here is the scene, as recalled forty-six years later by James P. Humphreys, in 1919 one of the lesser members of the *Stars and Stripes* staff, whose job it was to type the thousands of poems submitted by the doughboys so the editors could judge whether or not to run them in the paper.

"I shall never forget Woollcott," he said, "wearing a wig, and with his small mustache powdered so that he gave the appearance of having a large upper lip. He was short and dumpy while Baldridge was tall and thin.

"The scene was in a house in Belgium as the Germans were entering the city [1914]. The two ladies were feverishly walking up and down the stage indulging in a very funny dialogue. The German Commander finally entered the room, a fat little fellow, as far from a ferocious monster as one could imagine. Alexander Woollcott sidled over to him and gazed up at him with eager eyes.

" 'When does the raping begin?' he asked."

When Sergeant Alexander Woollcott was discharged from the army on the last day in April, 1919, he was already something of a celebrity in France and at home. His renown among the American soldiers could not be attributed to his articles in *Stars and Stripes;* these were all anonymous. His notoriety came courtesy of Wally Wallgren, who never stopped caricaturing him.

Aleck must have realized he would be a celebrity when he got home because of a practical joke created by Ruth Hale which resulted in a comedy of errors. One night at Bar-le-duc, when an air raid in the town had shut off all but candlelight and there was no going out to find companionship or a bottle of wine, Aleck had whiled away the evening by sending post-cards to friends, among them to Arthur Hopkins, the producer. He said after the war he intended to set off on a tramp steamer bound for nowhere in particular and spend a year at sea, after which he would present Mr. Hopkins with a play called *World Without End,* which was sure to be the ruin of Hopkins if he produced it.

Later, at Coblenz, Aleck received a cable from Hopkins: "Accept play and ruination," which amused him. Then, someone sent Aleck a clipping from the New York *Times* of December 2, 1918, in which the story was told, straightfaced. So Aleck *knew* he was a celebrity. At this time he began to develop the part he would play in public, the part of Alexander Woollcott, critic, iconoclast, deflater of bores, discoverer of unknowns, warm friend, and judge of all he surveyed. As for enmity, he achieved a reputation for making enemies, but mostly this was exaggerated. True, many people were to grow to dislike Alexander Woollcott for one reason or another—often his sharp tongue—but Woollcott seldom wasted much time or spleen on anyone. He might slash them with a phrase or a sentence but he was not interested in attacking further. He was far more interested in his enthusiasms than in negative matters. In a strange, negative book about Aleck written shortly after his death, Samuel Hopkins Adams dwelt heavily on Aleck's capacity for making enemies. One of the first was Burnet Hershey, he said, of the New York *Sun,* who published a remark that Aleck took to be unfavorable and "was never forgiven."

Perhaps, but at most, Aleck's dislikes occupied a very small part of his time or effort; he was far too busy living to worry much about the bruises to himself or others that occurred as he strode through life.

When Aleck stepped off the boat on June 3, it was to be interviewed by a representative of the *Times,* and to tell the world that the souvenir issue of the *Stars and Stripes* which was then to be published would be the last.

Aleck hurried from New York that spring to Clinton, for it was the tenth anniversary of his graduation in the class of 1909, and he was eager to visit with old friends. Already he was something of a legend on the campus. His comings and goings were chronicled faithfully in "The Lit."

Aleck did not go home because now he had no home. His father and mother were dead. His sister was married. Some relatives still lived at the Phalanx but the Phalanx without his immediate family was not home. His brother William, the one to whom he was closest, had moved to Baltimore, and his other brothers had scattered. Now thirty-two years old, and with no romantic interest in sight, Aleck was coming very close to being a confirmed bachelor.

Aleck went to stay at the City Club on West 44th Street between Fifth and Sixth Avenues, but within a few weeks he had knocked at the Truax door again, as he had promised he would, and moved into that apartment for a time. He needed money, because he had given away all he had, so he borrowed three thousand dollars from Al Getman, who had it to lend, and re-established himself as a civilian. Some of that money went back to France to Marie Louise Patriarche, the French orphan girl adopted by the *Stars and Stripes* staff, and some of it went to needy members of his family and to other orphans and victims of the war whom he had encountered in Paris. Giving away money was something Aleck always did very well. Ex-Sergeant Woollcott was not at all certain of the course he would now pursue in life. He was in no hurry to get back to work at the *Times*. He took some time off to look around and think.

In the fall, six of the old *Stars and Stripes* staff tried to establish a magazine called *The Home Sector,* but nothing came of it. Winterich drifted off to become editor of the *American Legion* magazine, Wally Wallgren tried his hand at producing a comic strip called Hoosegow Herman. Franklin P. Adams had come home early and was back at his old stand at the Conning Tower, as he called his syndicated column. Harold Ross fumbled with several ideas, took a job at *Judge,* and then came up with one for a sophisticated magazine to be called the *New Yorker,* an enterprise in which he was later joined by Hawley Truax, through Aleck's influence. Aleck collected his *Stars and Stripes* articles into a book—*The Command is Forward*—which was published that year by The Century Company. Then, for Aleck, it was back to work on the *Times* staff, in what he described as "a fog of the soul," where he resumed his old position as drama critic (he always referred to it as dramatic critic). John Corbin, the editorial writer who had taken on the task while Aleck was away, went back to editorial writing. By September Aleck was reviewing plays again, and writing his "Second Thoughts on First Nights."

During the summer of 1919, the Actors Equity Association had struck against the producers for more pay, and the strike shut down the theaters until September. Aleck did not take part in the strike or comment on it, although he might have done so if he wished. His position was that of critic, and as such he had friends on both sides of the footlights. Although he was taken to task for failing to live up to the radical standards established in his own life by his upbringing at the Phalanx, Aleck felt he had no business interfering in the strike.

In November he gave an old pal a leg up by reviewing LeRoy Baldridge's war book *I Was There with the Yanks in France.* Of course, in Aleck's fashion, it was a favorable review.

Aleck could live quite well on the salary the *Times* paid him, which was $100 a week or more, but his charities and obligations could not. He wrote two magazine articles for *North American Review* in 1919, one of them dedicated to explaining to those who had remained at home during the past two years why ex-soldiers were sometimes caught in the corner at a party looking into nothing and muttering softly to themselves "them damned frogs." The soldiers were not referring to bullfrogs, but to the people of France, who, the doughboys said, tried to skin them alive.

He attributed the American dislike of France and things French to many reasons, to different viewpoints about the war, to the uncleanliness of Frenchmen and the poor sanitation of the country. Yet, said Aleck, like himself, many Americans could say, with Laertes:

Yet now, I must confess that duty done
my thoughts bend again toward France.

So did Aleck's thoughts, and at Christmas time he was writing such old friends as ex-Lieutenant Ochs that in May he would head for France, and in January of 1920, he wrote a special article for the *Times* on the French war orphans adopted by members of the A.E.F.

He also got back to the serious business of playgoing and drama criticism.

Aleck was a more spicy critic in 1920 than he had been before he went to war. He wrote on many subjects: on the demand for plays with happy endings, for example.

Times policy had changed and Aleck was a featured writer, with even more freedom than Carr Van Anda had given him before the war. He was now apt to devote his entire "Second Thoughts on First Nights" to a single subject, as on January 18, when he discussed the revival of the Gilbert and Sullivan operetta *Ruddigore,* with assurance and ready opinion and a wealth of knowledge of the history of his subject.

Aleck did not confine himself to historical articles. He reviewed plays with even more vigor than he had reviewed them in the days of his battle with the Shuberts, taking the position that the reviewer had but one responsibility, and that was to the reader of the newspaper who examined the review of a play with an eye to attending the theater—to the playgoer, in short. In 1920, this was a radical viewpoint, and one not much appreciated by producers or the members of the acting profession. At the Lambs Club, Aleck was dubbed "The First Grave Digger" because of the harshness of some of his comments about some players. And yet—consider this review as it appeared in total in the New York *Times* as an example of Aleck's reviewing technique:

THE PLAY
by Alexander Woollcott

The Harvard Prize Play
MAMA'S AFFAIR, a comedy in three acts,
by Rachel Barton Butler, at the Little Theatre.

Tommy Hooper	Little Billy
Henry M.	George La Guere
Eva Orrin	Ida St. Leon
Mrs. M.	Katherine Kaelred
Mrs. Orrin	Effie Shannon
Dr. Brent Janson	Robert Edeson
Mrs. Bundy	Amelia Bingham

Take *Le Malade Imaginaire* from the theatre of Moliere or any other play on the wiles of the hypocondriac. Tap the vein of comedy that ran through *The M* of blessed memory. Add a smattering from the lore of the psychoanalyst. Stir violently and you will have the deft, original and uncommonly entertaining piece which, under the clumsy and inept title of *Mamma's Affair,* arrived last evening at the reopened Little Theatre.

Or let us call it the Somewhat Larger Theatre, for the onetime precious playhouse has been expanded to less intimate dimensions. In the days of the Winthrop Ames regime, it was just about big enough on opening nights to admit the Four Hundred, but with a couple of hundred seats added, Oliver Morosco had to let down the bars, which he certainly did. A curiously mixed audience was present, then, to applaud with a splendid impartiality both the very good acting and the very bad acting, jumbled together in the screamingly mixed cast of *Mamma's Affair.*

This is the Harvard Prize Play, for which Mr. Morosco, rather than Mr. Craig, offered the prize this year, and the new comedy by one Rachel Barton Butler is, by a considerable margin, the best product of English yet sent from the cloistered halls of Cambridge to try its luck in the hurly-burly of the commercial theatre. There is no more interesting comedy on view in New York today, and, if it were as well played as it deserves to be, it would be well worth going to see. As it is, you'd better see it. You might do a whole lot worse.

It required at least a surface knowledge of the Freudian explorations to write this play and playgoers with a bit of that knowledge will have the time of their lives as it unfolds. It is true that the Freudian playgoer lies in wait for the slightest lurking excuse to descend into the subconscious discovering clues and symptoms of which playwright, producer, and players are blissfully unaware. He sees an inhibition at every turn and with the slightest encouragement would talk about the Psycho-Analasis of Xenophon. But *Mamma's Affair* really invites his special attention.

It is all about the Oedipus complex. Or what is it called when the ingrowing bond is between mother and daughter? The Medea complex? Well, no matter—for, after all, the common thread run of us can relish the new piece at the Little Theatre and, as its somewhat uncomfortable story develops, will wriggle and chuckle with many a spasm of recognition.

Miss (or Mrs.) Butler's play is all about a docile daughter whose mother, wallowing in her bravely borne invalidism, has affectionately and sentimentally used her uncomprehending daughter until the latter is a self-denying, tortured neurasthenic. Mamma, in the sweetest, most self-deprecating way imaginable, has the vapors upon all occasions, and even, if needs must, swoons away in order to keep things moving just the way she wants them to. Things would go on this way forever if the daughter were not driven beyond her strength, and suddenly, in a complete nervous collapse, her love for her mother turns to bitter and spasmodic repulsion.

It is only a momentary spasm, but it lasts long enough to bring a wise and resolute doctor into the case. He sees through Mamma at one glance and vigorously cuts away her vinelike clutch upon the daughter. He isolates the daughter from Mamma, from Mamma's friend, and from the nice young man Mamma has picked out for a son-in-law. He keeps her isolated long enough for her to develop, for once, a mind of her own. Also long enough for her to fall in love with him. And he with her. But of course you knew that.

Having a few embarrassing ethics about the premises, he

is all for packing her off then, but that mind of her own has not been developed to no purpose. It is Miss Butler's purpose and is revealed in the clutch of the final curtain.

The cast of characters reads like the role of an old home week celebration, so many are the dear, remembered faces. Effie Shannon, Amelia Bingham, Robert Edeson, Katherine Kaelred—they're all here. Miss Shannon is delightful to behold and plays capitally the role of the languishing Mamma. Mr. Edeson is excellent, and Miss Bingham—as the Irish nurse—although often on the verge of considering herself in the presence of a big moment in a big play—adds considerably to the entertainment, even when she forgets and leaves her brogue up in her dressing-room.

Miss Kaelred is pretty bad, and the same must be said of George La Guere. Neither of them, with all their various accomplishments, appears to possess much of the comic spirit or any of the technique necessary for the touch of travesty in which the piece, in the present production, is invested. Then the use of the arrestingly adult Little Billy as a child is downright distressing.

Over against all these blemishes in the cast must be set the skillful and pleading performance of Ida St. Leon, who may be described as a Ruth Chatterton with salt, an actress of circus ancestry and "Polly of the Circus" memories, whose spirited, intelligent and appreciative playing bequeathes a deal of vitality to *Mamma's Affair.*

Aleck told his readers a very great deal in that two-thirds of a column. He told them that the play was a good play, much better than its title would indicate. He told them that the acting was spotty, some good and some bad, and he singled out both varieties of performance. He gave a synopsis of the play. What more could the playgoer ask?

He reviewed John Barrymore's Richard III that spring as a "magnificent performance." He chose Barrymore, at last, to fill Mansfield's empty shoes. He selected "the worst plays of 1919-1920" which some along Broadway took to be the unkindest cut of all.

As an incurable romantic, Aleck was always in love with some girl. This spring it was the novelist Edna Ferber, who called him Amoeba. They went to dinner. They went to parties, and Aleck took her to the theater. She did not like going to the theater with this distinguished critic.

"Going to the theater with you is, anyway, the most complete and skillful way of not seeing you, I've discovered," she wrote him. "My experience is that I meet you at the theater immediately before the curtain rises or just after it has risen. Between the first and second, second and third, third and fourth (if four) acts, you flee up the aisle, leaving me to appear as unconcerned and sheltered as I can stuck out in the third row center second seat. One has to be an Alice Adams to achieve the effect. Directly the play is ended you dash for the street, leaving me to follow or to struggle into my wraps as best I can. . . . Outside the theater I am hurled into a taxi (for which I pay) and am sent home alone. During the evening my entire association with you has consisted in the consciousness of a vague bulk intermittently occupying the seat at my right.

"Is that going to the theater, I ask you, Mr. Wolfstein, or is it bartering one's womanhood?"

They were very close, but they argued incessantly. One day in February Miss Ferber telephoned Aleck on the spur of the moment for dinner.

". . . silly sort of thing to do, because I mean to say don't you know why? But I had been out and bought two new blue candles—tall, thin, greasy-looking, dark blue ones, and I thought, now with jonquils those will look so pretty on the little table in my living room. And I'll give him a cocktail, Mother being out to dinner and the opera and all.

"But you weren't in and that's life. Still, we'd probably have quarreled anyway."

On one occasion in April, Miss Ferber gave a dinner party and asked Aleck and several of his friends, for 7:30 one evening when he had no opening. He and several members of the party were forty-five minutes late in their arrival, while their hostess and other guests stewed, and when Aleck arrived, he told her airily that they had been detained having cocktails here and there, and refused to take her complaint seriously or to show the slightest remorse. The next day she wrote him a furious letter. It was two weeks before he was forgiven, and then just on the eve of his trip to Europe.

This trip in the spring of 1920 was made for several purposes: to refresh Aleck's perspective on the theater by taking in productions in other countries, to preview some plays that would be brought over later in the year from London to New York, to write some magazine articles for extra income, and to have a vacation somewhere in Europe.

Aleck remained in London for several weeks, seeing plays and renewing old acquaintances, mostly with people in the theater. Then he took the boat-train from Dover to Calais, and to Paris. It was June, and he was in love with Paris and the world. He roamed the alleys and the boulevards. He met Neysa McMein, a New York illustrator and an uncommonly pretty girl who was beloved by half the editors and writers in New York City, and he began to assemble a crowd to go on a trip. He took them to his old haunts in St. Germain and to Montmartre. At the Café de la Paix one day he encountered the young violinist Jascha Heifetz, who had impressed him very much when Aleck heard him a few weeks earlier at a concert in London. He added Heifetz to the group and began showing him around the city. One night they all went for dinner to a smoky little café near Les Halles, a place called Le Père Tranquil. It boasted a three-piece orchestra. After dinner when the wine had flowed copiously, Heifetz arose and cajoled the violinist of the trio into giving up his instrument for a few minutes. Thereupon he gave an impromptu concert of gypsy music and love songs. The *patron* wept, wrung his hands, and offered Heifetz 100 francs on the spot if he would only settle down there forever. Rashly, he threw caution to the winds and told Heifetz he could, from that moment on, be *first violin* of Le Père Tranquil, if only he would stay.

The next day the crowd left Paris bound on a motor trip to the Pyrenees. They were a happy group, stopping for picnics in the shady grass along the sunlit roads, pitching pebbles at trees and gambling on the outcome.

At Pau they encountered rain, which meant that instead of

spending the evening at an outdoor café they must eat in the gloomy pit of the dining room. After dinner, they set out to see what amusement the town had to offer, but the rain had brought about a general rolling up of the sidewalks that night, and as the hotel clerk told them disdainfully, it was Monday and as all the world knew the movie houses were closed on Mondays so the projectionists might have their day off.

What to do?

Jascha Heifetz solved the problem. He led the crowd to his room, cleared the bed of pillows and a monstrous magenta comforter, and produced from one pocket a pair of dice, and from another a 100-franc note. He rattled the dice significantly.

"Faded," cried Neysa McMein.

"Aha," cried Heifetz with what Aleck described as "pathetic optimism." "The beeg deek."

And the game continued past midnight amid cheers and fierce cries with "francs fluttering about as they used to do in the big Casino scene in Camille."

Eventually the travelers returned to Paris, and then Aleck set out to fulfill a magazine commitment to *North American Review* for articles on France two years after the war.

Aleck traveled to the Aisne valley and to the old, battered village of Juvigny, where he discovered that two hundred people had come to live again amid the rubble of the crumbled houses and try to pick up the threads of prewar life.

> . . . Then, as you take another turn amid the rubble, you come upon another barrack and find within such hospitable tables and shelves of wine as glorify any *buvette* in France. A whopping big phonograph hums with some melody of Irving Berlin's and the patron shows you where, once a week, the tables can be cleared away for a dance or a picture show.
>
> There is the whole story of Juvigny. It looks disconsolately and discouragingly as it did when the Americans left. But children plug away at the tattered school books, babies are born, marriages are solemnized by the octogenarian cure, crops come in from the once bleak fields and they dance in Juvigny of a Saturday night. That is, after all, the real

message to the men who sweated in town when it shrieked and shook with the smash of shells. They are dancing now in Juvigny of a Saturday night. . . .

Something of all this must be on the mind of every American who starts back from Soissons to Paris and sees the desolate villages give way gradually to tidy clusters of red-roofed houses and garden land that never felt the scorch of war. . . .

Thus his thoughts run, and as the train slides along through Villers-Cotteret and he sees all the preposterous havoc and blight still in force, he finds himself thinking of pleasant suburbs back in America, comfortable well-fed America, of tidy lawns and overflowing Fords and children romping off to school, of country clubs and poker games and silk stockings and squandered wealth. And of people who say "Oh, forget about the war." And he begins to feel a certain tingling resentment at America.

But then the train wheezes into Paris and his taxi whirls him away to boulevards all gay with the bustling people and restaurants with groaning tables and such food and drink as only the old world knows. He sees luxury and ease and extravagance on every side and he sees that not all of it can be laid to strangers within the gates. He wanders on down into rich Touraine, a land flowing with milk and honey, where people, knowing only vaguely the hardships of the north fret and fume about their taxes and go on about their business.

And he realizes then that all the selfishness and forgetfulness in the world is not American. Whereupon he grows depressed and gives himself over to a low opinion of the human race. But even that fairly tenable position he cannot hold for long. For he keeps remembering something. He remembers that they are dancing in Juvigny of a Saturday night.

The war had affected Aleck very deeply, and he wrote about it and its aftermath with a seriousness that he did not devote to many other subjects at this time. He was doing much magazine writing in 1920: he wrote an article for the *Century* magazine telling the story of an old woman "of Margrivault farm" who had been found hanging, dead, by an American party during the fighting. The Americans had buried her. A year later they had come back to the area and had met her son, and the matter of her death had been carefully broached. They let him believe that she had died of a heart attack, when actually they knew she had taken her own life in fear and despair.

Aleck also was serious in an analysis of the theater, in the season just past, noting that "there had grown up an alert, discriminating, sophisticated public, numerous enough to last to make profitable the most aspiring ventures of which the theater's personnel is capable. This could not have been said ten years ago."

What had happened?

Aleck analyzed it as the growth of a big churning New York, "ten times more stimulating a place than any other community on this hemisphere," and he said that New York's new attitude toward the theater was due to "New York's seemingly greater response to truth and authentic beauty. . . . Whatever else may be said about the hundred-per-cent American of whom the platform orators sing there is no evidence that he has ever been a particularly discerning fellow at the play."

The season of 1919-20 had marked a great change. For the first time in the history of the American theater the experimental or brave or classical play could be put on and make money "without ever stirring a foot from Broadway."

He cheered the fact that "in New York, at least, we are less likely to hear the ravens of Broadway croaking as of yore: 'You can't put that piece on' and 'That's a great play but it won't make a penny.' If it is a great play, and it is well-staged, it will make money. That day has come."

Aleck's magazine success was even more notable in *Everybody's* where there was a Woollcott article published every month except August, September and October, representing the time when he was out of the country and too busy enjoying himself to write. In January it was *The Miracle of the Stars and Stripes.* In February it was an article on the child actor growing up, in which he paid particular attention to a girl named Helen Hayes, "an extraordinarily gifted and skilful actress who is just eighteen. Her technique is so remarkable that older and more famous actresses sit open-mouthed and wonder where and how she learned to do it." But where, asked Aleck, would she be at twenty-five? He was not seer enough to answer that question, just seer enough to recognize the great talent he saw before him.

In March he wrote about the grand old men of the American stage, and *Everybody's* announced that all during the theater season he would have an article in the magazine each month. He became, in essence, *Everybody's* theater critic as well as that of the *Times*. In April he wrote about John Drinkwater's play *Abraham Lincoln,* the hit of the 1919-20 season. In May he wrote a character sketch of the team of playwright J. Hartley Manners and his wife, actress Laurette Taylor. In June he wrote about John Barrymore.

In July his subject was Eugene O'Neill, and his remarkable *Beyond the Horizon,* which had been so successfully produced that season—and whose success was one of the reasons for Aleck's belief that the American theater public had finally matured, and, speaking of the newcomers to the theater, he said "of all these newcomers, none is of richer promise than Eugene O'Neill."

In November Aleck's article for *Everybody's* was of an entirely different turn, a pure feature about the "strenuous honeymoon" of what was then America's favorite couple of young lovers, Douglas Fairbanks and his bride, Mary Pickford. The first six articles had been thoughtful discussions of the theater—this one was a harbinger of the Woollcott to flower in the next decade, yet with overtones of the reporter in it: it was obviously a result of Aleck's summer trip and his observations of America's film stars. So was the last article of 1920, analysis again this time, however, a long study of the plays Aleck had seen in England and France.

The editors of *Everybody's* called Aleck one of the most prominent of New York critics—which he was, and they also referred to him as "the well-liked dramatic critic of the New York *Times*"—which he was. In his thirties, having done so much to raise the standards of the theater, even those for whom he had not always had words of praise began to respect and like him. This was true of such men as Booth Tarkington, who in September, 1920, objected bitterly to a not very favorable review of one of his plays. A month later Tarkington had this to say:

> The Woollcott-Broun entente was fair to Helen Hayes. I almost thawed to Woollcott recently when he described a play as one of those in which children are called "tots" and a house is called an "abode." He and Broun do a really fine service in increasing the consciousness of the vulgar to words: they raise standards, sometimes, but not when they kill *Poleloin* [his play] because its viewpoint was unsympathetic to theirs. I think Woollcott and Broun are the first drama critics in New York to be very sensitive to rotten phrases and absurd ones—I'll say that much for 'em.

This is the man who was to become one of Aleck's very best friends.

XIV

In *A Literary History of the United States,* Robert E. Spiller, Willard Thorp, and the other editors refer to Aleck as "one of the New York Wits along with Dorothy Parker, Robert Benchley, James Thurber, and E. B. White." Those "wits" of New York along with several others comprised the crowd called the Round Table, for the most part, and they gained their reputation from a habit of eating at the big round table in the main dining room of the Algonquin Hotel, an ancient house which had been discovered and patronized first by Aleck when he lived at the City Club a few doors down the street. He invited F.P.A. and Heywood Broun to lunch there one day and they liked it, and soon the Algonquin became their headquarters. The habit spread and the Round Table was formed.

The Round Table was famous among writers, editors, and the theatrical crowd as early as 1921. That fall Edna Ferber asked Aleck wistfully in a note, "Could I maybe lunch at the Round Table once?" It was famous for good reason. The people of the Round Table, most of them in their twenties and thirties, were making marks in the world of magazines, books, theater and even letters. The slight, acid Dorothy Parker, the lanky Robert Sherwood and the timorous, humorous Robert Benchley had worked on *Vanity Fair* until they were either fired or quit. Benchley went to the old *Life* as drama critic. Sherwood became a successful playwright. Dorothy Parker continued as magazine writer, and finally married and went to Hollywood to write films. At the Round Table the conversation of these and others tended to be brisk and airy and sprinkled with *bons mots.* It was always fair enough to repeat afterwards what someone else had said —some bright remark by Woollcott or Marc Connelly or F.P.A. One did not repeat one's own bright remarks; that and a certain devil-may-care attitude which all the Round Tablers had, plus an invitation to lunch from one of the regulars—these were the requirements for this membership that was no membership at all.

Heywood Broun was an original Round Tabler, but George Jean Nathan really was not. Nathan sat back in his chair and took potshots at all and sundry, with special attention to Aleck, at whose literary style Nathan sneered. In an article in the *Smart Set,* he called Aleck the Seidlitz Powder of Times Square. The article was filled with indirect jabs but that was to be expected of Nathan, and Aleck rather gloried in the publicity although he was not specifically named. Aleck, the public Aleck who was developing so rapidly, denied the sensitivity that the private Aleck felt. Once in a while that sensitivity was displayed, and when it was, it puzzled those who did not know the private Woollcott, but, for the most part, then and forever after, Alexander Woollcott took jibes and criticisms with the same jauntiness that he handed them out.

Aleck was very much a celebrity at Hamilton, the college described in Nathan's diatribe as a "small up-state college." Actually it had long been one of the finest liberal arts colleges in America. Each year Hamilton invited prominent men in the world of letters to come and speak in a series known as the Myers lectures, after the man who had endowed them, a member of the industrial family that was to build Bristol-Myers Corporation.

Aleck was invited to give the first Myers lecture of 1921, on January 8. He chose as his subject the circumstances of the writing and the production details of several plays, *Samson and Delilah, Enter Madame,* and *The First Year,* in order to give his youthful audience some feeling for the grandeur and promise of the theater. It was a most successful lecture, and a memorable occasion, because Aleck was the first alumnus of the college ever to be honored by such an invitation. His predecessors in this series were, among others, Walter de la Mare and E. M. Forster.

Aleck was asked to participate in many new projects in these years. Playwrights and publishers sought his introductions to the published versions of their plays.

That year the *Bookman* asked Aleck to write a "Literary Portrait" of his friend Heywood Broun. Some men would have backed away from such a task, concerned lest they write too favorably or too cuttingly; some would have accepted the chore and then written a literary puff. Aleck did neither, he wrote an honest sketch of his friend:

> Broun wears 13 shoes and is drawn to scale, a 230-lb. Barrymore, pretty discouraged about his appearance. As Mencken is the professional male, so is Broun the professional father, for out of the mouths of babes cometh copy. He is younger than Heywood, III, and personally much more timid. No one is so impotent that, meeting Broun face to face, he cannot frighten him into any lie. Any mouse can make this elephant squeal. Yet, I know no more honest being, for, when not threatened, his speech is an innocent emptying of his mind as a woman empties her purse, himself genuinely curious about its contents. And, threatened or not, he acquires all courage the moment he mounts a typewriter. When celebrating and serving the masses at that altar, he gives the truth til it hurts. Rich in his liking of his gang, he himself is non-friendly. Friendliness is an activity and he is the great inert. Broun is as young, as humane, as amusing, as brave, and as accessible as a set of Dickens—and just as likely to come running to meet you.

What that article did not say is that Aleck and Broun were close friends and shared a mutual respect as workmen. They had, shortly after Aleck's return from the wars, engaged a hotel room in the theater district, where they repaired each opening night to pound out their copy, beneath a sign that said "Minds at Work."

In the winter of 1920-21—at Christmas time to be exact—Aleck had encountered J. M. Kerrigan, a rolling, doughty Irishman and manager of the Abbey Theater in Dublin, while strolling on Fifth Avenue. It being the merry season, Aleck invited Kerrigan to visit various friends and speakeasies, and they spent the afternoon in that fashion. Kerrigan came home with Aleck around dusk, and they got to talking about Dickens. Kerrigan thought it was a cruel pity that Dickens' writings on the theater had not been collected into a single volume where they might be found by those in need of such restorative. Aleck agreed, but thought little of it in the midst of their wassail. Later, however, while poking around in the library on 42nd Street, he discovered no volume of this type existed and, abetted by G. P. Putnam's Sons, he set out to remedy that great lack in the English language's cultural heritage. All spring, he labored at night about the theaters, and worked in the morning on his book about Dickens and the theater.

Aleck was always a hard worker. He reviewed plays, and now he took to reviewing books, not just books about the theater, but books on other subjects that interested him. He was moving to extend his scope, to become an all-around critic of American social and cultural affairs.

One of his first efforts, outside the columns of the *Times* book section, was in the *Bookman* of March, 1921, when he reviewed a new book on Walt Whitman, compiled from Whitman's various newspaper articles, most of them dealing with the theater, and written when Whitman worked for the Brooklyn *Eagle*. The book was entitled *The Gathering of the Forces,* edited by Cleveland Rogers and John Black. Aleck objected to this title, to start off with, as far too pretentious for the subject and its treatment. After all, the material was nothing but a handful of musty old newspaper clippings that had been pulled from the files.

Aleck said:

> Among their many hypothetical explanations of why all this material had been neglected by Whitman's publishers, and biographers, they do not suggest either of two that must occur immediately to any reader of their collection —that the stuff was hardly worth the labor involved in its exhumation, or more positively, that its republication would be a distinct disservice to the reputation of a great name. Such republications are almost invariably of this effect, as you may verify by reading the dreary stuff by Kipling and Barrie, which, to their own intense annoyance, a later fame dragged forth from decent interment in old newspaper files.

The publisher could not have been very pleased with that review. And the publisher was G. P. Putnam's Sons, for whom Aleck was doing the Dickens book.

The summer of 1921, instead of traveling to Europe, Aleck chose to take leave from the *Times* and finish his book. He decided to go to Hamilton College because it was as much a home as anything he now had, and because it would be cheap to stay there. He boarded with the family of John Calder, who was also summering there, working on his book during the daytime, playing croquet in the evenings and sitting up late, talking or playing bridge.

Book complete, Aleck returned to New York to be greeted by the following in F.P.A.'s column, much to his delight:

> To A.W.
> Welcome home, welcome home!
> That's the theme of this here pome.
> For not excepting even my wife
> I never missed anyone so much in my life.
>
> F.P.A.

XV

In the autumn of 1921, Aleck returned to a busy season of play reviewing. It was a good season for Broadway, which meant it was good for Aleck, too.

He had a new assistant reviewer in the 1920's, young George S. Kaufman, who did everything on the drama page that Aleck did not care to do—except on nights when there were multiple openings, and then other members of the staff were pressed into service.

Aleck's reviewing showed the same restraint and sharp sense of the appropriate that he had always exhibited and which had made of him one of the two leading drama critics in New York. Helen Hayes was playing in *The Wren.* Aleck admired her. Booth Tarkington wrote the play. Aleck admired him. This admiration did not keep Aleck from pointing out that the play was slight and that Miss Hayes had yet to learn about the theater, but he did it with such gentleness that neither playwright nor actress could have been more than passingly annoyed.

He wrote:

> The author of *Clarence* has written a wistful, placid, gently amusing little comedy to nourish the oftsung talent of Helen Hayes.
>
> . . . What there is of it is charming and it is charmingly played—not only by the winsome Miss Hayes, who has foregone her naughty trick of insisting on herself too ardently, but by Leslie Howard, a singularly engaging English actor. . . . It is not possible to review *The Wren* even briefly and appreciatively without indicating that it is curiously short-weight. Here is a charming comedy, deftly and simply fashioned, artfully written, and warmed all the

way through by the kindliest humor. And yet—and yet it is a scanty play with a scantiness that is not quite accounted for even when you have looked at your watch and found that it took little more than two hours from first to last. You come away from the theater a little under-nourished, feeling that you have been permitted to peep in on some quaint and amusing people and that you have not been allowed to see quite enough of them.

No, neither author nor any of the players mentioned could object too seriously to this review, and yet it was far from selling. Aleck was living up to his billing: he was writing reviews from the standpoint of the people who put up their two dollars for a seat.

All the time Aleck was adding to his circle of friends. Edna Ferber moved alternately between Chicago and New York (working in Chicago and seeing editors in New York) and they saw much of one another early in the winter. They liked walking about the city, peering into shops on Sixth Avenue and eating in tiny restaurants off the fashionable avenues and cross-streets. Aleck gave parties—sometimes he cooked dinner for a mob by himself if the cooking didn't disturb Mrs. Truax in the 57th Street apartment where he still lived. Sometimes he and his friends quarreled, because Aleck was insistent that things be done *his* way and none other, as on the February day when he took Edna Ferber walking on Sixth Avenue in the snow when she wanted to walk on Fifth Avenue, which had been cleared. He had his way, but she caught the grippe and was flat on her back for three days, writing him chiding letters.

One of Aleck's friends was Otto Kahn, the banker and play producer of the 1920's who brought such cultural triumphs as the French *Vieu Colombier* repertoire troupe to New York. Aleck and Kahn often dined together, along with Neysa McMein and whoever else Aleck might have in tow on any given evening.

In the fall of 1921, Kahn brought to New York a production of *Chauve-Souris,* a Russian vaudeville show that dated back to 1908 when it had been assembled by members of the Moscow Art Theater for their own amusement. It was very successful. When Kahn ordered a command performance to be played at his own house Aleck christened him "Otto the Magnificent."

In the spring of 1922, when *Chauve-Souris* was at its zenith, the New York Wits of the Algonquin Round Table decided to stage a competing production of their own. For their single performance on the night of April 30 they secured the use of the Shuberts' 49th Street Theater. Their revue was called *No Sirree*! "an anonymous entertainment by the Vicious Circle of the Hotel Algonquin." It was written by nearly all assembled.

At its opening, Heywood Broun got on stage to announce himself as speaking on the Spirit of the American Drama, which he then did. A song followed by a choir consisting of Aleck, John Peter Toohey, Robert Benchley, George S. Kaufman, Marc Connelly and Franklin P. Adams.

Next came a skit, *The Editor Regrets,* played by Marc Connelly, J. M. Kerrigan, Donald Ogden Stewart, Harold Gould, Henry Wise Miller (Alice Duer Miller's husband), and Mary Brandon. It was set in the time of Dante, and involved the rejection of Dante's work by *Droll Tales,* a Venetian magazine.

After a satirical talk on the movies by F.P.A., came *The Greasy Hag,* "an O'Neill play in one act," which featured John Peter Toohey as a retired waterfront prostitute named Coal Barge Bessie, with George S. Kaufman, Aleck, and Marc Connelly playing, respectively, First, Second, and Third Agitated Seaman.

Robert Sherwood appeared in a drama called *He Who Gets Flapped* with ten "ingenues" including June Walker, Tallulah Bankhead, Ruth Gilmore, Helen Hayes and Mary Brandon. Then came a playlet entitled *Between the Acts*; Brock Pemberton played the manager and his brother Murdock played the part of the manager's brother. The following were listed as "first nighters": Dorothy Parker, Alice Duer Miller (the novelist who became a dear friend of Aleck's), Neysa McMein, Beatrice Kaufman, Jane Grant, Heywood Broun, Aleck, Robert Benchley, George S. Kaufman, Marc Connelly, Kelcey Alley and Arthur Bachrach.

Another playlet called *Big Casino Is Little Casino,* featured Toohey as James W. Archibald, a rich man, and Aleck playing Dregs, a butler, with Kaufman as an attorney, F.P.A. as a detective, Marc Connelly as a convict, and Robert Sherwood as the Governor of New York. Alice Duer Miller, Neysa McMein, and Jane Grant played the roles of "Guests." And while this three-act drama was in progress, offstage, fiddling his head off, was a figure identified only: "Offstage Music by J. Heifetz." Poor Jascha Heifetz: when he arrived offstage with his precious violin, he found there was no light, no place for him, no music stand. He solved the problem by standing near the electrician's cubbyhole, gaining what light he could, and pinning his music to the back of an indignant stagehand.

After a monologue by Marc Connelly there came one last play, called *Zowie, or The Curse of an Akins Heart.*

This was Aleck's own creation, written after seeing a series of plays that season in which the heroine was "ruined" sometime in the action, and particularly seeing two plays by Zoe Akins in each of which one heroine "kept being ruined and ruined and ruined."

Aleck's play had every trapping of a pretentious Broadway offering. It bore a subtitle:

a romanza in one act

It sported an obscure "theme."

—"Nor all your piety and wit"—From the Persian.
The Scene was: a Place in the heart of a great city.
The Time was: Printemps, 1922.

The Cast:
Marmaduke La Salle,
a stomach specialist .... John Peter Toohey
Lady Friend of La Salle's .... Neysa McMein
Another Lady Friend
of La Salle's .... Louise Closser Hale
Dindo, a Wandering
Busboy .... J. M. Kerrigan
Zhoolie Venable
a Suppressed Desire .... Ruth Gilmore
Mortimer Van Loon,
a Decayed Gentleman .... George S. Kaufman
Archibald Van Alstyne,
a Precisionist .... Alexander Woollcott
Lemuel Pip, an old taxi-driver,
who does *not* appear .... Harold W. Ross
Offstage Music by J. Heifetz.

Aleck's taste in theater was satisfied that year by one play that nearly none of his friends liked. A play called *Abie's Irish Rose* opened on Broadway in the winter of 1922, to be greeted by the jeers and catcalls of many of the drama critics. F.P.A. said it was the worst play he had ever seen. Robert Benchley, reviewing it for *Life* termed it "one of the season's worst," and Heywood Broun, critic for the *World* paid the play the worst insult he could give it: he did not review it at all. Aleck saw it, liked it, and said so in the *Times.* He liked it simply because he approved of the inter-racial theme of a Jewish boy marrying an Irish girl. It was not an artistic triumph, but called attention, in a pleasant, positive fashion, to an American problem, saying that it could be solved and would be solved. The appeal here went back to Aleck's basic natural support of the radical, and to the undisguised sentimentalism he had announced during World War I. The public liked it, too, and it ran for the longest period of any play that had ever struck Broadway.

John Peter Toohey, who had managed to snare the part of the leading man in three of the four playlets of *No Sirree!* was also the man who coined the name of the Algonquin Round Table's evening auxiliary society: the Young Men's Upper West Side Thanatopsis Literary and Inside Straight Club, or, more popularly, Thanatopsis. All the actors of the vaudeville review were more or less regulars at Thanatopsis, too. They assembled in a second floor suite of rooms at the Algonquin, and Frank Case, the owner of the Algonquin, made sure that there was plenty of food and liquor on hand—the Round Table crowd was worth a mint to him. By 1922 visitors to New York wandered into the hotel just to have a look at the celebrated Algonquin Round Table, and many of them stayed on to eat in the dining room or to book rooms at the hotel. There were some irregular members of the club, men like E. Haldeman-Julius of Kansas City who came to New York occasionally, and who published the forerunners of pocket books, the Little Blue Books, and Herbert Bayard Swope, the executive editor of Joseph Pulitzer's *World,* who with Harpo Marx and Ross would eventually bring about the breakup of the club. Thanatopsis lived for ten years, it floundered, then foundered for several reasons: Aleck outgrew it in time as his interests changed away from poker, much of the original crowd dispersed, married and moved out of the city into the suburbs, and, the stakes grew too high. Harpo did not come into the establishment for two more years—until 1924—but when he did he brought a gambling fever and plenty of money that was not shared by all the members. Swope, the big red-headed editor, was a ferocious gambler who always played for heavy stakes or was bored, and was known to bet $10,000 at a time. He had other unsettling ideas: one night when he was coming to the club he disdained the food and drink offered by Frank Case and ordered a caterer in from the pretentious Colony Restaurant. That did not break up the game or the club's relations with Frank Case, but it did give all the players pause.

That spring, just before he went to Paris, Aleck was asked to give a series of lectures by the Department of Journalism of New York University on dramatic interpretation. His reputation was growing constantly.

In Paris, Aleck called on Herbert Bayard Swope and his wife, who were staying in elegance at the Ritz. Mrs. Swope was in bed although it was noon, in a pink night gown and pink bed gown over it. Swope was being shaved by a barber and talking to foreign correspondents. Aleck and Margaret Swope shot craps while he talked.

From his meetings with the elegant, big-spending Swope, Aleck picked up a habit or two to fit his public character as man about town and bon-vivant playgoer. He adopted an opera cape and huge, black, big-brimmed hat and a stick, and these became his marks. It was not a ludicrous performance by any means, because first night audiences dressed in formal clothes for the evening. In fact, when *Strange Interlude* was presented on Broadway for the first time, and the very long play was split into afternoon and evening performances, Otto Kahn showed up for the afternoon performance in frock coat and striped trousers and gray waistcoat and winged collar and cravat, and then for the evening he came back in full dress. So Aleck's opera cloaks, many of them given him by actor friends, were not nearly so out of the ordinary as it might appear.

Aleck was back in New York, when his two books were published in the autumn. The first, *Mr. Dickens Goes to the Play,* was the compendium of Dickensiana on the theater. Aleck's contribution was to gather the material, arrange and edit it for brevity, and to write interleaf pieces to point it up and explain it. The *Bookman* called it "a delectable potpourri. Mr. Woollcott's own essays in the book are informative and altogether pleasing and his selection of Dickens anecdote and quotation is skilful. . . ."

Aleck's second book of the season also received good praise from critics and friends. This bore a title which Aleck explained very modestly in the foreword:

> And there sat in the circle at the Player's Club one who spoke always with the accent of authority, giving firmly the impression that his own story and the story of the theater were two inseparable strands of the same woof. Indeed, he sometimes referred casually and hazily to five seasons passed at dear old Drury Lane. But one day some one asked him point blank what his roles there had been. He had to explain then that his talent had always been devoted to offstage noises. Finally he showed a Drury Lane program, yellowed and creased and wine-stained. There his name was at the end of the cast and opposite it was the role assigned him—*Shouts and Murmurs.*

This book was composed of a selection of Aleck's Sunday columns as they had appeared in the *Times* and magazine articles that were published in the *Century, Vanity Fair,* and *Theater.* It contained poignant articles about O. Henry in the unusual guise of playwright. It included *Gunpowder Plots,* which had originally appeared in the *Century* as *Disarming the Drama,* an article of good humored chaffing about the tendency in the 1920's of playwrights to resort to firearms "to unnerve the audience."

> My favorite playwright is Euripides, because he wrote ninety pieces for the theater without introducing a gun in one of them. But, frustrated by the fact that it's not every evening one can find a piece of his being acted in my town, I then go by preference to plays involving the villainy of toreadors or to hot romances unfolded against Sicilian or Etruscan backgrounds. Even then the assurance is not ab-

solute but the chances are that whatever murder is to be attended to during the evening will be managed by a knife stuck quietly and modestly between the ribs.

I had hoped that the war would cure me of these weak tremors. I remember saying as much the night that the Argonne drive began. It was two o'clock on that momentous September morning in 1918, and up the road that led from Souilly toward Montfauçon three transported Broadwayites were plodding side by side, a quondam actor and two ex-dramatic critics, William Slavens McNutt, Arthur Ruhl, and I. Ruhl, as I recall, wore a shawl.* The guns were firing in concert from Alsace to the channel, a four-hundred-mile row of cannon all going off at one time, the heaviest artillery preparation the world had ever heard. I had been spending a considerable portion of the preceding three months under the guns and had soon become so used to them that I could sleep placidly, just as one gets used to a flat near the Sixth-Avenue Elevated or to a berth on a railroad train. And even to this monstrous redoubling of the ructions, this continuous blast at which the very earth twitched and trembled like a sleeping setter with a nightmare, we became accustomed, and by daylight were talking through it as though it were not there.

And I remember agreeing with Ruhl that at least the war would do one thing for us. The world might still remain a somewhat precarious place for democracy, but we could reasonably expect to attend an American crook-play without going through all the old pangs of the gun-shy. At one silly little revolver thrust suddenly into the suspense of a scene we would merely yawn and wonder where to sup after the play.

In my first week back home I went guilelessly to the Follies. There was an interlude, intended, I understand, to be extremely comic, in which that fine comedian, Bert Williams, had to sit in front of a shooting-gallery target, like a large black son of a latter-day Tell, and suffer an expert marksman to pick off the bulbs that formed an aureole for

* Other accounts, notably Heywood Broun's, have Aleck in the shawl.

his woolly head. Williams was supposed to turn as white as possible and to tremble with fear. He did. So did I. But *he* was acting. The war had been fought in vain.

He reprinted his selection of the ten worst plays of 1919-20, and he must have been right, for who has ever heard of *Katy's Kisses, The Poe Playlets, The Unknown Woman* or *The Blue Flame*?

He spoke out loudly against the terrible translations of French plays—knowing whereof he spoke because he had seen them in France.

> The translators usually engaged by American producers for such work are either men who cannot read French or who cannot write English. They achieve either a weird jargon that is half Harlem and half Montparnasse or they turn all the speeches into an Ollendorf idiom the like of which never found voice on land or sea. The heroines of such hybrids are given either to remarks like this: "Cheese it! Voilà le policeman!" or to remarks like this: "Is it not that it is necessary that the aunt of my friend assist?" My own discomforts at such productions have ranged all the way from the paltry jingles into which Granville Barker turned the lovely verse of Guitry's *Deburau* to the quaint adaptation of *Les Noces d'Argent,* which was credited at the time to Grace George. In it one important scene revolved around a coveted sideboard, which, because it had been referred to in the French text as a *commode,* was docilely and grotesquely called a commode in West Forty-Eighth Street.

He took umbrage at an issue with the claim heard all about him that the American drama was declining, and said:

> It is sufficient commentary on the whole mass of elegiac poppycock that if a publisher were to issue an honestly compiled volume of the ten best American plays he would have to take ten written in the twentieth century.

And the only American play of an earlier era that he could recall as having any worth was *Fashion,* first played in 1845, also the first American play to be presented on the other side of the Atlantic.

The arresting statement of Aleck's book was his appraisal of Eugene O'Neill:

> The most interesting playwright of the new generation in America is Eugene G. O'Neill. Short and long, experimental, a little undisciplined and exuberant, vigorous always and always somber, his plays have, by their own force, pushed their way up from the tentative little playhouses tucked away in Greenwich Village and have summoned imperiously the wider audiences of the pay-as-you-enter theater. Not one of them but has its blemishes that would catch the roving eye of any dramatic critic over the age of two. But they have stature, every one of them, and imagination and a little greatness. . . .

Then he recalled *Beyond the Horizon, The Emperor Jones,* and *The Hairy Ape,* "a fantastic play in eight scenes."

Neither Woollcott book hit the best-seller list but as with the Dickens book, *Shouts and Murmurs* was received well in the literary community. Edna Ferber, to whom he sent copies of both, was most complimentary. "That introduction to the Dickens book," she wrote him, "is one of the nicest things I've read in a long time." She asked him why he did not write a novel, because she liked the way he turned a phrase. He replied, as always, that he had no talent for the novel and did not want to write one. He said to her, as he was to say to many others, that he firmly believed himself to be the best writer in America—but he had "absolutely nothing" to say.

Around the time his books were published, Aleck left the *Times* for another job. He was not dissatisfied with managing editor Van Anda or with the management of the *Times* but he was dissatisfied with the money he was earning. He moved now in a rarefied atmosphere, spending many weekends at establishments such as Herbert Bayard Swope's home on Long Island, or the estate on the Hudson of W. Averell Harriman, Wall Street man and son of the railroad magnate, where he played croquet and indulged in repartee and card games.

Swope earned a great deal of money as an executive and more

on the stock market in those happy days, and he lived in the manner of a young prince. Frequent visitors and croquet players in Aleck's set included Neysa McMein, Richard Rodgers the composer and his wife, Dorothy Parker, and F. Scott Fitzgerald. Ring Lardner lived across a field from the Swopes' old Victorian mansion and commented that a house party was going on all the time. In clement weather the house party usually included a croquet match or two during the weekend. Such matches were carried out in deadly seriousness: the Swopes (and Aleck and his friends) used expensive sets with wickets made of cast-iron and the mallets of ash and hickory and bound with brass hoops, sets imported by Abercrombie and Fitch from England.

Aleck always gave Neysa McMein credit for adapting the gentlemanly game of croquet to the fierce competitive natures of the crowd of New York Wits. One day in 1920, out in the wilds of New Jersey, Aleck said, Neysa had suggested that the game be played without any bounds at all—which meant that if an opponent could knock your ball 150 feet from its lying place into a swamp full of alligators, you were to march out into the swamp and play the ball from there. This made for high scores, generally speaking, rather than low ones, but it also added zest and murderous initiative to the game. After 1920 this is how croquet was played by the Swope-Woollcott-Harriman group, and soon croquet became so important a part of the house party routine that all else paled before it.

In the autumn of 1922, Aleck spent many weekends "swoping," as Edna Ferber called it, and he felt the need to augment his income. At this time Frank A. Munsey, developer of a chain of grocery stores, was one of the most affluent of newspaper and magazine publishers. He owned the New York *Sun* and the *Herald* and with the *Herald* he had acquired the services of W. O. McGeehan, a sports writer and old friend of Heywood Broun, who had also been a sports writer before he turned to the drama. Through McGeehan, Aleck negotiated with Munsey and his editors, and secured a healthy raise in pay. So in October, for money and for no other reason, Aleck went to work as drama critic for the *Herald*. It was to be an unhappy experience for him, although the *Herald* treated him very well. He started off by fighting the battle of the underdogs, and continued it all the way. As with most of the New York newspapers, the *Herald* gave bylines only to its most highly-paid staff members. It had always rankled Aleck that George S. Kaufman did not have a byline on the *Times,* although Aleck had one after the Shubert fracas. Now he secured a byline for his *Herald* assistant, Frank Vreeland, simply by putting one on Vreeland's copy and fighting it past the managing editor's desk. Vreeland worshiped Aleck and said he created the best drama department in the city, which was quite possible, because all things considered, with the exception of Heywood Broun, Aleck had no peer in New York in interest or knowledge of the theater, and Broun's mind, in 1922, was beginning to turn elsewhere.

Aleck quickly settled into the routine at the *Herald.* He could not use the old title "Second Thoughts on First Nights," for this belonged to the *Times.* He called his column in the Sunday *Herald* "In the Wake of the Plays," not so striking a title, but the material and the essence remained the same.

Aleck could now be seen, year after year, arrogating to himself more authority on matters of the stage. He adopted the position that the true greats of the American theater were born to the theater, and made of this a theme for an article in the *North American Review.* There was, he said, "no art in which the heredity seems to play so controlling a part." The theater had an aristocracy "more deeply rooted than that which any other activity in American life can boast," he said. He referred learnedly to Eleanora Duse and he noted that "the two best plays of our time," *The First Year* and *Anna Christie,* were "the work of playwrights born of show-folks, the work of children of the theater born on tour. . . ."

He talked of "the tingle of the eternal renewal of the theater, the same tingle I felt one hot night in the summer of 1916, when I was watching some children in a settlement house on Avenue B, New York, perform with tremendous gravity the *Sherwood Forest* of Alfred Noyes. The boy who played Robin Hood was a striking, swarthy unexpectedly deep-voiced youngster who was later snuffed out in the war. The sight of his name in the programme had a little thrill in it for those of us who were out front. It was Richard Mansfield, 2nd."

Aleck's pronouncements began to annoy some of his peers. At the Lambs Club his name could be guaranteed to bring about ardent discussion if not louder noises. The *Bookman,* in reviewing *Shouts and Murmurs,* commented favorably on the book, but its reviewer felt constrained to say a few words about Aleck.

> . . . "that mountain might be brown," said the man, "or it might be blue"; and there was no arguing the matter, so I proclaimed it black. Alexander Woollcott is a man with whom it is well worth fighting, but timid souls should not enter the lists.

The change was gradual, but Aleck had come home from France as a drama critic in a very narrow sense of the word. By autumn he had become a public figure and had established a controversial public character. Very few people knew that the public Alexander Woollcott who was developing before their eyes was the artificial creation of an artist.

XVI

THAT AUTUMN THE Truaxes gave up the apartment on West 57th Street and Hawley Truax went into a real estate partnership with Harold Ross and his wife, Jane Grant, and Aleck. They purchased, on a cooperative basis, two old houses far west on 47th Street on Manhattan Island, in a neighborhood that Aleck described nonchalantly as "the Gas House District." In the beginning there were two other tenants, but they did not last long, because with Aleck in attendance, the establishment soon became a second Round Table, with much of the literary, artistic, and theatrical world making its way in and out of the establishment at various hours.

Aleck was now a confirmed bachelor. He was thirty-five years old and while he liked to think that he had prospects of marriage, he really did not have very many, because his affections were split in far too many directions. At this time he was in love with Edna Ferber, Neysa McMein, Jane Grant, Beatrice Kaufman, wife of his old assistant on the *Times*, and half a dozen actresses, whose feelings for him waxed and waned in relationship to his reviews and their roles of the moment. His fondness for good food and good wine caused him to grow enormously fat; and he weighed well over two hundred pounds although he stood only five feet eight inches tall in his stocking feet.

Part of Aleck's problem was undoubtedly glandular, but again there were two sides to him. He ate too much, but he was also a gourmet who loved food for its own sake. One could not say that his bout with the mumps had caused either his fatness or his ambivalence. All the elements of his character, except the love for good food, had been apparent in the early years, long before his illness. He was not effeminate in his nature, although he gave some outward indications of effeminacy.

Aleck was concerned about his extra weight and he spent some time in a New York hospital on a crash diet, losing some of it. This was a regimen he forced upon himself occasionally in the years to come. He knew he should lose weight, but his entire way of life worked against it, and so did his appetite for sweets.

At the West 47th Street establishment, which his friend and then bookseller Joseph P. Hennessey termed "a moist heap," Aleck arose early in the morning, donned a dressing gown over his pajama bottoms, and loafed around his apartment or those of one of his friends until noon. He might possibly eat lunch in their communal dining room, over which Jane Grant presided, but he was equally likely to go out for a sandwich or for luncheon. Dinner was ever his meal. During the week, when Aleck was going to the theater at night, there were not too many management problems in the household, except that he liked rich, heavy food and both Hawley Truax and Harold Ross suffered from ulcers and needed light, bland diets. On weekends it was different. The bootlegger was in attendance so regularly that Jane Grant said she narrowly escaped being called before the grand jury investigating violations of the prohibition laws, and one day, she said, twenty-eight unexpected guests arrived for supper.

The Wits met often, drank together, played Hearts which was then Aleck's favorite card game, called each other by the vilest names they could imagine, in a fashion Aleck had picked up in college and had never dropped. All this was enjoyable and it passed the time. Aleck's reputation as the Falstaffian leader of a section of the society of Wits increased and multiplied. He did not compete with F.P.A., who was sometimes regarded as the senior officer of whatever people believed the Round Table to be. No one among this group competed. Aleck attracted people around him because of his sparkling conversation and his obvious desire to have people by his side. As a bachelor, privacy to him was a vacuum which could only be filled by the company of his friends. To the Rosses, this became a trial, because Aleck took to coming home from the theater at night and marching into their apartment—even into the matrimonial chamber—where he would lounge around and give them a blow-by-blow description of his adventures of the evening.

Aleck was at this point going through a basic psychological change in life. He was moving past the age where marriage was important to him. He was soon to give up the idea of raising a family. His bout with the mumps had lowered his male drives and he found them easy to sublimate in the company of bright, witty people. He had decided that he would not seek to become a great playwright or artist, but would devote himself to the field of criticism, and yet he was not certain that this decision was merited.

Aleck was ever his own most severe critic in the altar of his soul. This winter of 1922-23 there occurred the death of a fifteen-year-old boy named William Duncan Saunders, son of Professor A. P. Saunders, who was the head of the Department of Chemistry at Hamilton College. Aleck had come to know the Saunders family well during the summer of 1921 which he spent on the campus finishing up his books. He had grown to like young Saunders, who first amused him by his insouciance, and second attracted him by his intelligence. The boy was bright. He wrote poetry, and for a youngster had a well-developed turn of phrase and thought. He entered college at Hamilton in the fall of 1922, and then was killed in an accident. Aleck was upset by this death, and it aroused in him so strong an emotion that he could not even bear to go to Clinton for the funeral, although he had made plans to do so and had farmed out his work before he lost courage.

Deep emotion brought Aleck to a high degree of self-analysis, which he exhibited in a letter to his old friend and classmate, Professor Robert Rudd.

> . . . I don't have to tell you or anyone who knew him that I feel incalculably bereft. But you cannot know, you cannot begin to know, how real my impoverishment is. No one will ever understand how fond of him I was. You must have suspected more than once that I'm a pretty trivial, rootless person, a fellow of motley and diffused affections, permanently adrift. Well, that's true, and this too is true. It just so happens that never in all my grown-up days before last summer had I known what it was to have a child's friendship and companionship. That was largely due to chance—

due for instance to the fact that not once in twenty years have I spent so much as a week under the same roof with a youngster. It was partly due also, I am afraid, to some inadequacy in me, some incapacity to hold their interest or to give them my own, some blind spot in me somewhere. Well, whatever of tenderness we all of us have stored up in us for some little chap, the love that in normal lives goes, I suppose, to a man's own son, had never been tapped in me. . . .

"A . . . trivial, rootless person, a fellow of motley and diffused affections, permanently adrift." This was Aleck's passing, rueful but acidulous appraisal of his own character, far more devastating than anything his enemies might say about him. It was an unfair appraisal moreover, and as such it would have been recognized by his friends, had he ever had the courage to ask them. Carr Van Anda called him "really a sensitive, sometimes almost a shrinking soul." Obviously Woollcott was that, this New York Wit who had not the courage to attend the funeral of a fifteen-year-old boy because he was "shattered"—to use his own term—by the youngster's death.

There were people in New York City who objected to the group to which Aleck belonged, "took a kind of resentful dislike to the group," as Edna Ferber put it. Aleck was made painfully aware of this attitude in the winter of 1922-23 when theatrical producer Richard Aldrich insisted that Woollcott ought to join the Century Association, a conservative club with some pretensions in the field of literature and accomplishment outside the purely business milieu. Aleck acceded to his friend's request with no particular enthusiasm, and his enthusiasm for extraneous clubs quite disappeared in January, when Aldrich wrote that there was such determined opposition to Aleck's membership in the club by a very small handful that if it was pursued he would be blackballed, and so Aldrich was withdrawing the nomination. Aleck never again let his name be put up for any organization; it was quite patently an indication of his personal sensitivity and feeling of inferiority.

Rebecca West, whom he met this same year, immediately noticed Aleck's feelings of disgust for the body into which nature had cast his soul. She met him, she said, "in disastrous circumstances, against which his peculiar gifts of character shone out like a beacon."

Miss West arrived in America that year seeking work and coping with many difficulties. She had come to New York as a feature writer. In England she had already established a reputation for excellence, particularly for her writing about political matters. When she arrived in America, however, she found that she was treated, not as a writer, but as a celebrity. She could not get work and she was thoroughly miserable. In the informal and careless manners of the time, Miss West was mistreated even by those who tried to befriend her. Scott Fitzgerald asked her to come to a party, but neglected to give her his address or telephone number. She dressed and waited. She waited all evening long and no one came for her. At the party, where she was to be the guest of honor, Fitzgerald became furious when she did not appear, and the hit of the evening's entertainment was his impersonation of a haughty Rebecca West who was deigning to visit the United States.

The misunderstandings and the stupidities continued. Swope made a great fuss over Miss West, socially, but he would not give her a job on any terms. In this terrible situation, ill, Miss West met Aleck, and she found him "always a sensitive, consoling, humorous, sturdy friend." She never had the slightest reason to withdraw that opinion. "Of course, he sometimes changed into what Shakespeare called the fretful porpentine. But one noticed it because he was so often the other thing—kind, loyal, understanding."

Some of Aleck's acquaintances always believed that the great love of his life was Neysa McMein, and that he chose bachelorhood in that summer of 1923 when he followed her to Europe only to discover that she had married a young mining engineer named John G. Baragwanath a few weeks earlier, but there seems very little to support this except that she was one of his favorite people, along with Alice Duer Miller. There were others. There were so many others that the old rule of safety in numbers seemed to insulate Aleck from a serious romance. Aleck's trip to Europe that summer was not taken solely to chase Neysa, but because it was his habit to go to Europe each summer, although sometimes he had broken his own rule. This summer he returned to the Meuse-Argonne, this time in the company of novelist Donald Ogden Stewart, and to call on the Canon Simonin, *curé-doyen* of St. Mihiel, whom he had met just a few hours after the Germans evacuated that little town in 1918. Aleck had learned on that joyous day in 1918 that the curé's mother had not tasted candy for four long years, and had rushed out to a Salvation Army booth and bought a box of candied fruit which he had presented to the lady, who was then eighty-eight years old. Five years later he and Stewart went to call at the curate, to see if the old priest was still alive.

> I supposed the old priest would scarcely remember one who was no longer clad in helmet and olive drab, and who had become—well, shall we say less gaunt?—since 1918. But I could tell him that I had been in Saint Mihiel on its great day, and we would have things to talk about. A few minutes later Stewart and I were tugging at the bell pull in the Rue Carnot. The same *bonne* took one look and clattered down the tiled hallway, beckoning us to follow and roaring through the half-open door of her master's study, "it is one of your Americans come back again."
>
> Older and more hawklike than ever, he arose and peered at me in the dusk of his study. Then suddenly both arms went out in the most heart-warming gesture that ever I saw in my life. "Mother of God," he said, "it is the fat soldier with spectacles who spoiled my *maman* with his American bonbons."
>
> It would be a most shoddy pretense to omit here an admission that I could scarcely see the old curé for the tears that filled my eyes. What a time we had that afternoon, the three of us—drinking up the Benedictine left over from the christening of the new *cloches* which had just been hung in the belfry to replace those the Germans carried off to melt into cannon. And his mother? Bless you, yes. There she was in the courtyard, telling her beads at a great rate. Her son knelt on the flagging beside her and roared in her ear that she was having another visit from the American who had once come a-sparking her with a box of candy.

I swore then that I would never venture into that house again without the precaution of bringing another box.

Jilted Aleck? Hardly. After the usual summer of touring the theaters of Europe, he came home again, to work on the preparation of a new book for G. P. Putnam's Sons. As with others, this book was a collection of magazine articles and newspaper Sunday articles. In it was an article in tribute to Neysa McMein, but the book was dedicated to Edna Ferber.

XVII

Much was said about the ephemeral quality of Alexander Woollcott's friendships, usually by persons who had little understanding of Woollcott or his friends. A Woollcott friendship had some similarity to a patent of nobility; the friend might be cast or go voluntarily into exile, but the patent was never really withdrawn, although all the appurtenances and privileges might vanish. Woollcott was bound all his life to his friends and they to him, no matter how much they might quarrel.

One of the best examples of this was the Woollcott relationship with Harold Ross, whom he met first in 1918 in Paris and with whom he was vigorously feuding, talking about and being talked about, cursing and loving up to the moment of his death. Scarcely a week would go by in all this time that Woollcott would not be thinking about Ross and talking about him, although in the later years Ross was more or less banished from the Woollcott circle. At least they went their separate ways.

But the autumn of 1923 was a part of the halcyon period. Ross was working for *Judge* and on the format of the *New Yorker*. Jane Grant Ross was managing the wild ménage on West 47th Street. Aleck was working on the *Herald* and writing magazine articles to keep up the style of living he preferred.

Spring, 1924, brought two noteworthy events to Aleck's career. First was the publication of *Enchanted Aisles* by Putnam's. As usual with Aleck's books, this one was well-received, although again it was more of a critical than a financial success. Still, Aleck could hardly complain. He was getting very good returns from his work, for he had the professional writer's habit of squeezing every use from each bit of editorial research he undertook. For example, Aleck visited the great French actress Sarah Bernhardt in June, 1923. He wrote about the visit in the pages of the New York

Herald, and had then used the material for a magazine article. Now, with some changes the magazine article appeared in *Enchanted Aisles.* In later years there would be some to sneer at Aleck for doing what his contemporary Bernard DeVoto boasted of doing, and yet, who could gainsay the value as well as the immense readability of this description of Bernhardt shortly before her death?

> We saw her in her last June. There she sat in her little, cheerful sitting room up in the musty, frowsy, old house in the Boulevard Pereire which belongs, they say to some South American government, but from which, since the day when an infatuated Minister had grandly placed it at her disposal, she had never been ousted. She was resplendent in a dressing gown of white satin with a saucy, fur-edged overjacket of blue Indian silk and there were blazing rings on the ancient fingers which now and again adjusted the jacket so that there should always be a good view of the scarlet Legion of Honor Badge on her breast. It had taken her so many years and so much trouble to get it. Her face was a white mask on which features were painted, but no craft of make-up could have wrought that dazzling smile which lighted the room. Just as in the glory of her early years, she had never suggested youth but seemed an ageless being from some other world, so now, in her seventy-eighth year, it was not easy to remember that she was old.
>
> There she sat, mutilated, sick, bankrupt, and, as always, more than a little raffish—a ruin, if you will, but one with a bit of gay bunting fluttering jaunty and defiant from the topmost battlement. There she sat, a gaudy old woman, if you will, with fainter and fainter memories of scandals, ovations, labors, rewards, intrigues, jealousies, and heroisms, notorieties and fame, art and the circus. But there was no one in that room so young and so fresh that this great grandmother did not make her seem colorless. She was nearly four score years of age and she had just finished a long harassing season. But she was in no mood to go off to the shore for her rest until she had adjusted her plans for this season. There were young playwrights to encourage with a pat on

the head, there were scene designers and costumiers to be directed, there were artists to be interviewed and there was need of some sort of benign intervention in behalf of a new play struggling along in her own theater. . . .

He spoke of Bernhardt's capacity for work, a quality he shared:

> Oh this passion and capacity for work—what Shaw in his essay on Caesar describes as "the power of killing a dozen secretaries under you, as a life or death courier kills horses"—the wanderer back stage in our own theater will find some stray examples. Maud Adams had it–a tireless general. Margaret Anglin had it. And Jane Cowl. Bernhardt had it supremely, and even as a sick and crippled woman of seventy-eight she could do more work any day than half the inert young people who litter up the French theater as they do ours. It has been said that she died in harness. That expression of a plodder overtaken by death is inadequate for so gallant, so defiantly twinkling an exit. She was a boat that went to the bottom with its orchestra playing gaily. In her final year she was aflame with that spirit which lighted the despondent blackness of the North Sea one ghastly and terrifying night when a transport carrying some American doughboys to the French battlefields was sunk many miles from shore. They went over the side into the rowboats, not chanting in the approved heroic vein but humming with incorrigible and facetious cheerfulness: "Oh, boys, say, boys, where do we go from here."

For those who read carefully, Alexander Woollcott's life was pictured in these pages, as in his description of Neysa McMein's studio, where he spent so much time.

> The spot itself is a bleak, high-ceilinged room, furnished by the process of haphazard accumulation. Its decoration ranges from a Briggs strip, torn out of the morning's paper and pinned askew on the wall, to an original Drian, respectfully framed. That splash of vivid color on the screen is a shawl sent by David Belasco and that stretch of gray-green fabric on the wall is a tapestry which she herself bought in

Paris and bore home in triumphant only to find that the greater part of it had come from the looms way back in the dim days of 1920.

The population is as wildly variegated. Over at the piano Jascha Heifetz and Arthur Samuels may be trying to find what four hands can do in the syncopation of a composition never thus desecrated before. Irving Berlin is encouraging them. Squatted uncomfortably around an ottoman, Franklin P. Adams, Marc Connelly and Dorothy Parker will be playing cold hands to see who will buy dinner that evening. At the bookshelf Robert C. Benchley and Edna Ferber are amusing themselves vastly by thoughtfully autographing her set of Mark Twain for her. In the corner, some jet-bedecked dowager from a statelier milieu is taking it all in, immensely diverted. Chaplin or Chaliapin, Alice Duer Miller or Wild Bill Donovan, Father Duffy or Mary Pickford—any or all of them may be there. . . .

As to Neysa McMein, Aleck's description tells it all:

Standing at the easel itself, oblivious of all the ructions, incredibly serene and intent on her work, is the artist herself. She is beautiful, grave and slightly soiled. Her apron is a shabby streaked remnant of a once neat garment. Her fair hair, all awry, is discolored from an endless drizzle of pastel dust. Her face is smooched with it. She itches to edge one of the pianists to the floor and join the concert herself. The poker game tempts her. But it is not until the daylight has dwindled to dusk that she comes wandering around the easel and drops into a chair, dog tired but sociable. Indeed, she brings to the party the kind of whole hearted laughter for which your true comedian will work till he drops. Few persons can tell a story better, but unlike so many who have that gift, she can listen, too. She listens with all her might, which, as those who know who have sat at the feet of Mrs. Fiske, is half the art of acting and almost the whole secret of good manners. . . .

This listening was also the secret of Aleck's affection for Neysa McMein, and of the close relationship that would last until the day of her death. Aleck, too, was an artist, and his favored instrument growing more important to him as the years drew on, was conversation. All Aleck's very closest friends were listeners; they were as important to him as are acoustics to an orchestra, or, more aptly, as is an audience to an actor on the stage. Here, in his character sketch of Neysa McMein, written in 1923, Aleck revealed a basic facet of his personality.

In the spring of 1924, Aleck met another who would become one of his most faithful friends, and, he too, a good listener. He was Harpo Marx, one of the then Four Marx Brothers, and in a sense their meeting was a mistake. Aleck had attended a meeting of the Thanatopsis and Inside Straight Club before the opening performance of *I'll Say She Is*. Somehow he had allowed himself to be dragooned into reviewing this performance and now he was regretting it. He looked around for somebody to take his place and write a review of "some damned acrobats called The Marx Brothers," without success, and he went off cursing to attend the show. The next day his review began:

> As one of the many who laughed immoderately throughout the greater part of the first New York performance given by a new musical show, entitled, if memory serves, *I'll Say She Is*, it behooves your correspondent to report at once that that harlequinade has some of the most comical moments vouchsafed to the first-nighters in a month of Mondays. It is a bright-colored and vehement setting for the goings on of those talented cutups, the Four Marx Brothers. In particular, it is a splendacious and reasonably tuneful excuse for going to see that silent brother, and sly, unexpected, magnificent comic among the Marxes, who is recorded somewhere on a birth certificate as Adolph, but who is known to the adoring two-a-day as Harpo Marx. . . .

Harpo was the one who appealed to Aleck, Harpo whom he termed a great clown in the manner of Joe Jackson and Bert Melrose of the past. Aleck was so impressed that he telephoned Harpo and asked if he would be received if he "barged" into Harpo's dressing room after the show that second night. Harpo later wrote his recollection of that meeting in *Harpo Speaks*:

> . . . Woollcott "barged" into my dressing room—literally. I had no idea what a "big New York critic" ought to look

like, but I didn't expect this. He looked like something that had gotten loose from Macy's Thanksgiving Day Parade.

I couldn't help thinking of Mons Herbert's old vaudeville act in which he blew up the rubber turkey. If Mons had blown up a plucked owl, put thick glasses and a mustache on it, and dressed it in an opera cape and wide black hat, this is what it would have looked like.

"The name is Woollcott," he said, and his voice didn't change my first impression. It was a voice that could have been reproduced by letting the air out of a balloon, a down-beat inflection with a whiny edge to it. Coming from him it sounded hoity-toity and supercilious, and I didn't like it a bit.

We shook hands. Woollcott sighed and settled his bulk onto a rickety dressing-room chair with surprising ease. He rested his hands on the head of his cane, blinked, twitched his mustache, then broke into a grin that wasn't supercilious at all. If anything, he was being shy. He had come to see me not as a critic, but as a starry-eyed fan.

"Well, Marx," he said. "So you didn't approve of my piece in the morning's paper."

Nope, I sure didn't, I told him. At least I didn't approve of the part I could understand. He laughed and said, "Might I ask what you disapproved of specifically?"

I had read the whole review by now. "You got us all mixed up, Mr. Woollcott," I said. "Groucho's not the oldest —Chico is. Zeppo's not the stage manager—he's the juvenile."

"And what about Harpo? Did I get him right?"

"Tell you the truth," I said, "I couldn't tell from the things you wrote whether you were giving me the raspberry or trying to give me a build-up, because I didn't know what half the words meant. If you're looking to give me a build-up, forget it. I don't work as a single. I work with my brothers or not at all."

He stopped smiling, and took off his hat, "My dear Marx," he said, "I was neither flattering your performance nor making light of it. I meant every word I wrote. You are the funniest man I have ever seen upon the stage."

I didn't know how to return a compliment like that, so I said, "What about my harp solo? How did you like that?"

"I still think you're the funniest man I have ever seen upon the stage," said Woollcott. "Consider yourself fortunate, Marx," he said, "that I am not a music critic."

So he was one of those characters. He made you a compliment, then jabbed the needle in. I had known guys like that, who couldn't help needling any more than a wasp could help stinging. It was a type of guy I loved to have around. They were the world's greatest patsies for practical jokes. I began to like this Woollcott.

He said he was sorry if he'd offended me, but he had an unfortunate social disease. He always spoke whatever came to his mind. "My friends will tell you," he said, "that Woollcott is a nasty old snipe. Don't believe them. Woollcott's friends are a pack of simps who move their lips when they read.

"Nevertheless," he continued, hoisting himself up off the chair, "I should like them to meet you, tonight. I should like to show them a true artist. You might bring some light into their grubby little lives. I take it you're free for what's left of the evening?"

I had to get out of this fast. If his "friends" talked the way he did I would have absolutely nothing to say to them. I didn't know the language. "Sorry," I said. "I've got a date I'm already late for."

Woollcott did not intend that I should refuse his invitation. He squinted down his nose at me and said, huffily, "A young lady, I presume?" I shook my head.

"Some business matter of great urgency?" he asked, with heavy sarcasm.

I nodded my head yes. "Poker game," I said.

His grin returned. "Bravo!" he said. "Precisely what my friends and I have in mind! Are you a good poker player, Marx?"

I told him I played a pretty fair country game.

He clapped his hands. "So be it!" he said. "The minute you're out of grease paint, come buckety-buckety over to the Hotel Algonquin. Shall we say eleven-thirty?"

I was trapped. "Okay, eleven-thirty," I said. "But first, would you mind showing me your teeth?" He bare his teeth. "Too bad," I said. "No gold. Well, I'll keep looking."

"No gold?" said Woollcott, waiting for the gag.

I told him I was still looking for another guy as nice to play poker with as Mons Herbert, who used to tip his hand by the number of gold teeth he flashed. This delighted Woollcott. "And what did this walking bonanza do upon the stage?" he asked.

"He played the 'Anvil Chorus' by blowing on knives and forks," I said, "and for a finish he blew up a turkey until music came out of its ass."

Woollcott laughed so hard he had to sit down again. He wiped tears from his eyes and said, "Dear God, why can't I have friends like that!" . . .

He put on his black impresario's hat, adjusted his cape, and stuck out his hand. "A rare pleasure, sir," he said. Instead of giving him my hand I gave him my leg, the old switch gag I had used since *On the Mezzanine*. He pushed my knee away in disgust. "See here, Marx," he said, with the full hoity-toity treatment. "Kindly confine your baboonery to the stage. Off it, you are a most unfunny fellow."

I liked him more and more.

Thus Aleck introduced Harpo Marx into the Thanatopsis and Inside Straight Club. Actually, at this time Aleck was no more than a casual member. He, Heywood Broun, and Marc Connelly had announced their intentions of resigning because poker was a waste of time. ("The persistent rumors," he said, "that we resigned from pique at our losses are unworthy of those who circulate them. It just happens to be true that Mr. Connelly (as always) and Mr. Broun and myself, for a change, did suffer some rather severe misfortunes; but as we always say, it all evens up in the course of a year.")

Thanatopsis lasted just about another ten years, with Aleck coming along when he felt like it and had the time, which was less and less as the years went by.

Aleck's review of the Marx Brothers' new show on Broadway had appeared in the New York *Sun*, also a Munsey newspaper.

When the failing *Herald* had been sold to the also tottering *Tribune* in the spring of 1924, Aleck had been transferred to become drama critic of Munsey's afternoon *Sun.* He did not like it much, for his entire experience in daily newspapers told him the critics of the morning newspapers were the important ones, the critics who made and broke shows. When the cast broke for the dressing rooms after an opening night, it was to rush out and wait for the late editions of the *Times,* the *Tribune,* the *Herald,* the *World,* the *American*—the morning newspapers—and for Aleck to occupy a second-string position as an afternoon newspaper critic was most uncomfortable to him.

Soon Woollcott was grousing in the meetings of the Thanatopsis at the Algonquin Hotel, and his complaints came to the ear of that other resigned regular, Heywood Broun, who was drama critic of the morning *World,* and that sometime visitor Herbert Bayard Swope, who was Broun's boss on the newspaper. Broun wanted to escape the chores of drama criticism and devote his efforts to a more general, more hair-raising column which would appear on the page opposite the editorial page, which Swope was making famous as the roosting place of important journalism. F.P.A.'s "Conning Tower" was also located on that page, as was Harry Hansen's column on books. For the moment nothing could be done, because Aleck's contract with Munsey ran until the middle of August, 1925, but Aleck had his eye on the *World* and Swope had his eye on Aleck.

XVIII

In the book *Enchanted Aisles,* Alexander Woollcott permitted himself an entire section which he titled "Resentments," for writing about some things he did not like in the theater. This willingness to stand up and be counted for his opinions was not unique with Aleck, but it was one of his strongest points as critic and writer. He was called treacly sweet and pursingly bitter by critics of his writings and public appearances, with the implication that he was all one or all the other—whichever facet the particular critic did not like. Aleck was both, but far more than this he was a very discerning man. What he had to say about the Marx Brothers, and particularly Harpo, was said later by millions of others in America and all across the world, just as what he had to say about Charles W. Chaplin was repeated by others long after Aleck began saying it. Aleck appreciated Charles W. Chaplin from the beginning and attributed to him a "kind of physical eloquence, a beauty of motion" which he had found only one other time among the players of the world, and that was in the work of Eleanora Duse. Aleck was not now talking about Chaplin for the first time—he had been among the original Chaplin discoverers in America, along with Mrs. Fiske. Indeed, he and Mrs. Fiske had sat down and talked about Charles Chaplin when Alexander Woollcott was a very young drama critic on the New York *Times* and Aleck had written about Charlie after he saw the early films produced by the Chaplin company. (Later Chaplin was to show his gratitude in his own way.) Aleck's articles about Chaplin always had that same breathless enthusiasm that he showed about Harpo.

Whatever profits there were to be made in *Enchanted Aisles* for the publisher, the author made little from it because he spent enormous sums for copies of his own book. He sent books to all his friends, and to some people whom he merely respected, such as Carr Van Anda of the *Times*, and Booth Tarkington, whom he wanted to know better. Van Anda found the book "pleasant." Tarkington wrote that it would be "discovered time and time again and should be." This was the same Tarkington who had so thoroughly disapproved of Aleck before the days when Aleck had given some praise to Helen Hayes when she appeared in his little comedy. And Helen Hayes? She was now so friendly with Aleck that she asked him to the parties she held at her apartment, 54 Gramercy Park. (Later he was best man at her wedding.)

This summer of 1924, the games of the Thanatopsis and Inside Straight Club were remarkable for the absence of Alexander Woollcott, for when the drama season drew to a close he disappeared from the city. He was working on a new book, *The Story of Irving Berlin,* which Putnam's would publish the following year, and this project had been put off, by and large, until summer when he would have proper leisure to devote to it. He needed leisure and a place to work that would be free of the constant atmosphere of party and play that permeated the Gas House settlement where lived the "moist heap." Forever Aleck was claiming that he "must get away from things" for some peace and quiet, whereupon he would repair to the Chatham or some other good-quality New York hotel for a weekend of absolute quiet—and then would telephone several dozen friends, telling them exactly where he was and what he was doing.

To write this book, he needed more quiet than he had allowed himself in the past because this was to be a biography and the longest sustained work he had yet written.

This time Aleck was in luck. A young New York lawyer named Enos Booth had acquired a wooded eight-acre island in the middle of a small lake near the western border of Vermont. The lake was called Bomoseen. It was seven miles long and a mile and a half wide. The island was Neshobe Island, once the center of Indian ceremonies, then the pig farm of a local Vermont settler, later an ice-fishing center and then a resort hotel. The resort hotel had been built in 1878, in a day when the lake steamer stopped at the island regularly during the spring and summer months. The hotel had burned down and when Booth acquired the island he built a small two-story summer house on it. He spent part of every summer there and invited a number of his friends up to use the island on a loan basis, sometimes communally. Through mutual croquet-playing friends from New Jersey, Aleck received an invitation to visit the island, and saw immediately that it was just what he wanted for the summer's work. He secured an invitation to use it.

In June, Aleck went to Hamilton College again to attend the commencement ceremonies. This was not unusual for him; he attended Hamilton's commencement whenever he was in the eastern part of the United States at the proper time. This year there was something unusual: he was to be honored by a degree of Doctor of Humane Letters. Following the ceremony he made arrangements for his summer work, and went to Neshobe Island for a month.

There he used part of his time writing to Robert Benchley who had appeared one season as monologuist in the Music Box Theater, which was built to house Irving Berlin's Productions.

He also wrote to John Alden Carpenter, the composer, and to Jerome Kern. What he wanted, he told all of them, was someone to bear witness about certain aspects of Berlin's character. Each man replied at length, and Aleck had, for the first time, established a research technique for writing that he was to use most successfully in the future.

The Story of Irving Berlin is unique among the writings of Alexander Woollcott in that neither the author nor his reminiscences appear in it. Irving Berlin—Israel Baline—knew many people that Aleck knew around New York and some that he did not know. Aleck talked to a great number of them, to Irving Berlin himself, and then he wrote his book. It was not a long book, consisting of some 50,000 words in 223 pages, and it could not be called a critical biography in any normal sense. It was, however, the story of Irving Berlin as he might have wanted it to be told, the story of a rags-to-riches rise of a young Russian immigrant on the sidewalks of New York. Aleck began:

> A dirty, little barefoot newsboy, already well enough known to the rival gangs of Cherry Street as Izzy Baline, stood on the edge of an East River pier, there where Cherry

Hill slopes down to the New York waterfront. It was his immediate mission in life to sell the *Evening Journal,* a gaudy gazette then adventuring for the first time those howling headlines of which the new vehemence was serving so well to usher in the war with far-off Spain. A discouragingly large number of copies rested still unsold under his skinny right arm. But, firmly clutched in the damp grasp of his left hand, five sticky pennies bore witness to at least some business done on this, his first day as a newsboy.

For a moment he had forgotten the dreary need of selling the remainder. For his large, dark eyes were happily occupied with a black and reeking ship which the waterfront tattle reported as about to set sail for an incredibly distant place called China. Over her rails there peered an occasional yellow face, just such a funny, yellow face as looked out at him from the window over by the Bowery when he scuttled by on his way to Chambers Street, where, it seemed, he could get the papers which an absurdly ordered world then expected him to sell at such a monstrous profit to passing strangers. It was pleasant to forget their almost universal indifference to *Evening Journal* in gazing at this craft which would soon put out for the mysterious east.

Indeed she proves so engaging a spectacle that the boy paid little heed to a crane which had been doggedly swinging to and fro all afternoon between a nearby coal barge and a row of carts waiting on the pier to carry its cargo to the cellars of the city. Thus the returning crane was able to catch him, sweep him through the air and drop him into the deep water of the East River which swirls littered and greasy there between the Manhattan piers.

There was laughter and shrill clamor along the rails of the big ship. There was much conscientious calling for the police along the bustling pier. But it was an Irish wharf rat of no official standing who parted recklessly with his shoes and jumped in after the small merchant. Afterwards the ambulance surgeon confided to the nurse in Gouverneur Hospital that the kid must have gone down for the third time, there was so much of the East River inside him. The newspapers were doubtless drifting soggily out to sea by this time, but some of Mr. Hearst's more emphatic tidings could have been read by anyone who had held Izzy Baline's shirt up to a mirror. And, as they stretched him out on a cot in the hospital, they laughed at discovering that his clenched left hand still held all five of the pennies. . . .

And yet, despite this Horatio Alger beginning, Aleck's biography was not a puff piece.

> It may be a shock to the ingenuous to learn that scarcely a song in all his long eventful catalogue was written because his heart was singing and the song could not be kept from bursting out of him. Nearly all of them were written deliberately and a little sulkily by one whose business associates stood around him in a reproachful circle and assured him that, if he did not give birth to something at once, the dear, old publishing house would go on the rocks.
>
> The artist in him may be tickled mightily by some neat, unexpected phrase in the chorus he has just written, but the publisher in him will ruthlessly strike it out in favor of some quite routine threadbare word with no disconcerting unfamiliarity about it to stick in the crop of the proletariat.

Aleck's biography of Irving Berlin gave a good picture of the day and the thirty-six-year-old man he was portraying. He made no pretensions for the book as finished biography.

> The tale of Berlin has a lilt in it for those who see it as a microcosm of this nation's history. If we keep green the memory of those gallant adventurers who first wrung a living from this resisting land, if there be a challenge for us still in the coming of the longboat that rescued the desperate settlement at Jamestown or in the gaze of the wondering priests who first sailed down the Mississippi,—well, here is a fresh reminder that the romance of America is an unfinished story. The life of Irving Berlin is a part of the American epic and the epic is still in the making.
>
> Then it is hard to write the biography of a man who is only thirty-six years old as you reach your final chapter. You are troubled by what Philip Guedalla calls "the studied dis-

> courtesy of a premature obituary," and there is always the plaguing notion that the subject of your narrative may, even as the presses are whirring with that final chapter, provide material for another one more eventful than all the rest.
>
> Perhaps after all, it will be decided in the perspective of fifty years that Irving Berlin was quite unimportant. Perhaps not. And if not, why here—sketchy, tentative, unfinished—is a source book for the convenience of the wiser historian who will put the facts in permanent form.
>
> Finally, it is never easy to tell the tale of one who, in time and space, lives just around the corner and may himself read the words you have written. In the gruff diffidence which is the American tradition of human relations, I cannot freely set down for his embarrassed eyes all the good qualities of the head and of the heart which the neighbors of Irving Berlin know are an essential part of the full story. I am not free to put into words how deeply I honor the true and gentle American who was carried out of Russia by that refugee Rabbi and who served for a time the drinks and the songs at Nigger Mike's.

As with every one of Aleck's lengthier literary efforts, the biography of Irving Berlin told much about the author and here it all was: Aleck's shyness; Aleck's reverence for the American past, kindled in the trenches of France; Aleck's diffidence and lack of pretense about the quality of the biography he was writing; his knowledge that he had prepared only part of the materials for a biography. This was the same man who speared Harpo Marx with a glance when Marx in his disconcerting and slightly vulgar manner, offered him his leg when Aleck had extended his hand. Aleck was a rare creature and even now, in 1924, there were very definitely two Alecks, the public character in the opera cape and the private Woollcott, a shy and lonely fellow.

XIX

In the autumn of 1924, after Booth Tarkington had read the pleasant chapter devoted to him and his plays in *Enchanted Aisles,* Aleck was asked to visit the Tarkingtons at their summer home in Kennebunkport, Maine. For protection and company in case the visit proved difficult, Aleck took along Alice Duer Miller. The visit was a complete success, although Aleck and Tarkington were almost as different as anyone could expect. Tarkington was of an older generation, and a conservative Republican in politics. Aleck's iconoclasm was matched only by his fierce loyalties and the radicalism he had inherited from the Phalanx group.

After that October visit, it was back to the serious work of assessing the dramatic offerings of the season. This was the year of *What Price Glory,* a war play written by Maxwell Anderson and Lawrence Stallings. Aleck discovered this play. He was lunching at the Brevoort Hotel on Fifth Avenue one day with Stallings, after having read the play and come to the conclusion that it was very much worth while. At the Brevoort producer Arthur Hopkins stopped by the table, perhaps to ask Aleck what had become of his own play *World Without End.* Aleck introduced Stallings and said he had just finished a play. Hopkins was polite. Aleck said that of course Hopkins never read plays because he was a producer. Hopkins, then, was badgered into reading the play, and having read it, he produced it. It became the most popular war play of the 1920's.

Aleck did not confine his helpfulness to budding playwrights. He helped actors, writers—anyone whose work appealed to him. Two years earlier, Aleck had encountered a young Negro named Paul Robeson, who had a minor stage part in a play, and in Aleck's way he had asked him, offhandedly, to come by the

West 47th Street apartment some time for a talk. Robeson had done so, and that was more or less the end of it for the moment.

But there was much more to the relationship in time. Aleck did not forget people he liked; he always went out of his way to do them good turns, and so it was with Robeson. As he wrote of Robeson later, in a statement as revealing of Alexander Woollcott the man as he ever made:

> In his [Robeson's] case I despair of ever putting into convincing words my notion of this quality in him. I can say only that by what he does, thinks and is, by his unassailable dignity, and his serene, uncorruptible simplicity. Paul Robeson strikes me as having been made out of the original stuff of the world. In this sense he is coeval with Adam and the redwood trees of California. He is a fresh act, a fresh gesture, a fresh effort of creation. I am proud of belonging to his race. For, of course, we are both members of the one sometimes fulsomely described as human.

At that 1922 meeting Robeson had told Aleck modestly that he had just discovered that he had a pretty good voice—one of the understatements of the century. Later Aleck helped get Robeson together with Jerome Kern, and from this came the production of *Show Boat.* It was so long delayed, however, that Robeson was abroad on a concert tour, and he actually first played *Show Boat* in London, then later in America. Aleck was to help a young actor named Coburn Proctor Goodwin secure stage roles in *The Ivory Door* and *The Jealous Moon.* He would help Will Rogers—whom he did not know then and never came to know well—begin a writing career. After seeing Rogers in vaudeville he suggested to Harold Ross that Rogers could write fine humorous commentary for *Judge.* Aleck was given credit for "discovering" Fred Astaire before the war, by calling him to the attention of several vaudeville stage managers.

That was one kind of help to which Aleck was addicted. There was another—pure financial assistance. Aleck was the softest touch along Broadway for anyone who needed cash. He had plenty of money, for his typewriter seemed to turn out golden manuscripts. The Berlin book was a good example of Aleck's penchant for earning money: not only was it successful as a book, but it was picked up by the *Saturday Evening Post* for serialization in five instalments. This bonanza earned Aleck as much money as he was making in an entire year as drama critic for the *Sun*.

He had long since paid back Alexander Humphreys of Stevens Institute the $3,000 on which he had based his college career, but when he was paying he was happily surprised to learn that Humphreys would take no interest on the money. Thereupon Aleck determined to help others. Shyly and quietly he was giving money to various youngsters in order to finance their way through college, and he was a donor to the causes of Hamilton College, whatever they might be. By 1925, he was among Hamilton's most distinguished and loyal alumni.

This year, 1925, was the year in which Alexander Woollcott left the *Sun*, where he had never been happy, to join the *World*, under Herbert Bayard Swope. He signed a three-year contract, which guaranteed him $15,000 a year and gave him special permission to write magazine articles. Heywood Broun went happily to writing a column in which he could deal with the greater social issues of the day, and Aleck became the *World's* drama critic.

This association with the *World* was never a very satisfactory one. Aleck did not like interference in the drama department, and Swope was a master at interference with everything in the newspaper. There was a basic difference in their approaches to journalism, too. Aleck had grown up on the *Times*, where the management took the position that it employed the critic and he said what he wanted. Swope was forever sending brusque memoranda to his staff members, and Aleck was no exception. On several occasions his copy was changed. At least once publisher Pulitzer complained to his editor about the acid writings of the drama critic.

It was scarcely an atmosphere in which Aleck could thrive or one in which he would long be happy. He was pleased with his two assistants on the staff, Alison Smith, who later married playwright Russel Crouse, and Jeffrey Holmesdale, who later became Lord Jeffrey, the fifth Earl Amherst. He protected them from the management, and they found him the most pleasant of superiors. It was always true of Aleck: he quarreled only with his equals and he countenanced no superiors in any way, shape or form.

There was no sudden breach between Aleck and the *World*. He was a good soldier, and if he had gotten himself into something he did not like, he had the sense to remember that he had left the *Times* for money and at the *World* he was earning as much as any critic in the United States. He could not expect to have everything his own way.

In the winter of 1925 the drama routine was the same as ever: one first night after another. Aleck went to the theater even when there were no openings, going back to see plays that he liked especially, and particularly returning to the Casino Theater on West 39th Street, where the Marx Brothers' *I'll Say She Is* ran for a solid year. One night, when he brought Mrs. Fiske to see the show, he tipped Harpo off that he was doing so, and asked that the brothers be especially on their toes. Harpo got Harold Ross to blow up a huge photograph of Aleck—taken at the Hamilton ceremonies when he was dolled up in his cap and gown to receive his L.H.D. degree, and planted this in the center of one of the lobby posters. Thus, when Mrs. Fiske swept in on Aleck's arm, the first thing she saw was Aleck, her "dear boy," surrounded by scantily clad chorus girls and looking very much part of the show.

Aleck was annoyed. There was no reason for Harpo to have known that Mrs. Fiske's Alexander Woollcott was not Harpo's Alexander Woollcott, but Aleck did not forgive quickly. He did not bring Mrs. Fiske backstage. He did not speak to Harpo when he saw him at the Thanatopsis next. But a few days later, when there came an opening of a new show down the street from the Casino, Harpo persuaded Groucho, Chico and Zeppo to get into their costumes early and appear under the marquee of the competing theater playing tunes on mandolins and singing while Harpo put on his pantomime act in the fright-wig. They knew, of course, that Woollcott would be there because it was an important opening.

Woollcott came walking by on his way into the theater, not cracking a smile, not noticing the strolling minstrels, until he passed Harpo, very close, brushing him with his cape. From beneath the Woollcott mustache came a loud stage whisper:

"Jew son-of-a-bitch."

And that was the signal of the truce.

On the other hand, there really never was any truce for the next nineteen years. How could there be, given Harpo Marx's propensity for practical jokes and Aleck's sharp tongue and instant furiousness when crossed?

One night Heywood Broun, Aleck, and Harpo went to the Colony restaurant for supper after the theater and then caught a taxi to take them home. Aleck and Broun became involved in a literary argument, each talking as fast as he could, and Harpo became mildly annoyed because he could not understand most of the conversation and they would not pay any attention to him. The cab stopped before his apartment building, and Harpo got out. Interrupted in mid-sentence Aleck spoke to Harpo in a lordly manner and asked him to tell the driver where to go.

"I did not like his condescending attitude," Harpo said. So he told the driver to take the other two to Werba's Theater in Brooklyn, which was a burlesque house in the flattest part of Flatbush.

Two hours later Harpo was sleeping soundly when the telephone rang. He picked it up, and sleepily said "hello."

Only one sentence emerged, a sentence covered with the frost of Brooklyn and the hoar of a broken down taxi, and the rime of a long cold January walk.

"You Jew son-of-a-bitch," the voice said.

Aleck spent much time carousing with the Thanatopsis gang, giving parties in his apartment, or Ross's or at Neysa McMein's studio, playing cribbage with Ross, whom he could always beat at this game, although Ross usually whipped him at poker, playing croquet in the spring in Central Park and moving out for house parties in the later months. He spent much of his time helping people, too. Scott Fitzgerald, who was living in Paris, wrote asking Aleck to help a writer named Harold Stearns if he could. Aleck looked into it and made some recommendations to Swope, then turned the matter over to Ross. Zona Gale, who had won the Pulitzer Prize in 1921 with her play *Miss Lulu Bett,* came to Aleck for a reading of a new play, and he showed her, to her immense gratitude, where she had gone wrong in several matters. For some reason or other, Aleck had quarreled with Walter Duranty, his old friend from the pre-war days at the

Times, but as with all Aleck's quarrels with his friends, he simply awaited a suitable time to make up again—at his convenience—and in 1925 Duranty was in New York, playing poker at Thanatopsis, complaining about "that villainous Ross" and glorying in Aleck's company.

One of Aleck's choice companions was George S. Kaufman, and Aleck was constantly pushing Kaufman to go into new theatrical enterprises. Kaufman, on the other hand, wanted Aleck to join with him in doing a play. They had one idea together: it was to be a play based on characters and situations drawn from the Swope household, which seemed to them to be one big houseparty, spring, summer and fall, lasting from Wednesday morning until Tuesday night and beginning over again. Oscar Levant, the young pianist, came to the Swope house for a visit and spent several years. So did Ruth Gordon. So did Joseph J. Hennessey. That was the kind of household it was, with a constant backgammon game or bridge game or cribbage game going on in one corner, the swimming pool filled with people who never were introduced to one another, and perhaps a no-bounds croquet game, proceeding out on the lawn.

In the summer of this year, Aleck went to Europe again, sailing in June, working in London, if one called it work, by seeing all the new English plays and dining his friends at his suite in the Carlton or at the Savoy. He met Irving Berlin there and many others from New York. Then it was on to Paris for a look at the French offerings of the season, and then to the south of France where he loafed at Antibes for a few weeks. Part of the summer was spent in the company of Charles MacArthur, former Chicago newspaperman, who, with Ben Hecht had written *The Front Page,* and in so doing had become one of Aleck's pets. When MacArthur married Helen Hayes that coupled two of Aleck's favorite people and gave him an immense feeling of satisfaction. Part of the summer was spent in the company of Edna Ferber, who came up from the south of France to see him in Paris, and then in July, Aleck went to Scotland for a visit before returning to the United States.

In the summer of 1926, Aleck formed a corporation with a number of friends to buy Neshobe Island from Enos Booth and make it into a summer club. They called it the Neshobe Island

Club, Inc., and sold shares for $1,000 each. Other shareholders were Neysa McMein, Alice Duer Miller, actress Ruth Gordon, songwriter Howard Dietz, George Kaufman's wife, Beatrice, Raoul Fleischmann, George Backer, Harold Guinzberg, a book publisher, and Raymond Ives, an insurance man. The idea was that no one would get in another's way; they would keep one another informed as to the dates when they wanted to use the club, and there would be no difficulties. They engaged a general handyman who was known as Bathless Bill. He lived in sin with the cook, and at night they fought and she threw crockery. At first, they were the only permanent residents. William Bull, who ran a fishing camp and resort on the east side of the lake, arranged to transport casual visitors to the island, to check in daily and go off to Castleton Corners or Fair Haven a few miles away to buy supplies, and to serve as a message drop and telephone center, because there was no telephone on the island. Several of the members of the club bought motorboats; they were relatively cheap and there was plenty of money among the crowd in the 1920's; Harpo at one time had *two* motorboats at the lake, for reasons he could not later remember, having won one of them, perhaps, in a crap game.

It was arranged that each member of the club would have the untrammeled use of the premises more or less when he wanted it. But that is scarcely how it worked out.

Aleck soon discovered that he liked the lake more than anyone else, and the others soon discovered that half the pleasure of being there was to listen to Aleck's perorations and challenges to conversation. The secret was that all of the other members were good listeners and Aleck was a marvelous talker. So, Aleck more or less took charge of the Neshobe Club and spent what time he wanted there, with the others coming and going as they pleased.

The use of the club, of course, like most of Vermont in those days, was confined to the summer and autumn months. The first frost came in September, the lake froze over in November and remained that way until perhaps the first of May. Only an ice fisherman would have wanted to visit Neshobe Island's eight wooded acres in the interim, only an ice fisherman with plenty of warm clothing and matches, because the clapboard clubhouse was neither weatherproofed nor centrally heated.

The autumn of 1926 marked the breakup of the pleasant but hectic household on West 47th Street in New York. It was done in a fury after a quarrel, and as he was wont and willing to do, Aleck turned on an embarrassing display of temper against Ross.

Ross, in spite of his ulcers, took the matter calmly enough. Aleck walked out, leaving the household furniture, for which he was to be reimbursed according to a formula fixed by Hawley Truax, and taking Junior, the son of the Ross's handyman. Aleck had been training Junior for several years to be general butler and factotum. Junior was slender and dark and self-effacing enough to disappear completely when Aleck was on a rampage—which made him the ideal servant for the time being.

The marriage of Ross and Jane Grant broke up, and Ross moved into an apartment with Ed MacNamara, sometimes known as "the singing cop," Aleck moved into the Hotel des Artistes on 67th Street, near Neysa McMein's studio.

In 1927, Aleck took over the Neshobe Island Club for most of the summer, bringing up guests as he wished, and keeping the clubhouse filled night after night. No one else minded at all for he was very careful not to offend the other members, and they were so fond of him that except for the continual quarreling over important matters, such as the spelling of a word or the outcome of a gambling game, there was little dissent.

One of his early guests was Harpo, and here is his description:

> The thing we cherished most about the island, along with its natural beauty, was its isolation. Whenever we stepped onto Neshobe, we left Western Civilization behind and entered our own primitive society. Aleck would have been content to keep the island in the Stone Age. The most modern appliances he would tolerate, at first, were kerosene lamps, a hand pump for water, and an outboard motor for the launch. Bit by bit, for the sake of his guests' comfort, he softened.
>
> Our privacy we fought for and protected at all costs. The mainland was only a quarter of a mile away, and near the

dock was a large resort hotel which we could see from the island. The natives, in true Vermont fashion, didn't bother anybody who didn't bother them, but the tourists were a pretty nosy bunch.

The rumor got around that there were "famous people living on that dinky island," and that there were "a lot of crazy goings-on out there." One day while I was waiting on the mainland for the launch to pick me up, two dames were sitting on the dock gazing at the island. One of them was looking through a pair of binoculars. I sidled over behind them, and heard the dame with the binoculars say, "Will you look who's there, in a bathing suit! It's Marie Dressler!"

"Marie Dressler" was of course Alexander Woollcott, taking his daily dip.

One day Alice Miller went for a walk and rushed back to report a harrowing thing. A group of tourists, she said, had rowed over to the island and were down on the beach having a picnic. I volunteered to deal with the interlopers. I stripped off all my clothes, put on my red wig, smeared myself with mud, and went whooping and war-dancing down to the shore, making Gookies and brandishing an ax. The tourists snatched up their things, threw them into the boat, and rowed away fast enough to have won the Poughkeepsie Regatta. That put an end to the snooping that season. It also, I'm sure, started some juicy new rumors about our crazy goings-on.

Alice Duer Miller, the novelist, was the only club member who did much serious work on the island in the 1920's. She kept a daily schedule. Neysa McMein did a little sketching once in a while. Aleck sometimes worked on a magazine article or pulling old articles together for a new book. The others loafed.

There were rules, however. One of them was Aleck's rule of the Morning Dip, which meant everyone had to be in the water before breakfast no matter how cold the lake was—and it could be freezing in August. Aleck was a fine swimmer, and with his layers of protective fat he seemed to be impervious to the cold. The others froze and swore and trembled in the cold, but they all went into the water every morning.

Then there was one other rule: no drinking before 11:00 A.M., and no drunkenness at any time. Aleck detested drunkenness, and several guests were surprised to have their stays shortened and never to be asked again when they imbibed too freely and made scenes.

There were many games, such as anagrams and parchisi at which Aleck was an expert—and Murder. This game was played by drawing lots first to see who would be the murderer, and second, who would be the district attorney.

One night Harpo was chosen as murderer (known only to himself) and Aleck was the district attorney. Harpo sneaked into a small bathroom used by the women, unrolled the toilet paper a little way, and wrote on it in lipstick the message that the person was dead, then rolled it up again. Alice Duer Miller came into the room and used the toilet paper, saw the message, and then obeyed the rules of the game. For five hours she sat in the bathroom, unable to get up and let herself out because she was dead. The game had begun before dinner, and the dinner had been ruined. There was no question about the identity of the murderer, because the message written in lipstick on the toilet paper told all. It said: "You are Ded," and there was only one person in this nest of anagram fiends and bibliophiles who would spell dead, d-e-d.

Harpo.

Aleck was furious. He was angry because his steak had been spoiled, but angrier because Harpo had fudged on the rules. The rule called for the murderer to come face to face with his victim, and Harpo had killed Alice Duer Miller, as one might say, by remote control. Aleck stalked off to bed that night without his supper.

At the lake during this summer, Aleck taught Harpo to play croquet, Neshobe Island style, which meant there were nearly no rules at all. The course was originally laid out on what might laughingly have been called a grassy sward, except that it was filled with stones, roots, stumps, trees, chipmunk holes, and was very long on sward and very short on grass. Further, it sloped nicely so that a good shot played away from the clubhouse side might well roll into the lake. And, of course, the object of every shot was to send an opponent's ball smashing into the lake. The Neshobe crowd played croquet in all kinds of weather, in storms and rains and fogs. In his first few days, Harpo managed to lose nine hundred dollars to Aleck in croquet, then won it back plus two hundred more at cards—whereupon Aleck took a cooling-off trip—which meant that he left the island for a day or so until his good temper was restored.

Here was Aleck's view of croquet and what he called "the new game" which he attributed to Neysa McMein's invention of the no-bounds rule:

> . . . . the new players also pass cheerfully (even scornfully) by the conventional sets of rules as issued from time to time by Spalding's.
>
> These ruffians prefer, instead, as big a field as they can get and not necessarily a smooth one. They then set their wickets up (slightly cockeyed as a rule) at such distances as make the shooting of two wickets in one stroke reasonable ground for suspicion that the player has sold his shopworn soul to the devil. For balls, they long since discarded as hopeless the brightly colored wooden ones because these skitter so roguishly on rough ground and because anyway they usually split in two halfway through the first game. Instead heavy composition roque balls do pretty well, though these begin to chip in time and even, in crises, fall apart.
>
> For a mallet, a short handled sledge hammer is employed —with a rough angular handle and a head made of snakewood, the latter strengthened with bands of metal and, in some cases, tipped with a rubber heel for long shots. With such a mallet and such a ball you can drive your enemy so far that there is time for light refreshment while the poor wretch is running after his ball, and since on reaching it, he is well beyond reach of human voice, a system of frantic signals must be devised to notify him when it is his turn to shoot.

At Swope's that summer, Aleck and Neysa McMein had played a match against Swope and Charles Schwartz, a banker, for $1,000 a side, best three out of five games.

The first game was played at Swope's estate at Sands Point, where the croquet course ran up hill and down dale so that at certain points the players could not see one another. Aleck won the first game. The second game went to Swope's team. Finally it was two games for each side and the rubber game was moved, at

Aleck's insistence, to the estate of Paul and Lilly Bonner. Aleck and Neysa McMein won. From the arguments that developed during the games Aleck and Swope were christened the Katzenjammer Kids, because they backbit and bickered and yelled at each other so loudly about the rules and ethics of the game. Aleck decided that Neysa McMein was "unquestionably the shrewdest, most powerful and most malignant" among the women players. He gave Kathleen Norris and Dorothy Parker high scores, and admitted that Alice Duer Miller brought a "certain low cunning" to the game. By this time Aleck also gave Harpo a very good chance of achieving second place. First place, of course, belonged to Alexander Woollcott.

Quite probably this was true, for Aleck put his heart and soul into croquet, witness Harpo:

> I knew Alexander Woollcott for eighteen years and eight months. I shared with him many moments of jubilation. I was beside him when he received awards and commendations, and when he got letters of tribute that brought warm tears to his eyes. Nothing, however, ever gave Woollcott a greater joy of pride and fulfillment than a good shot in croquet.
>
> When Aleck sent an opponent's ball crashing down through the maples of Neshobe Island, he would swing his mallet around his head like David's slingshot and whoop, "Buckety-buckety! Buckety-buckety! Buck-ket-ty-buck-ket-ty-in-to-the *lake!*"
>
> When Aleck pulled off an exceptionally tricky shot—hovering over his mallet like a blimp at its mooring mast, while he aimed with profound concentration, then hitting his ball so it sidled through a wicket from a seemingly impossible angle or thumped an opponent after curving with the terrain in a great, sweeping arc—he was in his own special heaven. He would dance around the court on his toes, kicking his heels together (unaware that his shorts were falling down), and singing in the exuberant soprano of a cherub in a Sunday-school play:
>
> I'm des a 'itto wabbit in de sunshine!
> I'm des a 'itto bunny in de wain!

In some ways the summer of 1927 must have been the most idyllic of all those Aleck spent on the island. It was new to them all, and the crowd was still quite young. Dozens of visitors came and went, actor Gregory Kelly and his wife, Ruth Gordon, and a score of others from the stage. In September, when the leaves began to turn on the birches and maples of the island, Aleck spent much of the last two days in the warm sunshine, on the lake in the island club's dinghy. The breeze shifted pleasantly back and forth from north to south as it always did on the lake, and the sun was at its September best, reminding him of the happy days gone by with no hint of the cold yet to come. Then the clubhouse was closed. The wickets of the croquet court were pulled up and stacked with the Abercrombie and Fitch croquet sets in their box in the barn. Next morning the clubhouse was locked and the remnants of the summer crowd took the last boatride to the dock, with Aleck sitting flatly in the boat and never looking back, not once.

XX

When Aleck settled down for the fall reviewing season he moved into luxurious surroundings. He bought a penthouse apartment in an expensive cooperative building at 450 East 52nd Street. Alice Duer Miller lived next door, and in one of the larger apartments on a lower floor was the New York City establishment of Ralph Pulitzer. It was a comfortable apartment for a bachelor, with a fine view of the East River from the study. There was a separate bedroom, although Aleck often slept on a couch in the study, a large living room and dining room, and a kitchen and bath. Junior, the butler and man of all work, lived out but was in attendance every morning by eight o'clock when Aleck arose to begin his day, no matter how late he had been up the night before.

Aleck started with a light breakfast. He did not dress until noon or after, but wrote on the typewriter and took telephone calls from his hundreds of friends and smoked cigarettes in a chair and drank coffee by the bucketful. (Once he estimated that he drank nineteen cups of coffee a day.) He sat in dressing gown, pajama bottoms and slippers, like an immense buddha, his white belly peering through the loosely draped dressing gown.

In 1927, Aleck was easily the most distinguished and most important drama critic in New York City. That year he was voted by Actors Equity as the "most discriminating" of all the critics.

He was known now for the pithiness of his reviews. Brock Pemberton, once Aleck's assistant and in 1927 a producer, had this to say about his old boss:

> His emotions overrode his judgment, making his hates and enthusiasms superlative. This amusing hysteria, a reflection of his personality, whipped up interest in the theater and was

therefore good for it, but it was hell for those on the receiving end.

That commentary came from a producer, the natural enemy of the critic. Aleck's friend Harpo long remembered one particular Woollcott review of a play which involved a pioneer airmail pilot who had crashed. In the first act the pilot dragged himself to an Indian wigwam where he was nursed back to health by the daughter of the Indian family. The mother of the family discovered the young pilot and the daughter in an embrace, and told the brave father who vowed revenge just before the first act curtain.

In the second act, the young couple wondered what to do. The father confronted them finally and accused the pilot of seducing the daughter. The daughter said he had done nothing. The pilot said he had done nothing. He confessed, then, that nothing could have happened to the daughter, because in the crash of his plane he had been unmanned.

Woollcott's review in the *World* was:

> In the first act she becomes a lady. In the second act, he becomes a lady.

This kind of reviewing angered many producers, and their argument was always the same: they had sunk money into these productions, and they were entitled to gentlemanly and dignified treatment.

Aleck was not above using a strong word or two, either, and from time to time the management of the *World* cut some of his language out of the reviews, which angered Aleck and provoked several arguments. Aleck and Swope were companionable enough at the Swopes, but the employer-employee relationship was not ideal.

Swope was not pleased that Aleck insisted on working outside as he wished, writing for *Collier's*, the *Saturday Evening Post*, *Theater*, *Pictorial Review*, and half a dozen other magazines, plus collecting these articles into a book every three or four years. Swope took the position that Aleck ought to devote all his efforts to the *World*. Aleck was being paid perhaps a quarter as much as Swope was being paid, and while it seemed normal for Swope to devote his full efforts to the newspaper, Aleck took the position that a job demanded only loyalty in the newspaper field and a good day's work for the pay—heresy to editors and publishers. Moreover, Aleck had been attending first nights for a dozen years, with time out for the war, and he was beginning to find the process restricting. He wanted more leisure to pursue his friendships, less interference than he was getting from Swope.

In the fall of 1927, someone in the business office of the *World* called Swope's attention to the fact that Woollcott's contract would expire the following summer and asked what Swope wanted to do about it. Swope sent the query to Woollcott, who pondered a little, but very little, and then announced that he did not wish to renew it. Swope offered him an increase of $1,000 a year to renew, but Aleck knew that if he continued, he would be subject to more control than ever and he liked it less all the time.

The negotiations dragged on past the first of the year, and then Aleck said flatly that he would not stay after the contract expired. He had enough commitments from *Collier's* and other magazines so that he had no worries about striking out on his own, and that would not have stopped him in any event. He was tired of newspapering and the daily grind of the drama critic.

Swope felt that he must have the last word, of course, and so he wrote in a letter on February 1:

> I see you leave the *World* with very real regret. I fear it will be a loss to the *World* and to you. Personally your departure makes me sad, for I have a deep-seated affection for you born of long years of close association. Though I am sorry it is the *World* you have chosen, perhaps it is not unwise for you to give up some of your activities. You were spreading yourself too thin.

Swope also suggested that Aleck might continue with the *World*, writing a syndicated column, or that he might do a weekly Sunday feature on the drama for the *World*. It was apparent that the outside work was the cause of schism, as far as he was concerned. The *World* wanted to keep Woollcott if it could.

Aleck toyed with the idea, but nothing came of it.

Oh, he went on for another few months, his contract called for it and Swope, in his best mailed-fist-in-velvet-glove-manner, insisted on it. And as long as Aleck was at the *World* he was subject to the memos, the furious spate of memos that Swope flung at the staff every day as he read through the newspaper, such as that of April 6, 1928, written just about a month before Aleck left the paper for the last time:

> MEMORANDUM FOR MR. WOOLLCOTT
>
> For God's sake see that the page proofs sent to my desk at least are readable. Page 3 is indecipherable.
>
> Incidentally, have some one look up the meaning of the word replica. Then it won't be used in the ridiculous manner in which it appears in "The King's Penguins."
>
> I thought your column ran too long. You could have well saved the space occupied by the unfunny Groucho Marx piece and in its place used personality stuff. We had 15 separate heads, including pictures, in 16 columns of space. I do not think that intelligent use of white paper. It showed no thought in its planning.
>
> Wouldn't it have been well to have used pictures of new shows, such as the Greenwich Village Follies, in place of old shows represented by Dorothy Stickney, Ruth Gordon or Charles Winninger?
>
> H.B.S.

So it was without any real regret that Aleck emptied his desk drawers and discarded his unwanted newspaper possessions and left Park Row and newspapering forever. The Critics' Club awarded him a silver-mounted cane for his services to the stage —but that was to be expected. What the Critics' Circle did not know, what Swope did not know, what Aleck himself did not know was that at this time, in choosing the larger stage of all life, Aleck was not deserting the theater, he was simply extending it. He would become both player and critic to all the nation in the next few years, and in both roles he would be eminently successful.

XXI

DURING THE SPRING OF 1928, Aleck was involved in several enterprises which interested him far more than anything Herbert Bayard Swope had to offer. He had rented the lodge house of the Emil J. Stehli estate in Long Island earlier: it was on this estate with the connivance of Paul and Lilly Bonner, the daughter and son-in-law, that the last game of the Katzenjammer Kids croquet series had been played. Aleck this year was half in love with Lilly Bonner, not to the exclusion of liking her husband, but with one of his usual and lasting affections. His attentions to Lilly were not upsetting to Paul Bonner, but they certainly were upsetting to her father. One day the previous summer Emil Stehli had come into a room and found Aleck and Lilly sitting on a sofa. He had gone out very worried, without saying a word, but convinced that they were up to hanky panky, and he never, never believed otherwise. Years later he told Lilly that he was glad she and Aleck were now growing middle-aged because he did not have to worry about them so much any more. Lilly asked him what he was talking about, and Stehli mentioned the guilty looks. He could never be convinced that Aleck and Lilly had not carried on a surreptitious affair that summer of 1927.

Aleck was delighted to add the Bonners to his list of very dear friends, and not knowing of Emil Stehli's suspicions, he was sublimely unaware of any difficulties. He went to Locust Valley to play croquet and escape from the business of the city on weekends. This year there would be no time for Neshobe Island, until perhaps, late in the season. Aleck had decided to celebrate his new freedom by renting a house in the south of France and spending the summer there, with a handful of friends, and, of course, conducting a continual open house for any of the hundreds of others of his friends who cared to call.

First Aleck used the transatlantic cable and rented a villa, the Villa Galanon on the Mediterranean coast near Cap d'Antibes. Then he picked up the telephone and called Beatrice Kaufman, Alice Duer Miller, and Harpo Marx. In his grandest manner he announced that he had taken the villa and that they were coming with him. He would accept no argument. They were coming. God had spoken.

And so it was. The party sailed on May 19 on the *Roma* to Naples, then motored up through Rome, Perugia, Florence, to reach the French Coast, and then stayed for several days at a small hotel while the villa was readied for them. Aleck proposed this summer to capture several important fish of the European world. Somerset Maugham, H. G. Wells, and Bernard Shaw. The Riviera was just the place to do it in 1928, for everyone in the combined international set came there for the bathing, the sunshine, and the gambling.

The establishment was operated in a covert partnership between Aleck and a combination chauffeur, chef and major domo called Guy, who fed them all summer long on *haute cuisine*, much to the worsening of Aleck's figure. There could be no croquet for exercise, because their villa was suspended on a rock over the ocean. They played badminton, on the terrace above the sea, badminton with specially weighted birds that would not blow over and down into the froth of the blue water. At night they entertained, and sometimes they went to Monte Carlo to gamble, with Aleck leading them in his lordly way and insisting on picking up all the checks.

As Harpo put it later, the summer divided itself into the Gambling Period, the Literary Period, and the Society Period. During the gambling period they all went to the casino at Monte Carlo. Harpo ignored the information that he should dress in dinner jacket and black tie, and appeared before the casino in polo shirt, blazer, and white duck trousers. He was turned away until he removed one of his black silk socks and tied it around his neck as a necktie.

The literary period opened with a visit to Somerset Maugham's villa on Cap Ferrat, where Harpo leaped into the swimming pool, nude. The next literary lion they met was H. G. Wells, whom Aleck had known earlier in London. Then G. Bernard Shaw came to luncheon one day with Mrs. Shaw. They met Harpo who appeared in a towel, which Shaw promptly ripped off him, then presented the naked Marx to Mrs. Shaw. They ate omelet and various vegetables and fruits in deference to Shaw's vegetarianism, and Harpo and Shaw hit it off so well that Harpo became Shaw's chauffeur for most of the rest of the playwright's visit to the Riviera that year.

Ruth Gordon came to stay with Aleck and the others for a time. She and Harpo went out together to costume and black tie and evening gown parties, while Aleck for the most part preferred to stay at his own villa and entertain such celebrities of the American stage as Otis Skinner.

Aleck's guests were his friends, but occasionally Harpo and the others got on his nerves, and then Aleck would simply disappear for a few days, to return when he felt more able to cope with the establishment. No chiding word was said, he simply went away. Harpo swore that one day after Aleck had been gone for several days, Candida, the black French poodle Aleck had acquired on a previous disappearance that summer led Harpo straight to the most luxurious bordello in Nice, and there Harpo and Candida found Aleck in silk robe and slippers reclining on a black velvet couch and being fed grapes by one of the girls.

Noel Coward, the English playwright, and actor, who was the prototype of Beverly Carlton in *The Man Who Came to Dinner*, announced that he was leaving America and coming to France late in the summer. Aleck and Harpo traveled to Paris to meet him. Harpo disguised himself as a street musician and as Coward stepped off the train he played on his miniature harp and then held out his hat for a tip. Without breaking stride, Coward dropped a sixpence into the hat and looked airily around him, called Harpo by name and asked where Aleck might be lurking.

Then it was back to the Villa at Antibes, for more summer entertainment and enjoyment. Aleck loved being in the center of the theatrical and literary worlds. But autumn came, and with it the time to go home. There was one last voyage down into Italy where Aleck and Harpo went to Amalfi and to a cliff restaurant where they played cribbage half the afternoon. But both were homesick, and it was time to be back at the wheel of fortune, so the party returned on the *Ile de France*.

Aleck settled down in his apartment on Fifty-Second Street, a celebrity who had passed the point of needing employment by others to sustain himself either financially or in the world of publicity. His apartment building, the Campanile, was expensive and pretentious: inside, his own modest apartment was termed Wit's End by Dorothy Parker and the name stuck tight. It was exactly the right name for an apartment occupied by Alexander Woollcott.

Aleck was very busy and very productive. He published another book, a very slight one—only 121 pages—devoted to three tales of dogs and dedicated to Neysa McMein. The first of these stories was an entirely new invention, a tale about a Long Island family that decided it needed a dog around the house.

The second story in the book was the now well-worn tale of Verdun Belle. It had changed a bit. In the original the young Marine had started off with all the puppies in his shirt and had then drowned four. In this new version he drowned four in the beginning and carried three in a laundry basket, before he moved them into his shirt. There was more detail and it was handled much more smoothly than earlier:

> An immensely interested old woman in the village where they halted at sun up, vastly amused by this spectacle of a soldier trying to carry two nursing puppies to war volunteered some milk for the cup of his messkit and with much jeering advice from all sides and by dint of the eye-dropper from his pack, he tried sheepishly to be a mother to the two waifs. The attempt was not shiningly successful.
>
> He itched to pitch them over the fence. But maybe Verdun Belle had not been run over by some thundering camion. If she lived she would find him, and then what would he say when her eyes asked what he had done with the pups? So, as the order was shouted to fall in, he hitched the pack to his back and stuffed his charges back into his shirt. Now, in the morning light, the highway was choked. Down from the lines in agonized, grotesque rout came the stream of French life from the threatened countryside, jumbled fragments of fleeing French regiments inextricably

> mixed with despairing old folks and little children, dragging and pushing along a goat, perhaps, or a baby carriage full of dishes or whatever else they had caught up in their flight from the heartsick homes. But America was coming up the road. . . .

The difference was the fleshing out of the story, the addition of detail and style that told the reader that this was a classic tale. After Verdun Belle was reunited with her pups, in the original version it had been enough to say she was given an old cot under a tree. Not in 1928, ten years after the war:

> The operating tables, with acetylene torches to light them were set up in what had been a tool shed. Cots were strewn in the orchard alongside. Thereafter for a month there was never any rest in the hospital. The surgeons and orderlies spelled each other at times, snatching morsels of sleep and returning a few hours later to relieve the others. But Verdun Belle took no time off. . . .

So the tale was spun to give a picture of the war itself—a needful change ten years later when Aleck was writing for homefront audience, most of whose members had no conception of trench warfare in France.

The third of Aleck's dog stories concerned Egon, a German shepherd belonging to an American friend, who had spent much of that summer on the Riviera along with the other Americans. The third story dealt with people he had seen that summer as much as the dog, the Archibald MacLeish family, the Charles Bracketts, Dudley Field Malone, the writer, and assorted others. Egon's neatest trick was to rescue every swimmer, whether he needed it or not. So all summer long the clustered humanity on the terrace of the Hotel du Cap was treated to the sight of the big German shepherd plunging in after some poor swimmer had dived into the sea, and dragging the human, willy-nilly, back to the shore.

All the tales were well told in Aleck's special style, a style he was using in writing for many publications, including the *New Yorker*. Harold Ross had finally assembled his magazine ideas and had secured backing for the magazine. Most of the backers were old friends of Aleck's: Hawley Truax and Lloyd Paul Stryker were both old Hamiltonians. Raoul Fleischmann of the banking family was also interested in the publication, and soon it was a going concern. Aleck was listed with a number of the other New York Wits on the board of editorial advisors. But Aleck did not like to allow himself to be listed as doing anything without doing it, and soon he began writing a column. From his book of 1922, he took the title *Shouts and Murmurs.* His column might deal with the theater or a reminiscence, or it might be a hodgepodge of anecdotes. He liked to tell risqué stories in print such as this one.

> Finally, from Quitman, Georgia, there reaches me the story of a refulgent blonde who, at the cashier's desk of a restaurant, was seeking to pay her check with a five-dollar bill when it was rejected as counterfeit. Milady paled visibly. "Counterfeit!" she cried. "My God, I've been raped!"

Ross had begun his magazine with the flat statement that it was not intended for the little old lady from Dubuque—or any of her relatives unless they had come to the big city and put on New Yorkers' clothes. Aleck, however, was a source of constant worry to the editorial staff, not so much with his earlier contributions, but later when "Shouts and Murmurs" began.

Aleck was never too busy to help out a friend. In 1928 the J. H. Sears Publishing Company brought out *The War Paintings of Claggett Wilson.* Aleck wrote the introduction, which was notable because it showed how smooth his style had become since World War 1 when he was writing so earnestly for *Stars and Stripes.*

> I first met Wilson during the St. Mihiel drive amid a deafening racket which made the little village of Thiacourt chatter. It was, I think, the afternoon of the day the Second Division had captured the town, if the word "capture" can be decently applied to so unresisted a taking over. By this time a reprisal bombardment was going on, and, as the shells fell in the narrow streets, the noise was earsplitting and blood-letting considerable.
>
> "Why, Sergeant Woollcott," exclaimed this huge lieuten-

ant who had recognized me from some libellous cartoon in the *Stars and Stripes,* "What do you think I have found here in this cellar, the most marvelous German Prince."

My news sense responded like a retriever at the thought of His Imperial Highness the Heir Apparent or even Rupprecht of Bavaria, thus left behind in an *abri.* But I had not understood the delighted Lieutenant correctly. My error. In fact my typographical error. The discovery he was gloating over was only the trove of some German prints. I shook with respectful laughter at the thought of a combat officer enjoying the quiet raptures of an art collector in the midst of that not inconsiderable hell and destruction. But I suppose that, after all, the pictures in this book could have been painted only by one, some part of whom, even as he retched with fear and panic in Belleau Wood, remained alert and sensitive to the beauty and the wonder and the horror of the world.

Aleck went on his way, having helped another friend, and having demonstrated, again, his growingly smooth command of syntax and expression that made his claim of being a fine writer a very real one. The demands on him were now so great, and in 1928, deprived of the assistance to be found in any organization, he employed a secretary. The first of these was a young man named Danton Walker, a young man because Aleck did not want the complications of a woman secretary when he would be traveling a good share of the time, and at least spending his summers at the Neshobe Island Club. A woman with romantic and familial attachments would be a nuisance.

So Danton Walker joined the ménage at Wit's End. He would come into the apartment in the morning and find his employer up, but not dressed, drinking coffee in the study. They would set to work, Aleck dictating letters, and then Walker typing while Aleck moved on to some other matter that had captured his attention—a book to be reviewed, a handful of telephone calls to be returned, or a stream of callers.

Walker observed his employer and wrote about him to a friend:

It may seem fatuous to speak of the dean of American drama critics as a case of arrested development, but this isn't as far-fetched as it sounds. For in the Alexander Woollcott of today, retired at 42 after 20 years of journalism, are traces of a little boy—a little fat boy, impish, disagreeable, even obnoxious at times, but one who creates amusement and wins friends. Brought up in the Mauve Decade, he is irrevocably stamped with its tastes, its ideals in art and its sentimentalities. Everything, in fact, but its manners, though he can be surprisingly tactful and courteous when he chooses.

Whether one page of his will survive in American letters it is hard to predict. His books are mostly reprints or rehashes of newspaper and magazine pieces, outrageous plagiarisms of his own works that have been sold once, twice, thrice to different publishers, and then, for good measure, broadcast over the radio—his uncanny sense of journalism tells him just what public he will reach and that one public seldom overlaps another. Most of his anecdotes were already stale when they achieved the dignity of Joe Miller's Joke Book, but there is this maddening thing about the man—he is a master of English writing, and can weave these ancient wheezes into such a spell of words that one not only does not resent such chicanery but, in his own language, clasps the threadbare anecdotes to his bosom and treasures them for what they are—literature.

His secretary (that's me) might tell you that he has the soul of a proofreader, can spot a typographical error at 20 paces and make it the subject of sarcastic comment for a week. His valet can and will tell you that the Boss has never admitted himself in the wrong about anything, whatever proof to the contrary. His cook and laundress are capable of even more lurid comment. But none of the people who work for or with him day after day, held to the job more by loyalty than anything else, can help admiring him for his punctiliousness and dependability, the honesty, sound character and fine mind that underlie an apparently flippant and frothy exterior. Petty, irascible and unreasonable he certainly is at times, but principally because he sets a standard for himself and expects everyone else to live up to it. He is fiercely intolerant of anything or anyone he dislikes, and like Heywood Broun, he has an "underdog" complex. His

> prejudices would furnish a field day for a psychoanalyst. Why, for instance, should he dislike Christmas cards?

The answer to that question was an easy one for any person who knew Aleck well—his dislike of Christmas cards was ancillary to one of Alexander Woollcott's most endearing qualities as a human being, his remarkable talent for friendship. One might say that Aleck always had this talent, but it became more apparent in later years; after the formation of Thanatopsis, perhaps; and certainly after he began life as a free-lance writer and critic of the American scene in 1928. Then Danton Walker was as much employed in writing letters to Aleck's thousands of friends as he was in transcribing commercial material for the magazines and book publishers and the business correspondence that was essential to keep the flow going. For years Aleck carried on a correspondence with Lucy Christie Drage, who was his sister Julie's best friend in the days in Kansas City. Now Aleck had left Kansas City at such a tender age that he could not possibly have known Lucy Drage as more than a friend of his big sister's, a friendly presence perhaps, but scarcely more than that. Yet particularly after Julie's death Aleck turned to Lucy to recount tales of the old days and to wallow a little in nostalgia. When Julie died, Aleck wrote Lucy Drage that he had a strong impulse to jump on a train and go to see her, simply because she was the only person left in the world with whom he might talk about his sister. And this was important in that spring of 1928. Aleck was rootless and he felt the need for roots. He lived in a rootless New York apartment. His friends of New York, many of them, were birds of passage. Aleck clung to the little shreds of the past because he was dissatisfied with the present and could not pretend to see into the future. That summer the one relative left in Aleck's life who meant anything to him was also taken ill—his brother William. Aleck transferred his reservoirs of family affection to that family, and thereafter did much to help the daughters of William Woollcott. This talent for loving was a shared characteristic in the Woollcott family; Julie had possessed it too, and as Aleck wrote to Lucy Drage about Julie's last few hours on earth, he portrayed a picture that might have been a self-portrait. All Julie's thoughts, he said, had run back to the years in Kansas City, forty years before her death, and to an even earlier time. Julie had talked of the day Aleck was born, a snowy day on which someone had to be sent seven miles to fetch the doctor who came in his cutter. She talked of the trip west to Kansas City so few years later, and of Rose Field, and of Lucy and other friends. One of Julie's last remarks to Aleck was that she must discover Rose Field's whereabouts and offer to keep house for him. One of Julie's last requests to Aleck was to write a birthday letter to Lucy Drage, because Julie could no longer hold a pen.

That had been Julie's custom every year, to write that birthday letter, and on Julie's death, Aleck assumed the responsibility and carried it on for the remainder of his life. This was a small sign of his talent for friendship, his sense of responsibility to people who had been close to himself or his family at an important time of life. Lucy Drage, one might say, became an "inherited" friend to Aleck; thereafter he never forgot her birthday; he never failed to visit her when he came within five hundred miles of Kansas City.

The birthday letter was a key to Aleck's attitude towards friendship, as much as his dislike of Christmas cards. His birthday letters always meant something, they always pointed up the personal relationship between Aleck and the recipient. Usually there was a birthday present. In 1928 for Harpo it had been a copy of the article in the New York *Times* which described the arrest and conviction of a number of persons on Long Island for the operation of a bawdy house, and for the operation of a burglary ring. The owner was a Mrs. Schang, and the place was called the Happy Times Tavern. Harpo played the piano while the girls cadged drinks downstairs and plied their trade upstairs. One night Harpo came down with the measles and had to go home. A few days later the place was raided, and had he not had measles he would have been convicted of playing a piano in a whore house, or of the charge nearest to this moral indictment. He had told the tale to Aleck amid tears of laughter from the latter and many happy cries, and now Aleck went to the considerable trouble of having the story tracked down from Harpo's vague memory of dates, having a photostatic copy blown up to a huge size, and then presenting this to Harpo on his birthday. That fall, when Harpo and his brothers took *Animal Crackers* on the road, Aleck gave his friend a parting gift: an RFD mailbox with his name painted on it. To one who had so special an idea of friendship and its responsibilities, the ordinary Christmas card, and especially the one with its printed greeting and printed name of sender could not help but bring resentments. To Aleck a Christmas card represented an insult by someone who should be his friend but was too lazy to write him a letter.

This year—1928—was the year of publication of *Going to Pieces,* another collection of Aleck's earlier magazine writing for the most part. The central piece was his farewell to newspaper drama criticism:

> . . . by a set of curious chances, I find myself engaged in the business—the business, mind you—of going to the theater. I do not write plays. I do not act plays. I do not even produce plays. I merely go to see them. By contracts between the party of the first part, the party of the second part and all that sort of thing my life is actually so arranged that in the past dozen years I have not only attended two thousand first nights in New York, London, Paris and Berlin, but far from paying for the privilege, am myself paid for the inconvenience. . . .
>
> Professional playgoing seems to me hardly a career which a decent man would deliberately map out for himself, any more than one would plan an exclusive diet of macaroons or lemon meringue pie. . . .

The collection was interesting, from another point of view, because for the first time Aleck manifested literary interest in crime and celebrated crimes. Lizzie Borden captured Aleck's interest when he came across her in *Studies in Murder.* What Danton Walker referred to as Aleck's "outrageous plagiarisms of his own works" was here too: one chapter of this book consisted of the reviews of six different plays of 1926 and 1927, done up in a neat package and described openly by the author as "a random handful of clippings from my scrapbook." Five of the reviews had first appeared in the New York *World,* and one was from *Vanity Fair.* Aleck was getting more than full mileage from his writing, by the standard of any other writer in the world. This talent came partly from what Harpo Marx termed his "nice sense of double-entry bookkeeping" and partly from what Harold Ross called Aleck's ability to mine a very thin vein of ore as a writer and make it pay brilliantly. The people who read Aleck's writings, other than the critics, simply did not mind. To counterbalance the understanding criticism of the professional writers (and here I include then-secretary Danton Walker) were such comments as those of Frank Lloyd Wright, Aleck's architect friend, in a letter in 1928:

> I have been reading *Going to Pieces.* I wish they might all go to pieces like yours. They have a very bad effect on me because they discourage me. Whatever you touch becomes fascinating reading, of course, but there is a quality of illumination in you, too.

This, perhaps was the point of appeal of Aleck's twice and thrice told tales—a quality of illumination shared by so few writers of the twentieth century.

Aleck knew better than anyone else that somehow he lacked the ability to turn his literary searchlight on subjects more worthy of treatment than those now treated. He was weary of the demands of the theater but not of the theater itself, and he was busy looking for subjects with a twist to satisfy the magazine market. He wrote extremely well about subjects he knew well, books and the theater and World War I and Hamilton and the delights of croquet and travels in Europe—and those were the subjects of the pleasant little essays in *Going to Pieces.*

Aleck was forever picking up people. Professor Robert Rudd, his college friend and forever after Aleck's companion at first nights and in Hamilton reunions, recalled that he always enjoyed himself at Woollcott's or in Woollcott's presence, because he met so varied a group of people. Aleck chose people because they were his friends and he expected them to meet and mix and be friendly with one another. In the 1920's at Hamilton he encountered a young Chinese named Henry Ke-an Yuan, son of Yuan Shih-Kai, once President of the Republic of China. The young man was badly confused by the American education, for it left in him a feeling for the freedom of occidental life, yet when he returned to the family household in Tientsin he was immediately dispatched to the interior to become an assistant accountant in the Kailan mining administration, and, unhappily, told to divest himself of his western ways. He wrote frequently to Aleck in the months to come and Aleck counseled him as best he could to try to accept the ways of his family and not to change China overnight.

Aleck never stopped his output of magazine articles, even when he was on the Riviera, and the proof of it began appearing in the autumn of 1928 and the winter of 1928-29. He was very much taken by a book published by Coward-McCann called *A Doctor of the Old School,* written by Ian MacLaren. He wrote favorable reviews of the book, and a foreword to go with a later American edition. Still the magazine was his standby, the manner in which he was amassing a large amount of money, about $100,000 before this year ended. In March, 1929, there appeared an article on "The Haunted House of Lunt" in *Vanity Fair.* He was to write many articles about his friends, Alfred Lunt and Lynne Fontanne, for this was one of Aleck's lasting friendships. The Lunts visited him at Neshobe Island and he visited them—very occasionally—at their house called Ten Chimneys in Genesee Station, Wisconsin. He carried on separate correspondence with them, writing in one vein to Alfred Lunt and a slightly different vein to Lynne Fontanne. Most of the correspondence was trivia, and much of it concerned the activities of the Lunts, but by keeping in touch, Aleck was always in a position to drop a note in a column or a review, the latest gossip about these increasingly prominent figures in the world of the theater.

Harpo, of course, was for nearly twenty years one of Aleck's favorite subjects; he honestly believed Harpo to be one of the greatest clowns in the world and thus suffered untold indignities from that clown that he would not have accepted from anyone he did not love dearly. One night when Aleck was backstage at the 44th Street Theater where Harpo was appearing in *Animal Crackers* with the three other Marx Brothers, Harpo switched hats on Aleck, giving him, instead of his black fedora, a five gallon Mexican hat covered with silver braid and spangles. Aleck wore the hat halfway down Broadway, strolling along nonchalantly and accepting the nonplused stares of passersby as recognition by the simple people of Broadway of that great character, himself. Only much later did Harpo receive a telephone call in which Aleck, with all the malevolence of his spirit repeated his favorite epithet for his friend: "You Jew son-of-a-bitch!"

Harpo recalled that January 1 of 1929 was ushered in by a New Year's Eve party at the apartment of the Herbert Bayard Swopes, a party attended by Aleck, Harpo, Neysa McMein, and the rest of the Algonquin gang. It ended in the morning with a croquet game in Central Park. Aleck immortalized the Algonquin that month in *McCall's* with an article about Frank Case and the Algonquin crowd called "Wayfarer's Inn." Again, he was making capital of a shared experience, but he did it with that sure, deft hand that no one else seemed to match.

Writing in the May 4 issue of *Collier's* Aleck went out on a limb, showing a certain editorial bravery not given every critic of theater or literature, and some six weeks before the announcement of the Pulitzer Prizes, predicted that Elmer Rice's *Street Scene* would win the prize for that year. That note was cast into the article casually, as if it was a matter of no question or controversy. The article was called "Elmer The Unexpected' and dealt with Elmer Rice's rise from the position of Elmer Reisenstein, immigrant boy, to the lofty perch of successful playwright. And again, in characterizing the playwright, he moved from the specific to drop the names of two other friends, Charles MacArthur and Ben Hecht, and then to the general—in a way that no other writer had yet managed:

> When the authors [MacArthur and Hecht] of that hard-boiled and delightful comedy *The Front Page* submitted their magnum opus they accompanied it by a note which ran: "we recommend this play as a great work of art, something like *Hamlet*" and thereto signed their names. Their intention was facetious, but so powerfully are we all hypnotized by our hopes that, though a writer may refer in conversation to his comedy as a little thing he has just dashed off, in his secret heart he does regard it as a great work of art, something like *Hamlet*. Only much better.

Aleck was still reviewing plays; now his audience was nationwide in *Collier's*, and his influence was greater than ever. He brought joy to the hearts of the producers of *Journey's End*, a British war play by R. C. Sheriff, when he reviewed that production on June 8 with his infectious enthusiasm ("*Journey's End* had enough theatrical guile in it to make a dozen thrillers").

With that same enthusiasm Aleck traveled to the twentieth reunion of his Hamilton College graduating class and participated with a tear in his eye in the commencement ceremonies. Then it was back to New York for a few more hectic weeks—then up to the Neshobe Island Club for the summer, following the birth of a young friend and one of his nineteen godchildren named Peter Hackett, who in the happy carefree gay days of 1929 was presented by Aleck with a share of stock in United States Steel as a christening present. It was, at that date, a gift worth well over $200.

Aleck could well afford the gift. He demanded—and received—the highest going rates for his magazine articles because he knew very well that his name on the cover of a magazine would sell several thousand extra copies on the newsstands. The editors knew it, too, and although they grumbled at his high prices, they paid them.

The money rolled in by the thousands of dollars that spring and summer.

At Neshobe Island it was another round of croquet and dinner parties, cribbage and guessing games in the evenings, swimming and sunning and work for Aleck in the daytime. While others drank or played, Aleck was writing "Lessons Between the Acts," an article on the professional children's school in New York City, which appeared in *Collier's* that summer, and another article on Harpo Marx, called "Harpo Smites His Lyre," which covered ground already traversed in newspaper and magazine articles—and yet there was no complaint from *Collier's* or its readers.

As always Aleck was helpful and crabbed, generous and pinchpenny. It depended on how he was touched. If he lost twenty dollars to Alice Duer Miller in a cribbage game, he would do anything to try to get out of paying it. One time, several years earlier, he had lost money to Harold Ross on the night before he sailed for Europe, and was so incensed that he said he had to rush to catch his boat—so he had no time to pay up. It was then shortly after midnight, and the steamer did not sail until 10 o'clock in the morning. The trouble was, with Alice Miller or Ross or any of his friends, Aleck could not bear to have anything go against him in the small ways of life. In larger matters it was a different story: one day he sent a letter to Henry Ke-an Yuan, suggesting that he write something of his impressions on returning to China after Yuan's western education, and offered to help the younger man market it. That autumn, when the Marx Brothers' mother died after a stroke, Aleck went to the Woodlawn Jewish Cemetery with them after the services. He made a wisecrack when he saw the name of Kelly on a nearby headstone. Harpo was irritated and upset by Aleck's apparent callousness, until he saw the forthcoming issue of *New Yorker,* in which Aleck had devoted his space to a eulogy of Minnie Marx. It had the usual Woollcottian touch, particularly at the end:

> She was in this world sixty-five years and *lived* all sixty-five of them. She died during rehearsals, in the one week of the year when all her boys would be around her—back from their summer roamings, but not yet gone forth on tour. Had she foreseen this—I'm not sure she didn't—she would have chuckled, and combining a sly wink with her beautiful smile, she would have said, "How's that for perfect timing?"

Aleck was up to something else that summer of 1929 and had been for several months. He and George S. Kaufman had been talking for years about writing a play. They did so, and it was produced at the Plymouth Theater. Kaufman, earlier, had worked up a comedy with Ring Lardner called *June Moon,* which was brought to the stage of the Broadhurst Theater by Sam Harris. Now, in November, he had two productions running, the Lardner show and this result of collaboration with Aleck, which was called *The Channel Road.* It was a play based on a short story called "Boule de Suif" by Guy de Maupassant, a story dealing with the German occupation of France in 1870, and the victory of a French prostitute over a German officer in matters of morals and patriotism.

Some reviewers liked it, among them Joseph Wood Krutch, who reviewed the play favorably in the *Nation.*

> Alexander Woollcott and George Kaufman have now turned it into an entertaining play which will doubtless never be as famous as the original, but which might reasonably be called a good deal more sensible. . . . The important thing is that with the change of little except the point of view the whole has been lifted out of the murky region of patriotic melodrama into the serene atmosphere of comedy. Messrs. Woollcott and Kaufman supply the lightness of touch which is necessary and the whole thing goes off with a ripple of laughter. Doubtless many serious persons will accuse them of having perverted the story but it was the original author who did that. "Boule de Suif" is startling, unforgettable, and preposterous; *The Channel Road* is slight and not tremendously important, but it uses intelligence to deflate a melodrama and it puts Maupassant's ingenious situation in exactly the category where it belongs.

Some reviewers did not like it. Among these was Francis R. Bellamy of *Outlook*:

> Woollcott is more a humorist than a critic. Else we doubt he could have perpetrated in the name of wit the crimes against human character which now stain the stage at the Arthur Hopkins Theater (Hopkins produced the play). The demon of the wise crack has been loosed by Mr. Woollcott on de Maupassant's simple tale of the German occupation of France. . . . The faces as they converse may be the faces of de Maupassant's people; but the voice is the voice of Mr. Woollcott, talking brightly to himself. . . . *Channel Road* is a hunchback comedy, wisecracked to death.

So the reviews were mixed, but much more important than the reviews was the timing of the play. If it was all that Krutch said of it and none that Bellamy charged it with being, it would have made very little difference. November, 1929, was not a good month for Broadway. Too few persons, including Alexander Woollcott, paid very much attention to what was happening to the Arthur Hopkins production at the Plymouth Theater. The authors, the producers, and undoubtedly the members of the cast were spending much of their time talking to their brokers or their ex-brokers or to each other about the debacle that had struck the stock market. The market opened in the first week of November, 1929, with some staggering losses which had begun during the previous week, and by the end of that first week, when *The Channel Road* was coming to the eyes of the public no one had any eyes for it, and very few people along Broadway could scrape up the price of a ticket. Aleck and George Kaufman and Arthur Hopkins could not have chosen a worse week to open unless they had chosen the week before. *The Channel Road* lasted fifty performances and then closed, but its epitaph might have been: "It never had a chance."

XXII

ALECK LOST his one hundred thousand dollars of capital in the stock market crash of 1929, and when it was all over and he and the Wits of the Algonquin met together to discuss their losses and recount their disasters, he discovered that so it was with nearly everyone else he knew, outside of Swope and the few really moneyed men in his circle. Harpo and his brothers had been on tour with *Animal Crackers* and they had been getting their market tips straight from an elevator operator in their hotel. Aleck took the position that he was not much better off; a broker, he said, was a man who took your bankroll and ran it down to a pittance.

Aleck's pittance became a debt of $7,000 he had to borrow in order to pay his current obligations and have spending money until his earnings could catch up.

It did not take long. Magazine articles continued. Woollcott might have lost his money but he had not lost his magic touch at the typewriter, and *Collier's* continued to pay him thousands of dollars every month for an article or two. Their readers said they were such good stories that he told, and they were told with such flair—as the article of November 23, 1929, about playwrights and the theater, called "The Child on the Garden Wall." It was a tale of Mrs. Patrick Campbell, that great artist and friend of Bernard Shaw's. She was opening, and this was her first major role, in London in *The Second Mrs. Tanqueray*, a play by the prominent playwright Arthur Pinero, a gentleman who knew his business.

Mrs. Patrick Campbell had gone through the first act of the play in a fashion so miserable that all the remainder of the cast was complaining. Her leading man was threatening that he would not respond to his curtain call. The audience was restive, cold to this lady who was mumbling her lines and missing her cues. Arthur Pinero, pacing up and down in the alley behind the theater, was apprised of this frightful situation, and he marched forthwith to the lady's dressing room to speak to her.

Suavely, he congratulated her on her playing.

"My dear," he said, "if only you can play the next three acts as magnificently as you have just played the first one, I will be a made man and your servant forever."

Whereupon Mrs. Patrick Campbell walked out onto the stage and made theatrical history. Her future and Pinero's was never again in doubt.

With such tales Aleck renewed his fortune. In the autumn of 1929, he came upon another medium of expression to which his peculiar talents were very well fitted, and he turned to this means of earning money and reaching a large audience, the commercial radio broadcast.

Aleck's first experience with radio broadcasting dated back five years to 1924 when he told the story of the adventures of an obscure American naval hero. It was apparent then that Aleck had a way with him that made itself felt over the airwaves. "Don't let anybody tell you that you can't write," Deems Taylor telegraphed him that day.

In the autumn of 1929, the Mutual Broadcasting System was looking for new talent, and someone suggested to the officials of WOR, the New York City outlet of that network, that Aleck would make a good radio personality. He had everything that anyone could want: a fine respect for the intelligence of the American audience which was not shared by all his contemporaries, an interest in the oddments of history, and the widest range of acquaintanceship among the great and near great of the literary and entertainment worlds of anyone in America.

So Aleck became a broadcaster, sponsored by the Colonial Radio Company, a manufacturing organization. At the end of thirteen weeks the original contract ran out. The Gruen Watch Company then picked up the option, and Aleck had another thirteen weeks of broadcasts. On his first appearance at WOR he was supported by Clifton Webb, Fred Allen, and Libby Holman, who were appearing in a show at the Music Box Theater. In later broadcasts he brought other actors and stage personalities to the microphone, or he reviewed performances, or he reviewed books, or he told tales from World War I or he examined the byways of history.

Aleck was now much in demand as author, broadcaster, and lecturer. As a lecturer, however, he was not always successful in these early years because he was not as careful with language or the prejudices of others as he might have been. On one occasion he was invited by Reverend Endicott Peabody to address the students of the Groton School for Boys in Massachusetts. Aleck was pleased to do so, and came to the old red brick quadrangle for the occasion armed with his best manner. He opened by telling the tale of his employment—or near employment—as principal of the high school at Hudson, New York, after his graduation from Hamilton College in 1909. He told how the head of the Board of Education had brought him to visit the school, and had instructed him in the duties of the principal. At the end of the tour, the president of the board had taken Aleck to a window and had pointed out several bulky young men in turtleneck sweaters who were passing the school grounds. Did Mr. Woollcott believe he could administer corporal punishment satisfactorily to these young men, he was asked. Aleck took another look, he said, and decided he did not wish to be principal of a school.

"I don't know why they ever asked me," Aleck told the Groton assembly. "I think they must have thought I was sort of cute."

The boys passed this remark, but the Reverend Endicott Peabody grumbled audibly, and Aleck was never asked back to that noble institution.

Aleck, obviously, was not everybody's dish of tea. Some magazine editors objected to his way of doing business, men such as Arnold Gingrich, new editor of the yet unpublished *Esquire,* who came to New York from Chicago seeking editorial commitments from a number of well known writers.

> I had somehow got hold of his phone number and gave him my pitch over the phone. When he asked what this proposed new quarterly was to be called, I told him "*Esquire,*" pronouncing the second syllable rather than the first This seemed to impress him enough that he allowed me to

come call on him in his apartment in the 50's on the East River. He had his coloured boy, Junior, fix me a drink and I occupied the lull by pulling out a checkbook and writing a check to Alexander Woollcott for $100. He was impressed by the fact that while I wasn't paying much, I was at least paying sight unseen and in advance of receipt of manuscript.

So he agreed to be one of the contributors to the first issue of the magazine. I gave him the deadline date and said I hoped he would do us something on the order of the story he did about the young cadet of *St. Cyr,* who spent the night with the famous courtesan, Cosette. He said something to the effect that that was a lot to expect for $100, but that he would certainly give me something by the deadline date.

He must have been feeling fairly amiable, because sometime in the interim he sent on to me a piece by Ring Lardner, Jr. I bought the piece, which was called *Four Years of Grace.* I changed that title to *Princeton Panorama,* because the title *Four Years of Grace* had been used by Professor Wenley at the University of Michigan for one of his lectures that had been printed frequently in pamphlet form, and which was practically used as a textbook. On the day of the deadline, I got a letter from Woollcott on his small, checkered stationery saying that he must "flagrantly default," and something to the effect that he did so without great harm to his conscience, because he was dealing with someone so cloddish as to fail to appreciate the great title that Young Ring Lardner had put on his piece.

I had to sit up that night and write a piece to fill the hole left in the starting lineup of the magazine's first issue, because I had literally counted noses and didn't have a spare manuscript in the house. I wrote something snotty back to him, though I have now completely forgotten what. He did of course, return the uncashed check with the letter.

He was such a rude and pompous little poltroon, so swollen with conceit that I carried a grudge thereafter. I never exchanged another word with him. . . .

On May 3, 1930, Aleck's *Collier's* article was devoted to *The*

Last Mile, a play suggested by an article that had appeared in *American Mercury* magazine. Article and play were to exercise a profound influence on Aleck's thinking and Aleck's life in a few years.

The article had been written by a convict in a Texas prison, a man named Robert Blake, who had been convicted of robbery and murder and was sitting in death row in the Huntsville prison waiting execution in the electric chair. Early in 1929 he had sent this study of Death Row to H. L. Mencken. Blake was electrocuted on April 19, 1929, the article appeared in the July, 1929, issue of the magazine, where it was seen by John Wexley, a playwright who then went on to do the play called *The Last Mile.* Aleck told this story in *Collier's.* He was much impressed by the play and much concerned about the cruelties of the American system of capital punishment.

At the *New Yorker,* associate editor Katherine White was appointed to take charge of The Gila Monster as Ross called his erstwhile companion on *Stars and Stripes,* sometimes laughingly and sometimes not so laughingly. It was all right to call Aleck names, for he did not really mind them from his friends. At the *New Yorker* some members of the staff regarded Aleck's weekly contribution as trash or mush or worse, but the fact was that in this early period Aleck was far more valuable to the *New Yorker* than the magazine ever would be to him. He was established and it was not. He could command $2,500 or more for an article from *Collier's* or another magazine; yet he wrote a weekly article for Ross for a sum that apparently never exceeded $400.

Aleck hated being edited, and as the years went by he came to hate it more and more, and finally, in his hey-day, to submit to editing only after emitting the outcries of a wounded coyote. Every few weeks he would resign from the staff of the *New Yorker* with cries of pain, and Ross would set out to placate him. As a staff member, Aleck seldom set foot in the premises, he sent his articles over by messenger from Wit's End, or by mail from Neshobe Island or wherever he happened to be.

In the summer of 1930, Aleck happened to be in Europe. He had remained at home during 1929, spending almost the entire summer at the island, but this year he felt it important to renew his European contacts, so he left in April, sailing with Noel Coward for England. They played backgammon all the way across the ocean, when they were not playing Russian Bank. This playing was done, in the inimitable style of a Woollcott-Coward comedy team, in the bar of the first class lounge. Occasionally the other passengers would stop at the table and make meaningful remarks about these two single-minded loafers. They developed a rejoinder. When anyone would stop at their table and say anything, the two would break into song:

We hope you fry in Hell
We hope you fry in Hell
Heigho
the-merry-o
We hope you fry in Hell.

It was not much of a song, obviously composed in a hurry, between moves, but it served to keep the elbows of loiterers off the board.

Aleck wrote modestly to Beatrice Kaufman on his arrival in London that he had not had much luck—he had just managed to win enough from Noel Coward to pay for his passage.

This season Coward, who was very much of a celebrity in London, took Aleck under his wing and helped him go places and meet people he would not otherwise have encountered, the dukes, duchesses, lords and ladies of the theatrical set. They went to the theater and Noel managed the use of the royal box. He was invited for a weekend at Coward's and went. He had his own friends in England, too, and he visited them. These were old friends, Lord Jeffrey Amherst, who had been his assistant in the drama department at the *World,* and Rebecca West, now coming into her own as a successful writer. Lilly Bonner came over from Paris, and joined the festivities.

After renewing acquaintances in England, Aleck sailed for France, and then to Oberammergau, the site of the famous Passion Plays where Anton Lang had played the Christ for so many years, between 1910 and 1922, to be succeeded this year by Alois Land, a master wood carver by trade.

Aleck was disgusted with the growing number of American tourists he found to be flocking abroad, even in this, a depression.

He felt strongly and he wrote strongly about Americans who disgraced their native land by misguided actions when they traveled abroad:

> I could cross myself before a stout, bespectacled matron whom I might see gathering lilacs in her blue-checked apron beyond the white picket fence of the Vermont garden, the while the wind bore the croon of a distant lawn mower and the fragrance of new-made bread sifting through the kitchen window. But I might run from that same woman if I encountered her abroad, trussed into traveling gear, her name changed to legion, her features sharpened by the suspicion that she is about to be cheated, her voice doubled in volume through the universal delusion that we can make foreigners understand us if only we speak loudly enough. No, I could not see Oberammergau for the Americans. I, too, will remember the Crucifixion scene as long as I live, but will also remember the less-studied scenes of the night before at the Hotel Wittelsbach. I will remember its great café, an endless room all lined with piteous paintings of Calvary but filled with beer-drinking tourists. In particular I will recall the three good souls from Baltimore whom I saw sitting beneath a painting of the bleeding Christ being lifted down from the cross. They were weeping softly into their beer, but it was because the jaunty little Bavarian orchestra had honored them with a rendition of Sonny Boy. I will remember, too, the woman from Boston who made such a scene that her sense of outrage could be heard for blocks when she found that there was no running water in her bedroom. She had a deafening attack of the vapors in the hotel lobby, all unconscious that this was odd behaviour in a pilgrim who had come four thousand miles to witness the chronicle of One for whose mother, in her great hour at Bethlehem, there was no room in the town at all.

"Oberammergau This Way" was the title of that article in *Collier's*. Aleck's shamed tourist baiting brought a lively increase in sales.

Home again in the autumn, Aleck was back at the radio,

this time with CBS, reviewing books, and all the rest. He had been on the air just about a year, but audiences, book publishers, and book buyers were becoming aware of a new phenomenon: when Alexander Woollcott took a book under his capacious and capable wing, the chances were very good that it would become a good seller, and the chances were at least even that it would become a best seller. One such in 1930 was *The Lives of a Bengal Lancer,* by a former British officer and very much an adventurer named Francis Yeats-Brown. This was one of Aleck's most stirring and most effective outbursts. It was written for *McCall's* magazine, in a regular column which he did for them monthly called "Reading and Writing":

> . . . In the most chuckling, mellow, and cosy volume of gossip which this season has added to the library—it is called *As We Were*—E. F. Benson looks fondly back through the now mist-enshrouded '90's to the time when the world was startled by a new voice lifted in that same mysterious East, the time when a short, beetle-browed young man with thick spectacles and a swinging, cock-sure gait came striding across the horizon. His name was Rudyard Kipling, and he had, as Mr. Benson says, "the glorious East and the British Empire rattling like loose change in his trouser-pockets." Not since then, I think, has a hand with so much magic in it held aside the curtains of India until this new one wrought the singularly beautiful tapestry of *Bengal Lancer.*
>
> It is the work of a war-worn, far-flung Englishman named Francis Yeats-Brown who, back in 1904, with his dogs and his rosy cheeks and his shiny new boots, went out from Sandhurst to begin his training as a subaltern of Indian cavalry. Much such a fellow he must have seemed as our old friend, Georgie Cotter, who has since entered into legend as the Brushwood Boy.
>
> But in time he was to keep such trysts as even the Brushwood Boy never knew.
>
> His ears were strained to catch sounds more delicate and elusive than the mere murmur of the jungle, the rattle

of musketry on some debatable frontier, or the sweet tinkle of all the temple bells from Rangoon to Mandalay. In the kit which this young lieutenant carried out to India there must have been an humble and a questing heart.

He has tried to hear the murmur of ancient days, the very voice of India. I suspect that he has heard it. At least, he has come from the feet of the contemplative Yogi sages, bearing with him an inalienable possession—the talisman of tranquillity. Since the days of his novitiate, he has known as a sky fighter both the exhilaration of great danger and the degradation of imprisonment, and learned, too, to treat those two external experiences with equal indifference.

I am afraid I shall have to ask you—either by purchase, theft, barter or whatever other method augments your library—to get hold at once of a copy of the Yeats-Brown book. If you now had it close to hand, I could point out to you the sorcery of certain passages. I could tell you to read the description of the young subaltern's first boar hunt, or the chapter on the feast of the Fish-eyed Goddess.

I could bid you note the beauty and wonder that fill two magical pages at the end of the chapter called "Christmas, 1918." I could ask you to meditate on that passage which begins:

> How I was condemned first to an underground dungeon with criminals (the forged passport had been found in my pocket) and afterwards to solitary confinement; how I stole a knife and fork from the prison restaurant and fused switches with them; how I made friends with a nephew of the Sultan, a prisoner like myself, who had been sentenced to a month's detention for blowing out the brains of his tutor; how this youth had a small black eunuch who used to bring me grapes and French novels; how Robin and I escaped again; and how, a fortnight before the Armistice was declared, we stole General Liman von Sanders' own motor-car (a Mercedes, which we hid in the back yard of the

> house we were occupying, and guarded with a performing bear), all sounds so improbable that I shall not write it down in detail.

> Think how rich an adventure the life of a man must have been who could toss all that away in a mere paragraph. I, too, hesitate to write down in detail his yarns of boar hunts, polo games, Constantinople intrigue, and Fakir miracles. I even hesitate to tell about the old men of Tughlakabad (one of them a spry lad of ninety-nine, by the way) who earn their keep by jumping down wells. But it is not from any base fear of skeptics. I hesitate because such a catalogue would give no real hint of this book's brooding peace, no notion of the sweet healing water Yeats-Brown draws up from the well of his experience and offers you to drink.
>
> In his discussion of India as a problem, he differs markedly from those vigorous journalists who, having spent a week-end in Calcutta, are now writing and lecturing on the subject in this country.
>
> On the subject of India, our quondam lieutenant of the 17th Bengal Lancers differs, I say, from these in one respect. He doesn't think he knows much about it.

In his review Aleck did not mention the price. He did not mention the publisher. He did nothing in the usual manner of reviewers—but very quickly *The Lives of a Bengal Lancer* became a best-seller, and Aleck's reputation as a critic of books was made to match that as a critic of the theater.

No one could understand it. This book was not an important book. As far as the public was concerned, Aleck helped greatly into making it an important book of the 1930 fall publishing season.

XXIII

ALEXANDER WOOLLCOTT WAS SHREWD enough to know that he could not rely on memory and reviewing alone to sustain him as a writer. He needed constant exposure to new experience. Thus when his correspondence with Henry Ke-an Yuan blossomed in 1930, Aleck planned a trip to the Orient for the spring of 1931. The Yuan family was one of the most distinguished in China and his welcome would be warm because he had befriended the younger son of the Yuans in America, and although Henry was showing signs of quite un-Chinese discontent and impatience, the Chinese family of the Yuan class never forgot its manners to strangers.

In the spring, then, he entrained for Seattle and sailed for Japan. First stop was Tokyo and the Imperial Hotel. Here he got out of his clothes and into a pair of silk pajamas and began receiving guests. He went to Kyoto, the ancient capital, and took every tourist trip he could imagine. He was entertained by Kikugoro, the master of the Japanese theater. He made a speech at a girls' middle school. He went to Osaka, to see the famous marionette theater there. He ate at tempura counters and enjoyed the food immensely, including raw fish and delicate fish soups which he had never before tasted. Unlike many Americans, Aleck had the soul of an adventurer, if he now had the general configuration of a Buddha.

He might have become a travel writer had he lived a quarter of a century later for he had a sensitivity to new sights and smells and sounds that showed through in his letters home. He wrote Lilly Bonner from Nara:

> . . . I've never seen so enthralling a country. Every waking minute entertains the eye. For sheer delight, I offer you

> this ancient and quiet town—so quiet that I hear all the bird-calls in the countryside and the rattle of a distant cart somewhere and the occasional boom of the gong at the Temple where some pilgrim must have paid five sen for the luxury of calling Buddha's attention to his prayers. I practically spent the day feeding rice-cakes to the sacred deer who drift by thousands through Nara and whose attentions, when they suspect you of concealing rice-cakes on your person, are even moister than Paddy's. It was a benign spring day and it seemed as if all the school children in Japan were out on the highways on a picnic. Sometimes I saw them trudging along through a very snowstorm of cherry blossoms. I invaded one Temple at a time when about two hundred girls were at prayer. Their shoes were ranged outside and how they ever get back into the right ones, is beyond me. . . .

On April 25, Aleck took a train to Kobe, and the next day he left by steamer on a four-day trip across the Yellow Sea to Taku Bar, and then to Tientsin, where he was met by Henry Yuan. Tientsin, with its trolley cars and busy downtown streets was part Chinese city, part foreign city. It was an important treaty port and the center of foreign concessions. Many notable Chinese families lived in Tientsin, but it had the atmosphere of a foreigner's city about it, and Aleck had already learned this before he came to China and had determined that he would spend nearly all his time in Peking, the old capital city.

So by train he and Henry Yuan went to Peking, to stay at the Hotel Pekin. There Aleck mounted in the open cage elevator to Room 303, donned his pajamas again, and held court for those who wished to call. The difference was that he drank tea instead of coffee while in China, and he had acquired a number of Japanese kimonos including a resplendent gown embroidered with a golden dragon.

He played poker with Mrs. Wellington Koo and was surprised to learn that the name was pronounced Goo. He visited Dr. Davidson Black, an archaeologist, and discussed *sinanthropus,* or Peking Man. He knew, as he visited, that he was seeing the end of an era. Aleck had a fine sense of place and for the changes in the world that swirled about him. After his visit to Peking he wrote this:

> Peking is the last retreat of the World's lost leisure, but one feels that the day of the huddled foreign colony is drawing to a close, not merely because in time the sulky legations will have to pack up and follow the national government to Nanking, nor merely because, in a short while, the truce implied in the Boxer Protocols will have run its course, but because, after all, there is a flood let loose in the world, and Peking lies in its path.

About Peking Aleck wrote with the wide-eyed enthusiasm which marked so much of his work, and which demanded a response in kind from its reader:

> My rickshaw boy, who stayed with me morning, noon and night, trotting cheerily off after breakfast to the bazaars or threading the sunlit enticements of Curio Street, and just as affably drowsing in the courtyard of some house until dawn if I was delayed overlong—my rickshaw boy, I say, charged me for these services the sum of seven Peking dollars a week. From this sum, I understand, he could put by a good deal each week for his old age, but in our money, since the fall of Oriental silver in the money markets, it meant a few cents over a dollar and a half a week. I tell you, you will be spoiled if you go to Peking.
>
> Speaking of dinner parties, I gave one the night before I left Peking, and it was a good dinner if I say it myself who paid for it. We were thirteen at table (no casualties as yet reported) and it was served at a famous duck-restaurant out beyond the grain market.
>
> We had the usual preliminaries of shark's-fin soup and hot broiled duck gizzards, the latter dusted with a powder made of salt, pepper and crushed lavender leaves. We had the white meat beaten up with something—milk, I think, or perhaps the white duck eggs—into a kind of soufflé. And we had the wonderful Peking turnovers—thin, unsweetened pancakes smeared with the tingling soy-bean sauce, garnished with young onions and stuffed with flakes

of glistening duck meat. And of course throughout there was a steady flow of rice wine.

The bill, including the tip and the second table supplied for the rickshaw boys, came to something less than eleven of our splendid dollars. You *will* be spoiled if you go to Peking.

He could write informatively, as the best journalists:

However, though it is my purpose dutifully to warn all casual wayfarers from taking the long road to Peking in these troubled times, it would be deceptive of me to leave you under the impression that, once there, you would have to remain cowering within the shelter of the United States Marine Guard.

There are, as a matter of fact, several feasible expeditions in the immediate vicinity of Peking. I know by hearsay that you could go by donkeys and river boats to one cluster of drowsy temples at a place of which you would find it even harder to pronounce the name were I to spell it out for you here. Or you could go by motor car (over roads rather like waffle irons) to the Ming Tombs, and, above all, you could go up by the Nankow Pass to the Great Wall of China which, as it follows the noble modeling of the naked hills in that leafless countryside seems like some such mad masonry as you would find traversing the burnished mountains of the moon. It is a soaring flight of the imagination forever transfixed in stone, and of all the wonders of the world that I have seen, this is the most breath-taking.

Yet, these are travel notes of one whose most uplifting experiences are always being chilled and complicated by dissonance. I had come up to the Great Wall by donkey from Nankow. Since that is a means of transportation for which I am not ideally constructed, I did not greatly enjoy the ride and I even have some reason to suspect that, after it was over, the donkey decided to go back to agriculture. Wherefore, when we left the Great Wall, I shifted to a chair and came down the rocky pass with only the pat-pat-pat of the chair-bearers disturbing the silence of the Maytime sunset. I was all prepared to enjoy this majestic ascent when, unfortunately I overheard the drawled comment of a young Chinaman as I went by.

"Ah," he said, "the yellow man's burden."

In that final paragraph, Aleck showed how well he could write with wry humor and self-deprecation, too.

During this period of his life Aleck planned his time as carefully as he must, but not very far in advance. He came home to America at the end of June, to San Francisco and then Los Angeles and New York. He wrote Lilly Bonner, who had gone to Europe with her family in his absence, that he might conceivably come across the Atlantic to visit them. But he did not go, because too many commitments appeared on the horizon—magazine tasks, radio broadcasts. He wrote an article entitled "Going to Pieces in the Orient," in which he described the theatrical people and theaters he had encountered on his trip, from Kikugoro, whom he discovered to be the sixth Kikugoro of the Japanese theater, to a visit to the Chinese opera in Peking. He had gone to see a performance that began at four p.m. and lasted until one a.m. Henry Yuan had told his party that the actor they particularly wanted to see would not come on in his particular plays until ten o'clock so they went to dinner and then to the theater at the intermission just before ten. During the intermission the stage director came out to announce that the star was ill and would not plav that night, which disappointed Henry Yuan, and led him to the point of leaving. Yet after all the hot face cloths had been thrown back and forth across the aisles from vendor to customer, and all the theatergoers were properly supplied with newspaper cones of roasted peanuts and lotos seeds, lo and behold, the great actor did come out. Saying he would not be there was simply his way of announcing that he was not feeling up to par and that the audience must not expect his best performance. Aleck suggested that some American actors might well adopt the trick.

Aleck could seldom resist a pun or a wisecrack when the opportunity presented itself, in writing or on the air, as that year when he wrote about his friend Alfred Lunt:

He had discussed Alfred Lunt's early career in Wisconsin. Then:

And now I find myself glancing into the dim future when Alfred Lunt will, I trust, be buried on his native heath. You see, as one of the pallbearers, I could relieve the gloom of the occasion by referring to the catafalque as the bier that made Milwaukee famous.

His criticism of theater and books, however, was not to be discussed lightly because he wrote frothily for *Collier's, New Yorker,* and other publications. He wrote frothily—but not always. Sometimes he wrote almost prophetically at least of trends. He wrote of Charlie Chaplin and Chaplin's 1931 silent movie, *City Lights*:

> . . . There must, I think, fall across each screen on which *City Lights* is shown a shadow not cast by any of the properties or puppets of the Chaplin lot. It is the shadow of a foreboding, an uneasy feeling that in this visitation we are seeing our Charlie for the last time.
>
> Well that is as may be. At all events, his like has not passed this way before. And we shall not see his like again.

The absolute proof of Aleck's good and strong literary taste came when he wrote of William Faulkner, virtually an unknown novelist, although he had published *Sartoris,* on the occasion of the publication of *Sanctuary* in 1931.

> I trust all those who care for sweet and sentimental books should be warned what a terrific experience awaits them within its covers. But I would not have you think it gross. Indeed, its great power derives all from the art of implication and understatement. Faulkner has a knack for filling his pages with a nameless dread so that his reader feels like an uneasy wayfarer who has found lodging for the night in some sinister house, where the corridors creak ominously and the darkness is alive with evil and mischance but dimly comprehended. . . .

A famous Woollcott feud—with Herbert Bayard Swope—began this year, and since Aleck was so often blamed for his part in this affair it is worth recounting in some detail. Aleck and Swope had been squabbling for years on those vast arenas that laughingly passed by the name of croquet courts, but these squabbles were always resolved in shouts and good humor, both by the gallery and by the Katzenjammer kids themselves. When Aleck left the *World,* Swope wrote him that "Margaret and I will always be delighted to welcome you as a guest in our home." When Swope left the *World* a few months later, Aleck wrote him: "If you ever take over the Great Neck (Long Island) *News* I can tell you one thing about its dramatic critic. His guts will be hated by your whilom underling Alexander Woollcott." Later Aleck wrote Swope "that your heart is God's little garden and that the indurated habit of loving you has lasted so long I shall probably never get over it."

But that was 1929. Swope, having made a considerable fortune in the stock market, turned to dabbling in international finance and began to see more bankers and fewer newspapermen, reformed or otherwise. He and Aleck grew away from one another.

A prominent figure in Swope's affairs was the financier John Hertz of Chicago, who ran a taxicab company and invented the drive-it-yourself automotive business. Hertz had lent Swope large amounts of money to finance his investments, and in 1931 Swope still owed Hertz half a million dollars, according to Swope biographer E. J. Kahn, Jr. When Hertz decided to move east to New York City, that year, Swope was obviously very much beholden to him and adopted the course of doing all possible to help make the move pleasant. He gave a dinner for Hertz at the Lotos Club which must have cost at least fifty dollars a plate, for fifty prominent New York business leaders. He also volunteered to help the multimillionaire with his housing problem, and there is where he and Aleck parted company.

In Aleck's building, the Beekman Campanile, lived the once wealthy oil speculator Joshua Cosden, who had gone broke and was now saddled with a 30-room apartment that seemed somehow suddenly to be too large for his family. Swope suggested to Cosden that his financial burden might be eased and Hertz's housing problem solved by a lease of the apartment to the Chicagoan.

Cosden accepted the suggestion happily and put Hertz's name up before the committee of owners of the apartments, for it was a rule in this cooperative building that no person could be admitted without the concurrence of all the apartment owners.

Aleck had met Hertz and did not like him. He found him personally obnoxious and he believed Hertz was a social climber. He objected to the change and it was not made.

Swope, a Jew himself, immediately leaped to the improper conclusion that Aleck was anti-Semitic and went about New York so charging. Aleck was truly shocked at this damaging intemperance by a man who should have known better. Nearly all of Aleck's best friends were Jews, and if there was ever a man whose character was tempered without the slightest trace of race or religious prejudice, it was Alexander Woollcott. Considering the fact that Swope was insulting him to everyone he knew, Aleck's response was most temperate.

He wrote Swope on November 30:

> I keep hearing rumors to the effect that you are denouncing me for discreditable behaviour in the matter of the proposal to install the Hertzes in the Cosden apartment. I am resting comfortably in the assumption that you do not express or even harbor unamiable thoughts about me without finding out from me just what mischief I have been up to and why. I don't know what tale you have heard, but to save time I might volunteer the information that I have done nothing I am ashamed of, nor that I would not do again on the basis of the same information.

Swope did not reply to this letter in writing. Rather, he did reply, but was persuaded for some reason not to send the letter. Instead, his secretary (according to biographer Kahn) read Aleck a stiff note, in which Swope said that he considered the Hertzes to be desirable tenants in any building.

> I do not say that the fact you met them several times in my home entitled them and me to any special courtesy. But I do say that while you have every right to view people as you wish, there is a price you must pay when you translate unkind thoughts into venomous action, and that price is my friendship.

Aleck did not wish to lose Swope's friendship, for whatever

it was worth to him at this time, but he would not back down on what he considered to be a matter of principle, simply because Swope had made the mistake of trying to push the Hertzes into the Campanile without a little diplomatic homework beforehand.

On December 2, he wrote Swope one last time, asking that before Swope broke off relationships he might at least hear Aleck's side of the story.

> Dear Herbert:
>
> If you are going to glower at me at parties, and write me terse notes which put me in the preposterous position of volunteering excuses for my way of conducting my affairs, I can not imagine what my next move should be—if any. But if you really have a friendly interest in my reputation for decency in human relations, and can remember to challenge me the next time I run into you, I promise to testify truthfully on any points that may still be troubling you. . . .

From Swope came deep silence.

Swope began blackguarding Aleck to their mutual friends, and Aleck responded in kind. The Katzenjammer Kids were no more.

XXIV

ALECK HAD LITTLE TIME to worry about Herbert Bayard Swope's new-found enmity. He was about to make his debut on the New York stage as a professional actor. It was the autumn of 1931.

This turn of events, which Aleck secretly relished, although he deprecated it in letters to his friends, had come about because playwright S. N. Behrman had written a comedy called *Brief Moment.* Katharine Cornell had leased the Belasco Theater for three years, and she and Guthrie McClintic had decided that their first production here would be the Behrman play, starring Francine Larrimore. One part was written with a Woollcottian character very much in mind. "Sigrist," Behrman said in his stage notes, "is very fat, about thirty years old, and lies down whenever possible. He somewhat resembles Alexander Woollcott, who conceivably might play him."

Aleck was approached. He read the play. He saw the part as that of a "stout, indolent, and unamiable creature who spends a large part of the play lying on a chaise longue and making insulting remarks." It was made for him, he saw, and after considerable discussion about what the appearance might do for and to his reputation, he decided to take the chance.

He would go into rehearsal for the part, and if it seemed to work out to the satisfaction of all concerned, he would go to Washington in October for the tryout. If no bombs were thrown, he would return to New York and play the part for several weeks—no more. He joined Actors Equity and began rehearsals, so serious about his stage debut that he refused all radio commitments for the early fall.

Brief Moment opened at the Belasco on November 9. The play was a flop but the performance, as an evening of entertainment, was adjudged worth while—and that was simply because Aleck was appearing at the Belasco, in the character of Aleck, thinly disguised.

Writing in the New York *Times,* Brooks Atkinson called the play "limp" and "apparently aimless" for at least half its length. He liked the dialogue and the characters, but what he liked most of all was Aleck's performance as the public Alexander Woollcott—lying on his chaise longue and making nasty remarks to all and sundry. "Mr. Woollcott tosses it across the footlights with a relish that the audience shares," he wrote. "If he enjoyed himself as much as the audience last night enjoyed him, he must have been having a very good time."

Gilbert Gabriel, the critic of the morning *American,* referred to Aleck as "the Cheshire Woollcott." The *World-Telegram's* critic said Aleck had run away with the honors of the evening. John Mason Brown, in the *Evening Post,* did not like the play, but he liked Aleck's performance because Aleck was not really a part of the play. "Indeed," said Brown, "he can disregard the action and concern himself with life." Percy Hammond in the *Herald Tribune* said that as an actor Aleck "proves to be as good an end man as any comedian he ever praised" and termed the Woollcott debut a victory.

Aleck did very well indeed. The play ran for 129 performances in New York City, almost solely on his momentum. When receipts fell off after the first three months, in order to keep going the rest of the cast accepted a cut in pay. Aleck asked for, and received, an increase on the basis (which all recognized) that he was keeping the stage doors open. Some, then and later, chided him for this "selfishness" taking the position that as a public figure he should be also an eleemosynary institution, quite forgetting that every day he played in *Brief Moment* he was sacrificing his radio career, which promised a great future. He wrote to Lilly Bonner two weeks after the opening:

> Well, I'm just a fool. Here I am sold down the river in so many directions that I practically have no private life. If you could see me dictating breathless [he wrote deathless but the secretary transcribed it improperly] prose

> while brushing my teeth in the morning, and correcting proof while applying grease paint in the dressing room, you would have some idea of my present demented state. . . . Of course I am having a robustly amusing time, and am really quite good in the play, thanks to the fact that it is an actor-proof part which fits me better than any suit I ever had did. . . .

Danton Walker, who had left Aleck's employment as secretary but remained his friend, came to call one morning at Wit's End and found Aleck being shaved by a barber (he had grown a goatee as well as a mustache), giving orders to Junior, the man of all work, directions to his new male secretary, and dictation to an extra stenographer (thus the errors like breathless for deathless) and instructions to the cook.

Considering his schedule and the dictating of letters and even articles for magazines, it is remarkable that Aleck would have had time for serious thought, and he never came to consider himself either pundit or sufficiently informed to comment on any special aspect of world affairs. Yet, an article in the February 20 issue of *Collier's* illustrated two points of Aleck's character that are worth exploring. The article dealt with his trip to the Far East and what he had found there. Among other things, in the black leather-and-old-oak sanctum of the Peking Club bar, he had found much talk about the day that the United States would go to war with Japan. He did not like the talk, and in this article in the early months of 1932 he said as much:

> I only hope that if ever there is such a war and we win it, we shall remember that we won it because we are larger, richer and more numerous, and therefore not feel too proud about it. For I have just seen enough of Japan and the Japanese to believe with all my heart that such a victory would be only another of history's insensitive triumphs of quantity over quality.

In this article Aleck also discussed the footwear of people in the Orient, and in so doing used one of his favorite archaisms which he swore should not be relegated to the past: the word shoon for shoes. Aleck often used the word, it was a part of one of his tricks of style, and truly very harmless if slightly affected, because no one in his right mind could mistake the meaning of the word. As an author, it was his prerogative.

No one at *Collier's* much minded, especially not William L. Chenery, the genial editor. But the copy readers minded and they changed Alecks *shoon* to *shoes.* When the typed copy of his article was sent to him, and Aleck saw that *shoon* had been changed to the prosiac *shoes,* he exploded on the telephone. Editor Chenery assured Aleck that all would be well and that he could have his *shoon* back. So it was—but only until the article reached the proof stage, and there it was changed from *shoon* to *shoes.* Aleck again remonstrated, but remonstrations did not carry well from New York City to the middle west where *Collier's* printing plant was located, and when the magazine was published, in Aleck's article on the far East, *shoon* had finally disappeared.

So loud were Aleck's cries and so anguished that after that day those who worked at *Collier's* editorial department in the period could recall the problem of the shoon, and the man who moved around the building offering to polish pedal coverings, invariably from that date offered *shoon-shines.*

In the fall of 1931, Aleck wrote something complimentary about Mrs. Laura E. Richards' memoirs *Stepping Westward,* and in the article mentioned others of her works, including *Captain January.* The response by readers of the *New Yorker* was everything he could have asked, just as the response from Mrs. Richards that year and the next was such that it began a long friendship which produced some of Aleck's most self-revealing letters, as this:

> You see, I am not a book reviewer at all. For too many years I was a dramatic critic, a post nicely calculated to rot the mind. After my flight from Times Square, I invented this page in the *New Yorker* where, as a kind of town crier, I can say anything that is on my mind. The trouble is that there isn't often much on it. But every once in a while I have the satisfaction, which is the breath of the journalist's nostril, of hearing bells ring all over the country.

> Then I know that I have had the good fortune to say something which a lot of people had wanted to have said. Said *for* them, that is. This happens just often enough to keep me going. It happened in the case of the piece I wrote about *Stepping Westward.* At the risk of seeming vainglorious, I must (because, after all, they are your affair, not mine) report some of these reactions to you. I do not think there has been a day in the past two months when someone has not written me about that piece. More often than not the note takes the form of someone thanking me for reminding him or her of *Captain January.* I get descriptions of angry hunts through the bookcases until the mislaid copy is run to earth in the spare-room closet. Then follows a fond reunion with a few tears for the story's sake, and for the sake of days gone by. . . .

Aleck then dropped into reminiscence of his own formative reading, in the days when he had towed a wagonload of books home to his rooming house every weekend from the Germantown Library, using the card of everyone in the household to obtain books:

> There would be candid juvenilia written for the slower-witted boys, sandwiched between books that I could and do read now for pleasure. But I think that even at the time, I knew there were those among my favorites which were good in a sense that the others were not. I think I knew, when first I read them, that I would always like *Huckleberry Finn,* and *Little Women,* and Kenneth Grahame's *The Golden Age,* and Howard Pyle's *Robin Hood* and *Captain January.* Mixed in with such treasures, and pretty much at the same time, was a good deal of addiction to Harrison Ainsworth and to Charles Reade. But above all, and through all, and to this day, my dear Charles Dickens. My father started me when I was ten by reading *Great Expectations* to me. I still think it is the best of the lot. I had read all except *Bleak House* by the time I was twelve. Later I took on Jane Austen, and one of the reasons why I am not particularly well-read today is because I have spent so large a part of the last twenty years re-reading

Dickens and Jane Austen. I remember Shaw admitting once to me that a concordance of his own writings would reveal the Dickens allusions as running four to one against any other writer. He told me it was a kind of shorthand, and I realized that that was what it had always been with us. If I had not known the people in Dickens as well as I knew the neighbors, I wouldn't have understood what the family were talking about half the time. . . .

During the spring of 1932, Aleck spent most of his time on various magazine articles, including the regular weekly "Shouts and Murmurs" page for the *New Yorker.* His book reviewing was now very much a part of his life—he could no longer write that he was not a book reviewer at all. He aired his enthusiasms for the most part but he was also courageous enough to state his case when he objected to the latest work of Ernest Hemingway, although the Hemingway cult had already been formed. Aleck had helped form it, and he had lustily beaten drums for every pearly word dropped by the professional male writer of the twentieth century.

A year or so ago, in one of these monthly discourses on contemporary letters, I spoke of those authors in whom I had such abiding faith and such deep interest that, sight unseen, I would want to read any book they might care to write. If memory serves, I named only three—Lytton Strachey, Willa Cather, and Ernest Hemingway. Well, Mr. Strachey, taken from the world at the height of his powers, will write no more. And now my confidence in Mr. Hemingway has been most grievously shaken. His new book, which he has sent forth under the beautiful name of *Death in the Afternoon,* is a muddled monograph on the aesthetics of bull-fighting, and it is so clumsy, so slovenly, so loutish a work that it really comes under the head of disorderly conduct. This, mind you, is the same Mr. Hemingway who, in *The Killers,* wrote as sinewy and potent a short story as ever I read and who, with *A Farewell to Arms,* earned a permanent place in the history of American letters.

I myself, am not much given to the innocuous and now somewhat *démodé* parlor-game that used to ensue whenever someone ventured to name the "great American novel." It seems to me that the solemn balancing of two such incomparable works as *Huckleberry Finn* and *Death Comes for the Archbishop,* for instance, is a little too much like fatuously debating which gives one the greater pleasure—the scent of mignonette or the taste of maple sugar. But if drawn reluctant into such a game, I could put up a good argument for *A Farewell to Arms.* It is not only lovely as you pass through it, but, seen as you turn your head for a last lingering look, it lies behind you as a complete landscape, fresh and delightful in its coloring, magnificent in its sweep, deeply satisfying in its unforgettable design.

I have read it five times, with ever increasing enthusiasm, and when the word went forth that at last its author had a new book ready, I was waiting on the doorstep of the publisher to catch the first copy as it fell from the press. Now, in the language which the lawyers use when their witnesses betray them, I claim surprise. I have all the emotions of the hostess who captures the most distinguished and fascinating visitor in town as her week-end guest only to have him pinch the waitress, fall asleep at the dinner table, and burn holes in the guest room chintzes. No crime, I admit. Just disorderly conduct.

According to his own account in *Death in the Afternoon,* it seems that when Mr. Hemingway was a young man trying to learn to write, he wanted to commence with the simplest things and, since one of the simplest and most fundamental things of all is violent death, he decided to inspect it. The war—a splendid laboratory for this course—was, unfortunately, over. Therefore the dependable supply of violent death was practically limited to the bullrings of Spain. So Master Hemingway crossed the Pyrenees, notebook in hand. This sounds to me a little too much like the advice one might find in How to Become an Author in Ten Easy Lessons, and it is my dark and now strengthened suspicion that it would be followed only by a disastrously humorless young man.

However Chatauquan his first visit may have been, once he had seen the toreros at work under the Spanish sun, he became consumed with a passion for bullfighting, and perhaps it is just as well that he has now unpacked his mind of all his jumbled thoughts on the subject.

In the process he has planned (as a by-product) to affront a good many readers by dragging in, as by the scruff of the neck, certain words which usually appear in print only when some normally smutty little boy with a piece of chalk finds an inviting fence to write upon. Their use by an author is, like spitting on the floor, a question of manners and a matter of fashion.

I would be quite willing to let Mr. Hemingway have his fun with his piece of chalk if only he could be persuaded to pause for breath in some of his more shambling sentences, and if only he would cut down a little each day in his use of the word "very," with which his text is as much a-twitter as the gush of an ingenue at a tea-party. Indeed, I mention his coarse speech only because it seems part of an attitude which is maintained throughout the book. I should describe that attitude as a somewhat sedulous virility. Every now and again in *Death in the Afternoon* I seem to detect the weak violence of a pudgy young man, standing with his feet wide apart and spitting tobacco juice through his teeth, in the hope of striking us all as a pretty tough customer.

From a vantage point of thirty-five years the Woollcott review of this particular work and his estimate of Hemingway's basic attitude toward life stand forth bright as a beacon; Aleck was working without benefit of the biographies, memoirs, and reminiscences that have exposed Hemingway's personality to a later generation, and his clarity of thought and expression in this matter show why he became the most effective book reviewer in the United States and the critic read most and followed most by Americans from one edge of the continent to the other.

In the summer of that year, it was back to Bomoseen for house parties on the island, with occasional business trips to New York; that was always the pattern of his life; he stayed nowhere very long at one time for he was far too busy and far too restless.

Late in the autumn, just before winter set in, Aleck went to Europe. His plan was to stop off in Paris, go to Berlin, then to Moscow, and then to London, to collect more material for his writings and to look in on "the great experiment" from the point of view of a descendant of a much earlier form of communal or socialist society.

In Berlin Aleck made his last minute arrangements for the trip to Moscow. Walter Duranty, correspondent there for the New York *Times* was his old friend. He cabled Aleck that he had found himself a new apartment and that he had laid in a supply of whiskey and other rarities for the occasion of Aleck's visit.

Aleck, for his part, laid in a supply of gifts for friends and people he expected to meet in Moscow. He asked various people who had traveled or lived in Russia recently what people there would appreciate most, thinking in terms of cosmetics and luxuries, perhaps. He was told, and he went out and bought: he arrived in Moscow with a large supply of toilet paper, and to each and every host who treated him, Aleck gave a roll.

So Aleck was in Moscow in October in high good humor, to spy for his readers on the Russians. Here are snatches of his reports:

> I am just back from Leningrad and the manager of the hotel has gone off again with my passport. He will brood over it for a week, entering all its fascinating vital statistics in a series of ledgers and in the process discovering—I should think without great surprise—that, although I have been away from Moscow three whole days, nothing has happened in the interval to alter the previously noted fact that I was born in Phalanx, N. J., of all places, on January 19, 1887. It is depressing to contemplate the amount of clerical labor and white paper which, during the past ten years, has been wasted in solemnly recording for the police archives of various countries a date of such scant historical significance.
>
> There is one aspect of travel in the Soviet Union about which no one thought to warn me. . . . How disconcerting would be the daily experiences of a fat man in the Soviet Union. . . .

Now every foreigner is used to being stared at in Moscow. It is his clothes which betray him and it is no uncommon thing for him to be stopped in the street and asked politely, wistfully, even desperately, where he got them. But it is my unfailing and often embarrassing experience that all Russians, young and old, whom I pass on the street not only stare but halt in their tracks as though astounded and then grin from ear to ear. The custom dislocated almost to disruption one detachment of the parading workers on the anniversary of the revolution. The good citizens nudge one another and hold hoarsely whispered conferences about me. The less inhibited ones burst into shrieks of laughter. Of course there be those among my friends who would say that the man in the street of other countries is similarly affected by the sight of me and is merely more self-controlled. Local commentators are inclined to suggest that I owe this mild but constant commotion to my striking resemblance to the capitalist as he is always pictured in Soviet cartoons. But I myself am disposed to ascribe it more simply to the fact that in the Soviet Union a man of girth is an exotic rarity. . . . The other evening while I waited on a windswept doorstep for a friend to pick me up, one of a trio of young communists—a lad of fifteen perhaps—reached out and patted my facade as he passed by. I feel sure this was not rudely done at all. The grin he gave me over his shoulder as he went on his way was somehow both envious and amiable. Not fond, exactly, but appreciative. That's the word for it. It was an *appreciative* grin. It seemed to say: "Ah, comrade, what a sequence of juicy steaks, what mugs of good beer, what mounds of lovely golden butter, what poods of fine white bread must have gone into the making of that!

* * *

Moscow, November, 1932 . . . I have been here long enough to learn what the major industry of Soviet Russia is. It is printing pictures of Stalin. You cannot walk ten minutes in any direction here without encountering twenty. His formidable image is so omnipresent as to provoke in all naturally mutinous hearts an impulse to go out into the Red Square, yell "Hurrah for good old Trotsky!" and see what happens. I myself am half disposed to make this instructive experiment tomorrow, and if you do not hear from me again you may assume that I did try it. . . .

To any American setting out for these parts, all his neighbors come around and say loftily: "Of course you will see only what they want you to see." . . . Now I object to such warnings not only because they happen to be false, but because they are intolerably smug. . . . It would be a truer thing to say that when you go to Soviet Russia you see only what *you* want to see. At the frontier the customs officials may check up sternly on the amount of good coffee, cockroach powder and American tobacco you are sneaking into the country, but they never think to examine your prejudices. You bring them all in with you. . . .

Except for a few such men from Mars as Walter Duranty, all visitors might be roughly divided into two classes: those who come here hoping to see the communist scheme succeed, and those who came here hoping to see it fail. . . .

Aleck concerned himself very seriously with the Soviet drama, and went to a number of plays. Along with a cousin of Captain Dreyfus, the son of a Chinese father and a dusky mother from Trinidad, and a Russian girl, he went to a production of Eugene O'Neill's *All God's Chillun Got Wings,* played in Russian, under the title *The Negro.*

. . . In the intervals for scene changes there would also be American songs to create the proper atmosphere. With a perceptible start I recognized one old favorite of my childhood even when disguised as "Onnie Roaney." But if you have never chanced to hear Russian troubadours lifting their voices in Negro spirituals, the more pensive ballads of Irving Berlin, and "Bon-Bon Buddy, the Chocolate Drop," let me console you with the assurance that you have not suffered an intolerable aesthetic privation.

In four weeks Aleck went to a dozen theaters. He met director Alexander Tairov who gave him tea and raisin cake and asked for the libretto and score of *Of Thee I Sing*, to be sent by Aleck from America.

His conclusion:

> The Russian stage, with such superb organizations as the Kamerny, the Vakhtangoff and the Moscow Art Theater, is, I suppose, the finest and most flexible instrument of its kind in the world, just awaiting, like the bow of Ulysses, for a great dramatist to come along and bend it to his uses. But there is, I think, no such dramatist even in sight, and, as things have been and still are, there could not be. Without going into the anxious question whether, as the Russians say, our own boasted freedom means nothing more than the poor privilege of starving to death on a park bench, it is impossible to characterize the theater in Moscow without mentioning as its most salient characteristic the fact that it is not free. . . .

Aleck attended a matinee performance of *Uncle Tom's Cabin*, along with hundreds of children from the Moscow schools who were as delighted as he was when Simon Legree met his comeuppance in the end. "The most fanatical Marxist could scarcely ask a more satisfying picture of private property at its foulest," he said.

He became aware that the Russians in the theater were playing a system, stacking the cards he called it. This came upon him as he went to see the *Hamlet* staged by Akimov, "the Belasco of the Vakhrangov."

> Since *Hamlet* is a play of court intrigue with all its leading characters either royal or the hangers-on of royalty, they must have been mean swine without a single, creditable motive in the lot. . . . It was Akimov's direction of Ophelia's mad scene which made me recognize him as a man who was playing a system. [Akimov changed the play so that Ophelia was not mad, but she was tipsy, and fell into the brook and drowned while drunk]—and not him alone but all these Kremlinites, who with the grim relentlessness of Calvinists, still have a great milling multitude in thrall. I suppose we are all holding our breath with some prayerful

anxiety, mind you, because for weal or woe, the outcome concerns us all. The least we can say is that the hapless Russians are the guinea pigs of a great scientific experiment and whether we are to profit from it by positive or negative example, whether the remedy discovered by those doctors be a deadly poison or another insulin, is the question to which only children yet unborn will really know the answer.

After his month in Moscow, Aleck went to London, where he had promised himself a month's visit, rolling in luxury, to reward himself for all that he would have to endure in Russia. He found, in retrospect, that he had endured nothing in Moscow, and enjoyed his visit very much.

Hardly had Aleck returned from Europe when he was again plunged into controversy, this time with Kathleen and Charles Norris, with whom he had been very friendly in the past. Aleck had written a human interest article about Kathleen Norris, novelist, for *Cosmopolitan.* He had written about her early life, mentioning the word "tenement." He had written about her tenderness toward their foster son. He had made certain mentions of their parties ("ghastly receptions") and of Charles Norris as Kathleen's husband as well as writer. All this had been shown to Kathleen Norris and she had read and approved the article. In fact, she had thanked Aleck for writing so beautifully about her. Then, when the article appeared in *Cosmopolitan,* she and her husband took violent objection to it.

Aleck asked them to dinner to try to pacify them. They refused to come. They sought legal counsel, but Aleck had Kathleen Norris' letter which said she "loved" it, and that the parts about "the ranch and Bill brought tears," so there was no legal recourse open to them. Aleck listened to their recriminations and read their angry letters, and finally wrote an angry letter to Norris.

> The letters from you and Kathleen about the article in the Cosmopolitan, when read in their proper sequence, constitute an extraordinarily interesting exhibit. I think there is only one point in your letter which I am obligated to answer. This is the point contained in this sentence, which I quote:

> Especially I resent the impropriety of which you are guilty in betraying and publishing Kathleen's confidences regarding our foster son which can only hurt and humiliate him.

It seems to me that you paint a quite dreadful picture of Bill Norris if he would be hurt and humiliated by the beautiful story of his childhood. However, I naturally could not be sure on such a point about someone I never met. That is why I took the precaution of asking Kathleen's permission to use the story as she had told it to me, and receiving such permission in writing from her. I am glad, in case this has slipped her mind, that I kept the letter in which she told me it would be quite all right.

Then there is the question whether the article should have been shown to Kathleen before publication. I was informed three months ago by Mr. Berlin of the Hearst publications that he *had* shown it to her, and that she had approved it highly. It was only the other night when we met on the sidewalk after the Coward show that I learned from her that no such advance glimpse had been vouchsafed. I am, of course, delighted now that it was not shown to her if, as I am forced to conclude, it would have involved turning the subject of my small sketch into the kind of shopwindow dummy I must assume is your ideal in such public appearances.

Another friendship gone. In later years Aleck would be accused of turning on his friends viciously like a snapping turtle. Sometimes Aleck's friends turned on him, as well.

People wondered why Aleck's book reviewing had so much impact in America, and the reason was not only because he was brave—as in his criticism of something of Hemingway's that he detested—but also because he gave such eminently sensible advice to readers. In June, writing in his book column, Aleck listed six carefully selected books about life in the Soviet Union. His point?

> If, in a magazine at your dentist's, you were to read how all American workmen wear silk shirts, gamble in

stocks, own two cars apiece, and give over their leisure to midget golf and Mah Jong, it would probably dawn on you that your dentist was careless about keeping the table of his waiting room freshly stocked from the newsstand. It is well, in taking a library course on Soviet Russia, to remember that life in that vast and variegated federation during the past fifteen years has been at least as fluctuant as it has been in our own, and that much water has gone over the Dnieperstroy Dam since some of the most frequently quoted works on the Great Experiment were written. I have heard enough Congressmen railing at the Communists for doing something they had quit doing ten years before to make me suggest to each inquiring reader that he never ponder a report on the state of things in Muscovy without keeping the date of its authorship in mind. The best of those reports have just as much finality as the daily fever-chart of a patient who has been ailing for some time and is not yet out of the woods.

Then would it be asking too much to suggest that you try reading dispassionately? Few people have even made the attempt. Wherefore all over Soviet Russia one runs into grievously disappointed visitors who are naively shocked by discovering the existence of conditions—such as the fostered persistence of inequality, let us say, or the ruthless suppression of individual freedom—which had, as a matter of fact, been explicitly and repeatedly reported to the outside world by all the first-rate correspondents stationed in Moscow. I suppose that such visitors, having encountered so much venomous nonsense in the early diatribes against the Soviets, had had their minds permanently immunized against the acceptance of a single unwelcome fact.

Let me suggest then that, with a mind watchful and at least half open, you seek a picture of Soviet Russia by reading these books in the order named:

Ten Days That Shook the World
by John Reed
The History of the Russian Revolution
by Leon Trotsky

A Short View of Russia
by John Maynard Keynes
Soviet Russia
by William Henry Chamberlin
Red Bread
by Maurice Hindus
The Little Golden Calf
by Ilf and Petrov

He then, of course, reviewed each book succinctly. He was not simply preoccupied with Russia. Few people realized it but Alexander Woollcott, bon vivant, man-about-town, wise-guy and professional character, was also a man of thoughtful mien, who in his own way worked unceasingly for the public good, both in his private actions and in his public posture. That autumn of 1933, he displayed his avid concern in matters of public affairs in reviewing a book with which he disagreed in principle, yet advising Americans to read it:

> When Bernard Shaw had been three score years in the land he sat him down and contemplated the fact that though Jesus of Nazareth was first executed by his contemporaries as a dangerous anarchist and blasphemous madman, and then rejected by posterity as an impractical dreamer, there did still survive, after two thousand years, an irresistible impression that he was greater than his judges. Shaw even went so far as to suggest mildly that the economic heresies preached by the Nazarene may have been sound after all, that before giving Christianity up as a failure it might be a good idea—if only as a desperate last resort—to try it.
>
> I find myself minded to make a similar suggestion every time I read one of these new books which announce, with the professional gusto of an undertaker, that democracy has failed. Such a book is this glib, cocksure and faintly condescending piece of Spenglerian, historical panorama called *The People's Choice*, written—with the perspective afforded by a snug berth in London, I believe—by one Herbert Agar. I think you might (and probably will) do worse than read it, if only for its value as an irritant. Ah,

Agar, Agar, we need the sheer roughage of your thought, after the soothing doses of American history—the positively sedative doses—administered to most of us in school.

What Mr. Agar offers us is a hasty glance at the men the American people, with varying luck, judgment and illusion of free-will, have selected as Chief Executive. When the late Viscount Bryce wrote his *American Commonwealth* thirty years ago, he pointed out quietly that it was the tendency, if not the invariable rule, of American politics to summon second-rate men to the White House. Mr. Agar makes it painfully clear that to call most of our presidents, from Jackson's time on, second-rate would be to flatter them grossly.

"The important point about the Harding regime," says Mr. Agar, "is the indifference of the American people to the scandals that resulted. Vice-President Coolidge, who sat mum while the evil work was done, was elected President in 1924. And the man who succeeded him, in 1928, had been a member of Harding's Cabinet, and had not felt called upon either to draw attention to what was going on about him, or to resign from the little group of thieves to which he had been appointed."

Now that, I submit, is true talk. But I have no words for the violence of my dissent from the bland conclusion to which our author arrives next. "One feature of a money-bossed democracy," he says, "is that good men learn to refrain from public life. But it is wrong to blame those who hold aloof: *their action is the result, not the cause, of the degradation in politics.* Since the Civil War, for example, good men have merely been wasted in Washington."

The italics are mine, the defeatism Mr. Agar's. When we are badly governed in city, state and nation, it is the fault of all who hold aloof, not only of those good men who learn to refrain from public life in Mr. Agar's sense, but of every one of us who, week in and week out, think of the public weal as somebody else's business. One day a man of means and deep culture in the humanities sat in my house and filled it with scornful description of our misgovernment. He would have lingered longer to explain this sad decay to me but he had to hurry down town. He had to look up a Tammany chief and get himself relieved from jury duty. I am tired of hearing the ineptitude and poltroonery of Congress spoken of as some unavoidable phenomena of nature, when the speaking is done by those neighbors of mine who could not name their own Congressman, forgot to register at the last election, and have not therefore contributed the decent minimum of citizenship to the hazardous venture of making this continent an Eden after all. I am tired, in short, of hearing it said that democracy doesn't work. Of course, it doesn't work. It isn't supposed to work. We are supposed to work it.

The important part of the foregoing sentence is the personal pronoun. Indeed, I think that the hands of the present occupant of the White House might best be upheld if a few million of us were to forego, for the period of his administration, the corrupting use of the seductive pronoun "They." No mysterious "They" put Mr. Harding in the White House. We did it. The crime of those thieves Mr. Agar mentions—a crime far more despicable even than those committed by Leopold and Loeb and the evil men who stole the Lindbergh baby—was not merely a shame. It was our shame. When we have a sense of that—when our toes curl and our scalps crawl with our sense of it—we will be on our way to the Promised Land. Until then we will be misgoverned, and richly deserve to be.

I know a woman who stays in a hotel room and cries all day over difficulties from which she could, with an atom of spunk, extricate herself in ten minutes. She reminds me of a heroine sitting on a railroad track in tears at the dark prospect that a train will probably run over her. It probably will, and what of it?

It should perhaps be pointed out that *The People's Choice* was written before the present incumbent was sworn in. Since March 4th there has been a tremendous reawakening of public interest in public affairs. How long that interest will remain alert deponent sayeth not, not knowing.

Since the days when Aleck had been a drama critic for newspapers, he had never really lived in New York City—he had merely roosted there. During the week he stayed at the Campanile apartment, but he took long weekends in the country. For several seasons he had rented that gatehouse on the estate of the Bonner family, but this was sold away from him (shot out from under him, as he put it) and then he had no particular place of his own in the country for fall, winter, and spring when it was far too cold to go north to Neshobe Island. In the summer of 1933, without a compunction, Aleck lured Joseph Hennessey away from the Swopes. Hennessey had been working at Swope's as an estate manager for several years and was becoming restless. Considering the state of the Swope-Woollcott relationship there was no conscience to be consulted in hiring Hennessey. The purpose was to employ an estate manager of his own, a combination leg-man for reportorial chores, advance man for trips and tours, travel agent, purchasing agent, and manager of whatever property Aleck happened to be interested in at the time.

Jo Hennessey was sent to look for a house that could be made into a sort of club, which would belong to Aleck, Beatrice Kaufman, and S. N. Behrman, the playwright and author. Aleck, of course, would preside when he was on the premises. A house was found out at the northern end of Westchester County on the Harlem Valley line of the New York Central railroad, near the pleasant little town of Katonah, to be held from October until June. From June until October, of course, the Woollcott ménage was domiciled mostly at the Neshobe Island clubhouse.

In the autumn of 1933 Aleck began broadcasting twice a week on a sustaining basis over the Columbia Broadcasting System network. Later he described this experience in a letter to Laura Richards:

> . . . someone casually asked me if I wouldn't like to broadcast a little in the Fall—only fifteen minutes twice a week. It sounded so easy. I was a fool. I didn't know it would spread to a network of eighty stations, that I would be talking to people in the West Indies and Southern California and

in lumber camps in the far West. I didn't know it would mean engaging several people to open and answer my mail. I let myself in for things so casually. One night, for instance, I did a nostalgic broadcast about The Gibson Girl, ruminating on the days when all the young women I knew made horrid copies of the Gibson drawings in India ink, framed them in passepartout and gave them away for Christmas. I told of my own fruitless quest in the secondhand stores for a copy of the 1894 edition which used to repose on the chenille table-cover of a gnarled and horrid cherry table we had out in Kansas City. If anyone had an unwanted copy in fair condition, I would like to buy it. I shall never be able to describe the ensuing bedlam. There were telephone calls and telegrams coming in all night. A messenger boy arrived with the book as a gift before eleven o'clock. It took an office to acknowledge the more than four hundred copies offered for sale. There was one woman living in Eureka, Minnesota, who offered to sell me the first Gibson book by Howard Chandler Christy. Eureka, indeed! She further confused the issue by offering to bring the book into Minneapolis to show me. There were more than eighty people who said the book had been their mother's and they couldn't sell it, but they would like to give it to me for Christmas. These had to be headed off somehow. Well, it's been getting worse and worse. I have been torn between sheer pleasure as an exhibitionist and a troubled sense that millions of Americans had me prone on the ground and were kneeling on my neck. When I tell you, as I do, with uncomplicated pride, that the kids of the seventh and eighth grades in the School for Crippled Children in Toledo wrote me a round-robin letter telling me they were being allowed on my account to sit up a half-hour later on Wednesday and Saturday nights. . . . I am docile from exhaustion.

On the national hookup Aleck was an instant and huge success. His Crossley ratings never matched those of Fred Allen or Jack Benny or the Maxwell House Coffee Hour, but for a single performer on what was basically an intellectual program they were very high, say 6 as against 40 for someone like Jack Benny. A rating of 6 was very comfortable in 1933.

The autumn of 1933 was also the year that Frode Jensen came down to Columbia University's medical school to study, and the year in which a new play, *The Dark Tower,* by Alexander Woollcott and George S. Kaufman was produced by Sam Harris at the Morosco Theater. It was easy to understand, then, why Aleck did not get around to paying much attention to young Jensen until the following spring when he landed in the hospital for what he termed "minor repairs."

The Dark Tower was a melodrama. It was also a disaster, or rather, several disasters. The first came on the morning after the night the play was produced, November 25, 1933. Brooks Atkinson found this murder mystery a very badly written play which would have been much better left as a Woollcott sketch in the *New Yorker.* But the most devastating review came in the *Commonweal,* by Richard Dana Skinner. He called it "a comedy of errors in taste and judgment." The authors, he said, "have given the play a dose of degenerate verbiage and implication which has nothing to do with the plot but a great deal to do with a vaguely foul atmosphere . . . *The Dark Tower* . . . is not in fact, about much of anything at all," he said, and it merely wasted the large talents of—here the angry reviewer listed the cast.

Of course the *Commonweal* was a moralistic magazine, but it appears that in staging a merry murder (which this was) and expecting the audience to react to it laughingly, the authors had expected too much. Howard Lindsay and Damon Runyon did only slightly better the next year when *Anything Goes* was produced and enjoyed a brief run. That play, like Aleck's, was dedicated to the principle that good clean murder could be fun.

The second tragedy of Aleck's life that year concerned an old and valued friendship with Edna Ferber. Aleck had, of course, invited her to the opening, and she planned to come. But she was coming with Stanton Griffis (later American ambassador to Poland) and a party which would first dine at the Griffis apartment and then go to the theater. Some guests were late, the dinner dragged, and they arrived late. To add insult to all this, Gary Cooper was in the party, and outside on the street he was mobbed by a group of young women who made so much noise there and in the lobby that the performance suffered and the audience turned to crane heads as this large, disheveled group straggled in noisily.

Aleck was very angry. The next day Edna Ferber wrote him an apologetic note (although she was hardly at fault). The incident, coupled with the critical failure of the play, rankled him deeply and he glowered about it publicly. After that there were insults on both sides, stated publicly in conversations with others. Aleck wanted to make up with her, and she with him, and they might have, except that he chose to offer the wand of friendship by offering to review her autobiography. He planned to do so splendidly, with fanfares perhaps, on the radio, but it turned out that he did not like the book. No matter what anyone said of Aleck, no one ever claimed that his literary opinions could be bought, or that he ever failed to be true to the greater concepts of literary morality. He found it impossible to review the book well. In his own mind, although not in Miss Ferber's, of course, he did her a great favor by not reviewing it at all.

XXV

IF 1933 HAD BEEN a bad year for Aleck in the matter of quarreling with friends, at least in 1934 one of these quarrels was healed. This was the unpleasantness with Kathleen Norris. Aleck was the doctor who healed the friendship, although after a few months Mrs. Norris had realized that her pique should really not be taken out on Aleck, but on her own bad judgment in letting herself be the subject of a profile without exercising more care in controlling its nature.

The crux of the matter was really none of the things that the Norrises had spoken about it; it was Kathleen Norris' reading public and one casual mention by Aleck, really a stylistic, gossip bit. He had been speaking of her as the type of "ideal lady president of all the women's clubs in the world," and then:

> But you did not chance to see our Mrs. Norris on that night when she and I missed the entire first act of *The Black Crook* because we had become involved in a singularly bitter cribbage game with Madge Kennedy and Harold Ross in a Hoboken saloon.

Those words—Hoboken saloon—had created havoc in Kathleen Norris' life. Her public had arisen—the WCTU section—and had demanded explanations. What was she doing in a Hoboken saloon? If she ever expected them to buy another copy of a magazine with a Kathleen Norris serial therein, she had best explain, and well.

Aleck did everything he could to ease Kathleen Norris' pain. In the spring of 1934, when *While Rome Burns* was published by Viking Press, at least two readers were pleased to discover that Aleck had added a lengthy footnote to the Kathleen Norris profile.

Footnote:

In behalf of Mrs. Norris's vast following among the members of the WCTU, if that organization has survived its recent encounter with the Juggernaut, further details should perhaps be offered about the aforesaid cribbage contest in a Hoboken saloon. Mrs. Norris and I were partners. Our opponents were Harold Wallace Ross, formerly of Ogden, Utah (who is editor of the *New Yorker* and probably the greatest cribbage player since the late Charles James Fox pegged out), and Madge Kennedy, who must, I think be so disassociated in the public mind with ruffianly behaviour and raffish disposition as to render the further contents of this footnote a work of supererogation. However the game was staged on the night when all the writing folk of Manhattan were swarming across the Hudson for the premiere of Christopher Morley's *The Black Crook*. The insensate cribbage players could find a table only in the bar of one of the more teeming restaurants. If soaped mirrors and brass rails can make a saloon, I suppose it *was* one, but if any members of the WCTU were present that evening, they can testify that, when it comes to a question of liquor having soiled any of the players' lips, the game might as well have been played in the basement of the First M. E. Church.

Which, of course, could hardly have been the truth, knowing Aleck and knowing Harold Ross.

So it might be said here that Aleck came as close to telling a lie as he ever had in his life in that footnote, in the interest of the preservation of an old friendship.

Friendships do die out, and why so much was made during Aleck's lifetime and after his death about his friendships that ended in quarrels can only be understood by acknowledging that Alexander Woollcott lived a life as public as if he took his baths every day in the 59th Street fountain at Central Park. If Aleck quarreled with a friend everyone in the theatrical and literary world knew about it immediately, it seemed. Some, who were not even friends of Aleck, boasted that they had "quarreled" with him just to establish their own position. Such quarrels might have meant that he had sent back to them their what-ever-it-was-they-wanted with a terse remark or no remark at all. Aleck was constantly bedeviled by people who wished to show him photographs or paintings or Great American Novels. Even his best and dearest friends imposed on him thus, and from them he took this imposition, but not always without protest.

Friendship meant much to Aleck, and yet he was never confident that he attained and held the respect and love of those around him who professed friendship. He once said, when discussing the illness and death of a loved one, that he was made sick by the thought of "what swinishness and poltroonery and malice the spectators would find if ever *my* guard were dismissed and I could not longer edit myself for my neighbor's inspection."

So Aleck's guard was almost always up, and the face he turned to his friends was not the face he turned to the pillow.

In this period—the 1930's—Aleck set out to capture the imagination of what Elsa Maxwell had established as café society. Aleck could not bear Elsa Maxwell, she had tried to lord it over him—if a woman can do so—on the Riviera that summer of 1928 and he had developed one of his few sincere enmities toward her. Nonetheless he entered her circle and made it a point to become a public character. Soon he was one of the most sought-after of dinner guests, because he could always be relied upon at large showy dinners to capture the conversation and either by use of four letter words or insult he would shock the assemblage, and all the guests would go home to tell their nearest and dearest friends the awful remark that Alexander Woollcott had made the night before. In college days Aleck and Robert Rudd and others of their group had developed the habit of addressing one another by insulting terms which were really terms of endearment. "You Idiot" was common enough. "Emptyhead" was another term. As the others grew up and went into life they stopped the practice. Aleck never did. In *The Man Who Came to Dinner,* when Banjo appeared in Sheridan Whiteside's presence for the first time, he was successively addressed as "you mental delinquent," "you reform-school fugitive," "you idiot." In an earlier telephone call Whiteside addressed Banjo as "you faun's behind" and "Hollywood

In the 1920's and 1930's, Neshobe Island was the scene of some of the most ferocious croquet contests known to Western man. Aleck particularly relished lining up his ball on that of an opponent, smashing the ball carefully, and chortling gleefully as his opponent's ball plopped into the lake. Here Beatrice Kaufman watches with trepidation and Harpo Marx with the calm benevolence of an innocent bystander as Aleck lines up on Bea's ball.

Back from the service, Aleck took time out from his newspapering to write a glowing, if somewhat sugary, biography of his friend Irving Berlin, shown above with the author in the 1920's.

A group from the Round Table of the Algonquin, or the New York Wits, as they were sometimes called, in the 1920's. On the left is Art Samuels, raconteur and bon vivant; seated are Charles MacArthur, playwright, with Dorothy Parker; and standing behind them, the inimitable Harpo. Aleck is in a typical pose at right.

A typical 1920's summer day in front of the clubhouse door on Neshobe. Aleck, Neysa McMein, Alfred Lunt, Beatrice Kaufman, and Harpo.

Aleck, in the late 1930's, playing one of his favorite roles—Aunt Aleck.

Aleck and Harpo always said they would play the starring roles in *Yellow Jacket* and in 1939 they did, in summer stock.

riff-raff." These were all typical and usual Woollcottian forms of address to his acquaintances. His friends took no offense, but strangers did not know how to take him, and sometimes, merely for show, he would be rude and vulgar, particularly to women he encountered at various parties and dinners.

Alice Root Nichols, the Alice of Aleck's college days, and one of that select circle of old friends who could say what they pleased to Aleck, took him to task once for his bad public manners.

She did not understand New York, he said.

Decency and good manners were the same everywhere, she insisted, and he had done the same thing in college. Now he was no longer a college boy.

Aleck refused to listen. He said that New York was filled with phonies and the only way to keep oneself in the public eye was to keep shocking the public. So there it was. The public Aleck was a fraud, by his own admission.

Unfortunately, for Aleck's own peace of mind, he was proved to be absolutely correct. The worse he behaved in public the more popular he became as a centerpiece of conversation at dinner parties and the more often his name appeared in the gossip columns of the newspapers, and the more magazine and radio value he seemed to have as a public character.

The difficulty of Aleck was that he knew this was a pose, and fraudulent, and it took something out of him to carry it on. Beneath the fat and the layer of contumely was a very sensitive man, suffering seriously as he had since his college days from feelings of insecurity and inferiority. Before college Aleck did not so suffer, except when he was boarding around Philadelphia. His problem stemmed back to what was in effect a very much broken home, and the lack of family ties colored his existence forever after childhood.

At the core Aleck had many elements of greatness, and they showed through the pose. Stripped of the pose his work might have been assessed quite differently than it was, for his rudeness made the professional assessors of society reluctant to grant the credit due, and since his most effective prose was written either for ephemeral magazines or even more ephemeral radio broadcasts, the proof of his abilities was widely scattered and hard to muster.

The title of Aleck's new work—*While Rome Burns*—was presented to him by one of his *New Yorker* readers, after he called publicly for suggestions in his page in that magazine. It was, again, a collection of Aleck's articles and essays. The Norris article was there, newly dressed as noted. There was an article about Harpo, one about Father Duffy, the World War I chaplain, an article on Paul Robeson, one about Dorothy Parker, another about Charlie Chaplin, one about G. B. Shaw, and then Aleck's writings from abroad. It was broken into a general section, one called Legends, which included the famous story of the cadet from Saint-Cyr who spent the night with Cosette, the most famous courtesan in all France (which Arnold Gingrich had coveted); the story of two ladies who discovered a ghost all dripping in seaweed, a story of pain and mystery called "The Vanishing Lady." Aleck had recently taken an interest in such stories—begun collecting them from among his friends—and he passed these along in fine style. Later he was to improve tremendously on these tales and make an art form of the telling of them. But in 1934 it was already art and successful art: *While Rome Burns* sold more than 120,000 copies.

The year 1934 was the one in which Aleck rose to his pinnacle as a reviewer of books and as an influence on the nation's literary taste. That was the year that he took Somerset Maugham to task for misusing the words imply and infer. "The female implies," Aleck said, "and from that the male infers." Maugham, signing himself William, which he did only to his friends, accepted the rebuke gracefully. "I am not yet too old to learn," he wrote Aleck, and said he was grateful for that sort of criticism, which he, as a successful commercial writer, seldom received.

One of Aleck's successes in the reviewing field came in April, when he wrote about a book called *God and My Father*, by Clarence Day. Aleck described the book. "My first impulse," he said, "is to fill a wheelbarrow with copies and go from house to house in quest of converts." The book, which had been languishing on the market with sales well under five thousand copies, suddenly began to spurt in sales and soon had earned a considerable sum of money for author Day and his publishers. From that point all kinds of subsidiary sales and successes began piling up. Aleck, and Aleck almost alone, was responsible for Day's continuing success.

An even greater success came later that year. Jo Hennessey, in leafing through a copy of *Atlantic Monthly,* came across a long short story by James Hilton, a story about a superannuated, gentle teacher in an English boarding school. As he read, Hennessey recognized the story as material for Aleck's mind and pen, and he called it to Aleck's attention, knowing full well that it would appeal. It did appeal, indeed how it appealed, and Aleck made it a point to begin beating the drums for *Goodbye, Mr. Chips.*

First he persuaded Little, Brown to publish the story as a book. It appeared in June and was reprinted twice that month. It was reprinted twice in July, again in August, twice in September, twice in October, twice in November, and twice in December. By December, 1934, more than 106,000 copies of *Goodbye, Mr. Chips* had been sold, and it was still selling marvelously well.

James Hilton knew how this tremendous success had been achieved, by Aleck. He wrote on November 2:

> I want to tell you how well aware I am of the extent to which my present American reputation (let alone book sales) owes to your enormously influential advocacy, both in print and on the radio; and I count myself the most fortunate of writers to have had it so happen. Your review of *Goodbye, Mr. Chips* in *McCall's* magazine (to take but one instance) contained not only the best things I have ever had said about my work, but the most sympathetic understanding of Mr. Chips and all he signifies that I have read, either on your side of the Atlantic or mine.

Nineteen thirty-four was passed as usual by Aleck, with many short trips and much of the summer spent at Lake Bomoseen playing croquet and word games and dining well in the evenings, swimming and sunning in the daytime. One day while Harpo Marx and a new protégé of Aleck's named Charles Lederer were talking about Aleck in Los Angeles, they decided to pay him a quick visit, so they dropped whatever they were doing and flew to the East, came quietly to Lake Bomoseen, and approached the island by boat. From onshore they heard the clicking of mallets and croquet talk, so they knew Aleck was there with a party. Harpo and Lederer landed the boat at the landing, which is some way from the croquet field, and retired to the bushes. They stripped off all their clothes and then appeared, stark naked, to see Aleck, in tatterdemalion shorts and a sweatshirt leaning on his mallet.

He looked up, saw these two nude wretches, and turned to Alice Duer Miller.

"I believe it is your shot, Alice," he said, and turned away.

The two deflated savages went back to the bushes, put on their clothing, took their motorboat back to Bill Bull's fishing dock, got back in their hired car and were driven to Whitehall, New York, then to Lake Champlain, caught their private plane, and flew back to Hollywood. The croquet players did not even halt to wave good-bye.

Aleck and Alice Miller visited Booth Tarkington again that year, and also that other writer resident in Kennebunkport, Kenneth Roberts. Aleck was constantly sending gifts to his friends: he sent so many detective stories to the Tarkingtons that Tarkington said the Kennebunkport public library suspected him of no good intent when he presented dozens of books concerned with mayhem. He sent hams and other delicacies to Roberts. He gave Roberts a dog. (He was constantly giving away dogs to friends, and eventually settled on standard French poodles as the best companions of all.)

Aleck was very busy with writing and lecturing, and the radio. He wrote a number of articles for the *Saturday Evening Post* and other magazines, on Katharine Cornell and other Broadway celebrities. He joined the faculty of the Columbia University School of Journalism briefly. He continued to write "Shouts and Murmurs" for the *New Yorker*.

A great positive change came to him in radio. The Cream of Wheat manufacturing company decided to sponsor his radio broadcasts, three times a week, at $500 a broadcast. Aleck now began taking radio very seriously, for it was to bring him to the attention of millions of Americans.

In November, Aleck became involved in a controversy which was widely heralded because he took on as an opponent a publicist who was well-versed in public opinion, perhaps his equal in the arts of verbal warfare, and his master in grudge-holding. This acquaintance was Bennett Cerf, head of the Random House Publishing Company, and the fight was, of course, over a book.

In "Shouts and Murmurs" one day in November, Aleck took a potshot at Frederick A. Blossom, translator of the last volume of Marcel Proust's *Remembrance of Things Past.* Aleck had met Proust and felt that he knew him well. The argument he offered was that the rendition of some French *argot* was not faithful to the intent of Proust in his original text. It was a very delicate question, one of the kind that can begin a literary argument that continues for years.

Random House, the verisimilitude of its translation questioned, and thus the value of the book threatened, rose in anger and took Aleck to task. Frederick Blossom, the translator, wrote an angry letter to the editor of the *New Yorker.* Others leaped into the fray, including Malcolm Cowley, who in the *New Republic,* sarcastically called on Aleck to have undertaken the job himself if he did not like the way it was done, or to come forth with a better translator than Blossom.

Aleck answered these complaints in a "Shouts and Murmurs" column in the *New Yorker* headed "Merry Christmas to Bennett Cerf." Cerf responded, he wrote years later, by cutting Woollcott off the Random House reviewers list; Aleck thereupon refused to review any more Random House books, and the feud continued past Aleck's death: while all others seemed to lavish benediction on Woollcott's ashes, Cerf demurred publicly in an article in *American Mercury,* insisting that Shakespeare be served and that the evil that Aleck did must live after him.

Nearly a quarter of a century after Aleck's death, Cerf still spoke harshly of Woollcott's memory, even though he was reluctant to admit it.

"I disliked Mr. Woollcott intensely," he wrote this author in 1966. "In literary matters, he was a consistent champion of the second-rate and worse, and the charm that he turned on for the people he considered important was singularly lacking when he was dealing with people he considered his social inferiors. This is not my idea of the way a gentleman acts.

"However, he has been dead a long time, and I don't see much point in digging up all these unpleasant memories. Obviously, Woollcott had a very fine side, as evidenced by what he did for Dr. Frode Jensen, a gentleman whom I respect very highly indeed."

Aleck had a quality of arousing some people to heights of fury, it was the arrogance he pretended in public, and only his friends knew that it was an act.

Bennett Cerf never knew or suspected that the private Aleck, the kindly, helpful, loving Aleck could exist. He saw the public Aleck, and like many other persons he was repelled. Only in 1966, when talking one day with Frode Jensen did he learn of the other Aleck. That was a little late.

XXVI

In the summer of 1934 Aleck began to make major renovations of the clubhouse at Neshobe Island, all out of his own pocket. He put in electric lights, refrigeration, new beds, and many other niceties. He intended, then, to spend a good part of the year at the lake, coming in the springtime and leaving after the maples had turned in the autumn. His entire orientation was moving north: that summer Aleck gave three lectures at the Bread Loaf writer's conference at Middlebury College, a few miles north of the lake. He wished and firmly intended to make his home in Vermont.

The time was not yet ripe for semi-retirement. True, Aleck had been ill and he had not been sleeping well. He was having some trouble with his circulation, and he consulted Dr. Al Getman, his old friend from Hamilton and New York days. Dr. Getman put him on a strict diet, which he kept to for three months, losing fifty-five pounds. The doctor also prescribed sleeping pills and blood vessel dilation medicines for Aleck, and he took them without much whimpering. One of Aleck's major troubles was the pace of his life. He was only forty-seven years old, but he was wearing himself out, sleeping relatively little and engaging in furious activity, and then overeating and overdrinking. Only part of this activity was involved with his writing. The reviewers, by and large, liked Aleck's *While Rome Burns,* but in a sense, they tended to review Aleck more than the book. This was exactly what Aleck hoped for, because the book was merely one aspect of the production of Alexander Woollcott. That year, for example, he had written and starred in a movie short which was made on Long Island. His radio broadcasts were attracting millions of listeners. He had fully achieved his position as Public Character.

"Alexander Woollcott is celebrated as a dramatic critic and one of the chief figures of the *New Yorker,*" wrote Raymond Mortimer in a review of the book in Britain's *New Statesman and Nation.* "He is himself as specifically New York as Jean Cocteau is Paris. Like all books of collected journalism, this should be read interruptedly, not more than ten pages at a time—you can not take the measure of a champion sprinter by making him run a marathon. Mr. Woollcott is, as a journalist, simply stunning. . . ."

Not in relation to this book, but in relation to Aleck's creativity as a whole, critic John Chamberlain had this to say:

> At his worst, and it must be said that he occasionally puts his worst foot foremost, Alexander Woollcott is something of an intellectual crooner, bearing about the same relationship to literary criticism that Rudy Vallee or Kate Smith bears to music. At his best he is an invaluable connoisseur of minor key perfection—which is the sort of perfection whose existence many people of supposed Catholic tastes are constantly forgetting.

And yet Aleck was cutting down a bit on his writing. He had decided to drop the "Shouts and Murmurs" column in the *New Yorker.* For years he had been resigning irregularly as he objected to the very heavy editing that Ross imposed on his writers. Aleck really did not like to have a word changed in his copy, and like G. B. Shaw, from whom he learned the trick, he could present copy that was justified for typesetting, which eliminated the need for the slightest editorial change. Aleck regularly turned in his page of "Shouts and Murmurs" so that it fit almost exactly the space allotted. This posed a difficult problem for editors who might wish to delete some portion of the column as unsavory. Aleck and Katherine White, his editor, were forever fighting over niggling changes and big changes, and Ross was growing weary of Aleck's ways as Aleck was growing weary of the weekly deadline.

That summer of 1934 Aleck was subject to a parody in a novel written by Charles Brackett. The novel was called *Entirely Surrounded.* Many months earlier Aleck had seen Brackett and suggested that a novel be done about the island and its people, and Brackett had seized upon the idea with glee. Aleck read the book and approved thoroughly. Charming, he called it. As for the portrait of himself, he wrote Noel Coward: ". . . the owner of the island is a repulsive behemoth with elfin manners whom you would be the first to recognize." (Later a friend, David Lamson, read the book and did not recognize Aleck at all.)

By fall, Aleck's plan for the island had changed completely. Enos Booth, who had allowed Aleck and his section of the New York Wits to move in on him at Neshobe Island and form the club, had steadily been pushed into the background as Aleck made of Neshobe *his* island, and grew yearly more demanding about its uses and his time to be spent there. Booth had been careful enough when the club was formed to reserve half the island for himself, and this year, he set out to build a house which he might be able to use at his convenience rather than Aleck's. In the middle of the process he tired of the project, and Aleck bought him out. Aleck then put Jo Hennessey to work drawing plans to complete a year-round house, where Aleck could come whenever he felt like it without worry about the snow and ice that covered the lake.

Back in New York in October, 1934, to begin the new broadcasts for Cream of Wheat, Aleck became the *Town Crier*. His program opened with the ringing of a handbell of the kind that town criers once used in the village streets, and Aleck then came on with that mellifluous, *sincere* voice, and announced to the audience "This is Woollcott speaking." From that point on he might launch into anything. He gave one talk on Stephen Foster early in the next year that brought him and CBS thousands of congratulatory messages. He gave another on Dr. MacLure, a Scottish country doctor, whose story he had told time and again in one way or another. Indeed, more, he made a promise that each year that he broadcast, it would be part of his task to tell again the story of "Weelum" MacLure and his patients in the highlands.

More than three decades later it is nearly impossible to explain properly the impact that Alexander Woollcott's broadcasts, particularly the Sunday evening broadcasts, had on the American nation. But consider these factors: all the nation, by and large, was poor in 1934 and 1935. The depression was the worst in the nation's history and it was continuing, with very little end in sight for the average man—although the economists argued for hours on this subject every day in every conceivable way. So, the nation, at large, was at home on Sunday nights, families clustered around their hearthside, reading the Sunday papers, and listening, in these days before television, to the hugely varied fare of network radio.

Aleck's broadcasts played every string in the human emotional orchestra. He offered hope, in his stories of men like Dr. MacLure. He offered nostalgia for a better, happier day, in the story of Stephen Foster, tragedy though it was. He offered life on a platter, love and gentleness. He showed the American people moments of their greatness, moments of sadness, moments of beauty. He had such command of the pictorial aspects of the language that he could, aided by the public imagination, draw a sharper picture than any artist of the brush. He told of courage when the nation needed courage, and he talked of kindness when Americans thirsted for the milk of kindness and he appealed to all that was bright and shining and purely American in the souls of his listeners. He was corny, he was magnificent, and he attracted the largest audience of any critic in history. Men on the street wrote him admiring letters, and so did United States Senators. Crusty old William Edgar Borah, Republican Senator from Idaho, complimented Aleck on the "perfectly beautiful" Stephen Foster broadcast, and gave Aleck material for a story about a heroic doctor of Idaho. Thousands of lesser citizens did the same. He developed one trick which endeared him to audiences and friends—he arranged serenades by a studio chorus for his friends, surprising them with selections of music they liked. He did this for Laura Richards one night in December. He did it for Irving Berlin and for a dozen others.

There exists in America an undercurrent of opinion-forming, not public opinion itself, but the movers and shakers of the newspaper, magazine, radio, and other portions of the world of publicity. Book reviewers, syndicated columnists, and editorial writers also make up a portion of this crew. Taking some idea, such as the concept of the public character played by Alexander

Woollcott, that soft, mushy, and preposterous figure that paraded about the stage that was New York, shocking matrons into choking on their champagne and caviar and alienating the gentry by rude gestures and noises, these opinion-makers could create a climate that had nothing to do with the facts. Facts, in the United States, have always run a poor second to emotions in any given race. Now Aleck found himself, so to speak, hoist by his own petard, and accused of foolishness and uselessness at a time in his career when he was beginning to exhibit some elements of greatness.

The Cream of Wheat broadcasts were devoted to many subjects. Aleck reviewed books. He reviewed *Paths of Glory* by Humphrey Cobb. He reviewed *Life With Father* by Clarence Day, *North to the Orient* by Anne Morrow Lindbergh, *I Write As I Please* by Walter Duranty, *Death and General Putnam* by Arthur Guiterman, *Mrs. Astor's Horse* by Stanley Walker. Not least, he reviewed his own *The Woollcott Reader,* which was published in 1935, an anthology of the writings of seventeen authors who ranked high in Aleck's opinion.

Most of these were hard books and some of them were harsh books. His anthology, which after all, represented his personal taste, included works by J. M. Barrie, Thornton Wilder, William Allen White, Saki, Richard Harding Davis, Lytton Strachey, and Evelyn Waugh. The point of his anthology was to assemble works that Aleck thought ought to be saved for posterity, but which had either slipped into obscurity or were so slipping.

In reviewing this anthology for the *Nation* at the end of 1935, Louis Kronenberger struck the note that was common in the worlds of publicity and letters, the note that had been brought about by Aleck's own public actions. "Down with Woollcott" was the title of the article:

> Mr. Woollcott is not only a best-seller in his own right, but with a sentence or two he can make best-sellers of other men. At present he is by far the most influential salesman of books in the United States, and consequently looms larger on the cultural scene than even Dr. Eliot's Five-Foot Shelf. Mr. Woollcott's ascendancy means, indeed, death to the Five-Foot Shelf and all its analogues, for Mr.

Woollcott is no friend of difficult and stodgy classics: he is skeptical of their worth, or at least of their readability, and prefers the readier laughter and tears of writers not in the pantheon. He has had much to say, here and elsewhere, about the snootiness and pedantry of people who play safe with the names which somehow live on in his despite. If he has not quite aspersed their sincerity, he has wiped up the floor with their sense of humor.

Now there is perhaps no better way of attracting followers than by suggesting that they, like oneself, have a superior sense of humor, and I have no doubt that Mr. Woollcott's ripe appreciation of anecdote has helped pave the way for his dictatorship over literature. But he is by no means one-sided, and if he has a lively turn for laughter, he has an even livelier turn for tears. I even suspect that weepsiness is his true love and that he would rather have a good cry than a good laugh. And I further suspect that literature has no meaning for him beyond providing one or the other.

It is very seldom, of course, that a critic who becomes widely influential with the general public is a good critic. He is usually its superior in articulateness, not acumen. If he has virtues, they are only tolerated for the sake of his vices. Thus Mr. Woollcott's immediate predecessor in the land, Professor Phelps, really liked good books as well as bad, but won his spurs entirely through recommending the bad ones. Professor Phelps's chief critical characteristic is a low boiling-point, so that he is as quickly bathed in steam when reading *Anthony Adverse* as when reading Aeschylus. But Mr. Woollcott is a very different kind of critic. He is vastly harder on dull books than Mr. Phelps, and vastly harder on good books. He does not like a great many things, and all the things he likes have points in common. Thus the prose had better be more like French pastry than bread, the sentiment bountiful and lush, the characters exceedingly wicked or noble or salty, the scene distant if not downright exotic. But Mr. Woollcott will not approve of such productions if there is anything naive or blundering about them: they must be executed with all possible cunning and sophistication. Their true character must not be obvious; it must only steal upon you that they are hokum.

Yet hokum they are, high-grade, streamlined hokum if you will but hokum. There is not much in *The Woollcott Reader* that any well-known critic of our time except Mr. Woollcott will wish to see preserved. Here is, I say boldly, second-rate taste at its most formidable and deceptive, tricked out in its Sunday best, beckoning and easy to take. It is second-rate in a number of respects, but I am satisfied to rest my case on the fact that there is scarcely a thing in this anthology which does not, at bottom, falsify or run away from life. Like all sentimentalists and easy scoffers, Mr. Woollcott can be quickly spotted as an escapist; and in this compilation of modern writing he has escaped to the strongholds of all those who bruise easily and think with difficulty—to the world of children and animals and triflers and people easy to laugh and cry over. I count it of some significance that in a book of 1,011 pages, exactly 72 are laid in the United States. I count it of some significance that in a volume running over with pathos, there is exactly one story that might by any standards be considered to treat of tragedy. I count it of some significance that Mr. Woollcott's leviathan does not include one living writer interpreting the current scene.

It would no doubt be more than enough if Mr. Woollcott sent this book forth to his hundred thousand or so admirers merely with the statement that it contained things which he had enjoyed. But he is at all times the critic: these selections are called "minor masterpieces"; one of them is "as simple and modest and perfect as a Vermeer" and another is "the most moving and uplifting tale ever told in the English language." His critical dicta, furthermore, are set down in a prose which I do not hesitate to describe as nauseating. Mr. Woollcott loves perfumed words, but knows no better how to use them than certain women know how to use an atomizer. This sentence from one of his recent indorsements may indicate what many times awaits a reader of this book: "You, I think, will find Carrie mysteriously warming to the cockles of your foolish heart." When such a writer comes along and compiles such a book as *The Woollcott Reader,* I am not afraid to put my own sense of humor to the torch and get up in the pulpit as a reformer. While Rome, by Mr. Woollcott's bland admission, is burning, I should like to see practically everything that he has written and most of what he has compiled and recommended thrown as further fuel upon the conflagration. At least while Rome is burning, let it fumigate.

This acid review was not very well justified either by history or by Aleck's works, yet it represented a prevailing opinion. It seems quite apparent in the review that Louis Kronenberger objected to Aleck in principle, the tone is not that of one who complains about a work, but one who complains about a state of affairs in which the American people were being led down the garden path by a fool and a boor. When Kronenberger said so sarcastically that Aleck must be compared to the Professor Phelps who recommended only bad books, he disagreed with the later judgment of Messrs. Specter, Thorp, *et al.*, who said in their *Literary History of the United States* that Alexander Woollcott succeeded Christopher Morley "as what might be called a caresser of books, choosing the radio as his means of access to the public," and that the best of his books, *While Rome Burns*, did not tell the whole story on Aleck. John Mason Brown, not entirely an easy man to please, called Aleck one of the finest writers in America.

The point is not whether Aleck was a fine writer or not, but that by 1935 he had achieved an unwanted reputation for softness and appeal to the equivalent of the lower vulgate in America.

This attitude was not confined to the bright, brittle critics who brooded in New York City, but spread across the nation, and to even such healthy American territory as Omaha, Nebraska, where apple pie and good thick steaks were perhaps invented, where people said they went to church on Sunday, whether they did or not, where motion pictures and the radio were the major means of entertainment, and where one would have expected Alexander Woollcott at his most tryingly serene and most sonorous to be applauded.

But no, in December Aleck was the subject of an intemperate attack of the variety that had begun to disturb him because it was all of one piece and it was repeated very frequently. He realized that it could cause his destruction as an artist.

The attack was based on Aleck's taste; the substance of the editorial in the Omaha *World Herald,* as he put it in a letter to the editor, was that "as a recommender of books over the radio, I take advantage of a nation-wide network to further the sale of soft, sentimental works." "Marshmallows" was the term employed.

Aleck listed the books he had recommended, which included those mentioned above. "If these be marshmallows," he said, "then I am the Grand Duchess Marie."

Then Aleck could not refrain from exhibiting his growing lack of restraint in dealing with public and private persons. The power he had gained in the past two or three years was most certainly affecting his self-control:

> What interests me in this instance is the apparent lack of journalistic conscience manifested by the editorial I complain of. If that editorial was written by someone who would think of that list as so many marshmallows, it was the work of a fool. If it was written with someone who was not even familiar with what books I had recommended it was the work of a knave. Neither alternative is agreeable for a colleague to contemplate. Of course, there is always the third possibility that our editorial writer is a nicely balanced mixture of the two.

That last sentence undid any good that Aleck's argument might have done for him. It was more and more his way, to satisfy himself by flaying his enemies with words, to pierce them with sharp thrusts and deflate them, but the fact remained that there was a growing opinion that Aleck represented something mushy in America, and it was not confined to editorialists.

One day Arthur Guiterman, author of *Death and General Putnam,* wrote Aleck to tell a tale he had heard at the Author's Guild meeting not long before. One member had heard a group of high school girls discussing literature, and she caught the following interchange:

One girl was just saying, "Yes, you know—Alexander Woollcott."

"Oh yes," said the other, "He wrote *Little Women.*"

Aleck's followers knew better, but his detractors were gaining much ground in this period, and one reason for it, quite aside from his sharp tongue and honeyed ways on alternate occasions, was the breadth of his activity. Until 1935 he wrote for the *New Yorker,* and he did not quit "Shouts and Murmurs" quite soon enough. His radio commitments had become so demanding that he did not have time to do a good job on the column and the last few essays suffered from this inattention which was quite unlike Aleck. He also spread himself into other activity. He joined Noel Coward to act briefly in a new picture written by Ben Hecht and Charles MacArthur. He also took on a stringent regime of lecturing.

Between lecturing and traveling, Aleck and his secretary and various hired stenographers read and answered thousands of letters, and Aleck planned his broadcasts and arranged for the research that would make them accurate. He took infinite pains in his reportage, and while this seldom showed through the veneer it was one of the most important elements of his success.

This year he interested himself in the legal case of David Lamson, a young Stanford University faculty member who had been accused of killing his wife, convicted, sentenced to death, held in death row for months, before he was granted a new trial. Lamson had brought himself to Aleck's attention by writing a book on life in Death Row and his case. Aleck wrote him, showing the depth of his research and interest, and his understanding of his position and Lamson's and the delicate maneuvering that was required if he was to be of help:

> . . . All I want to be sure of is that no glib broadcast or platform utterance of mine should, for all good intentions, do you more harm than good. I suspect that a good many emotional commonwealths have a not entirely unreasonable hostility to those mouthy New Yorkers who, from tea rooms in Greenwich Village, issue caustic comments on their judicial proceedings. I have myself been known on occasions to shoot my mouth off without really knowing what I was talking about. In your own case I have made a careful study of the brief on appeal but am really guided by an instinct as undebatable as a sense of smell.

> It is fatally easy for a distant outsider to be bold and critical. . . .

Aleck went to California on other business, and he visited Lamson. He did make broadcasts about this case, and created a Lamson defense fund, to which he donated the proceeds of several of his lectures in California. He had been told that if he mentioned the case, he would offend a great many dear old ladies, and this became a matter of discussion between Aleck and a reporter for the *San Jose Mercury Herald* in an interview.

"That's jake with me," said Aleck. "There are people in every community whom it is not only a duty to offend but a positive pleasure."

And that was the high point of the interview, as reported in the newspaper.

Aleck could not get away from the Smart Aleck treatment in the press, no matter what he did. What he could and did do, however, was investigate thoroughly, satisfy himself as to the justice of Lamson's case, and then begin beating the drums for him.

At Christmas time Aleck broadcast the story of David Lamson, while reviewing the Lamson book. Here, in Lamson's words, were the results:

> . . . you in fifteen minutes did what we had failed to do in two and a half years—threw the weight of public opinion completely. Those who had been neutral or unconvinced are now definitely friends; the band of loyal friends are exultant and triumphant and rearmed; what the enemies think no one knows, for they have had no word to say. The care with which you thought out what you had to say has disarmed them; criticism is impossible, for you anticipated and met it at every point. There is no least whisper of an ulterior motive . . . your reputation, together with the manner and matter of your utterance, is far beyond that. So far as the case is concerned, the effect you have had is monumental and utterly good.

The effect on book sales was immediate. On Monday after the Sunday night broadcast the New York City stores began phoning in large orders to the publisher, editor Whitney Darrow reported. By Tuesday, San Francisco stores alone had taken 2,000 orders for the book. A San Jose friend of Lamson's went into a local book store and heard three orders for the book given in twenty minutes. Some bookstores had earlier refused to stock the book because of public opinion against Lamson. Now they clamored for it. By Monday noon there was not a copy of the book anywhere in the San Francisco bay area, at least not one available for delivery. By the first of the year the first printing of 5,000 copies was exhausted and new printings were being ordered. (So much attention was focused on the Lamson case that he was later retried, and acquitted.)

There was a victory for the helpful Woollcott.

That autumn Aleck was engaged in a friendly argument with the manufacturers of Cream of Wheat and their advertising agency. The argument lends much honor to Aleck and none at all to the business firms: they were objecting to his "caustic references to people like Hitler and Mussolini" because they might offend large racial groups. Unless Aleck agreed to refrain from including in his broadcast "material of a controversial nature which, in our opinion, would be offensive to individuals or groups in the radio audience," Cream of Wheat did not wish to continue to sponsor Aleck.

For one whose sharp tongue flashed at those who disagreed with him, Aleck was surprisingly mild. He refused to allow himself to be censored in this fashion. He would allow the agency to cut any joke, anecdote or phrase which they considered to be coarse or suggestive (Katherine White had taught him, finally).

He would not accept political censorship.

He sympathized, he said, with Cream of Wheat, and if the company believed that he was antagonizing old customers or driving away new ones it would be folly to continue the program. He offered a few reasoned arguments against censorship, but there was nothing unpleasant or upsetting in his letter.

Aleck said here that he did not think he would find another sponsor, and that since all the best time on the air was pre-empted by advertisers, he would drop out of national broadcasting altogether. He would be glad to do so, he said, and return to the printed page.

And that is what Aleck did. Without rancor, without a whimper, he gave up a radio contract that brought him $80,000 a year and went back to writing for magazines. The Town Crier was off the air.

XXVII

In the sense that he had no further responsibility to fill the airwaves, the year 1936 opened for Aleck with a great feeling of freedom. He had no worries about making money—no writer ever made money so easily as Aleck for so long a period. His lot was made happy by favorable reviews of Aleck, as in a journal that ought to have counted with publicists: the *Yale Review*. He had not a care in the world, it seemed.

> There are two main difficulties in writing about Alexander Woollcott, even after one has mastered the spelling of his name. The first is met when one tries to write at least half as well as he does, and the second in searching for things to say about him that have not already been very well said by himself.
>
> Mr. Woollcott is one of those persons for whom we should like to lift the adjective "elegant" out of the gutter and cleanse it as best we can; and in him, as in all such persons, there is always an echo and a reflection of that most ancient irrecoverable time called yesterday. His wit, his air of omniscience, his imperturbable poise, and most of all the beauty of his fastidious prose, relate him to certain English writers who adorned the last age of literary style; but he reminds us of the Nineties with a refreshing difference. When his expert care for prose rhythm has made us think of Walter Pater, we soon find that his cadences are never languid and that his eyelids are not even "a little weary." Compared with Max Beerbohm, he is far gentler and more neighborly. He has a head grown old in this wicked world, but a heart as young as any sophomore's, stuffed with enthusiasms, and wholly American.

Not the least American trait in Mr. Woollcott is his regret for a day that is dead—for some golden American day, of rather uncertain date, that comes not back again. He has an eye for spring and summer beauty, but the faces that he most loves are autumnal. At the World's Fair, meant to celebrate what we still call a "century of progress," he looks with a yawn at the marvels of modern transportation, and chooses for himself a rickshaw. At the dance of life he prefers, like young Romeo, to "be a candleholder, and look on." So always he manages to be up-to-date in a charmingly old-fashioned way.

This effect is due, partly, to his prose style. The elegant Englishmen named above never wrote a prose at once so brilliant and yet so even in texture as this of his, so meticulous and nicely calculated and yet so free of mannerism. To find in our raucous America a man who writes by ear, using every delicate chime and nuance of which the old rich language is capable, is a delightful surprise. Mr. Woollcott's prose is as expert, in its very different kind, as Santayana's own. He has captured his large audience by the ear, and his fame reveals in us certain unsuspected traits of civilization.

Or perhaps it is not so much his prose style as his great skill in the art of the raconteur that explains his reputation. *While Rome Burns* contains a score of stories not very remarkable for the events narrated but nearly perfect in the skill of the narration, and *The Woollcott Reader* has some fifteen tales from other pens in which this same skill is everywhere apparent. It is clear that the man who wrote the one book and selected the other is definitely turning away from the "objective reporting" of much recent fiction towards the elegant old fashion of telling a story with all the art and all the charm one can muster. Often his stories are little more than anecdotes, but there is a finish and finality about them that promises long life. Other storytellers of the day may delve in coal mines; Mr. Woollcott cuts diamonds. And yet his work is not hard, and it does not glitter. In the book that he has written as well as in the one he has compiled the outstanding characteristic is

> not brilliancy but tenderness. Human courage and gallantry, human patience, human love, are what touch him most deeply and hold his lasting admiration. These books of his have been made by an agile, witty, and well-stored mind, but already they have been taken home to the American heart.

Not many writers received such fulsome praise, certainly few others who were so roundly castigated in other quarters.

The leisure that Aleck acquired by giving up radio was really no leisure at all. He simply devoted more time to pursuits that interested him other than making money. *While Rome Burns* and *The Woollcott Reader* were making money while he played, so he could afford to do so.

He joined the board of trustees of Hamilton College and was president of the Hamilton Alumni Association. He had established a prize in English writing, along with Grace Root, in honor of William Duncan Saunders, and he renewed this prize. He gave a series of lectures at the New School for Social Research in New York on American journalism. He made speeches and gave lectures elsewhere.

This year, for the first time, Aleck took a personal interest in a national political campaign. He had gone to Washington for the first Roosevelt inauguration, but he had not moved very deeply then into political life. Now, in 1936, when what he considered to be the social gains won by the Roosevelt administration, were threatened by what might be a Republican resurgence, Aleck moved into the campaign with his usual vigor, assailing his enemies hip and thigh, annoying some friends and losing others, attacking all who disagreed with Roosevelt and Aleck.

It was not that he liked Roosevelt so much, he disliked FDR's opponents more, and suspected publicly that the Republicans who had coined Landon were the same who had brought Warren Harding into the White House. Aleck's politics were noticeably left of center, but more than that could scarcely be said. When he wished to shock someone he told them he was a communist. Several young communist sympathizers he knew, including Essie Robeson, wife of Paul Robeson, were abjured to stick to their guns when he wrote to them or talked to them. Sometimes, when he wished to shock but not quite so much, he would declare himself a socialist. Actually he was only slightly left of center in his beliefs, and perhaps amazingly to his enemies, he really believed in something very much like Christian behavior, although as a child of the Phalanx he wanted no part of organized religion.

In the spring of 1936 Aleck went to Europe, where he visited friends: Rebecca West, Lady Sibyl Colefax, who liked to entertain celebrities, Mrs. Belloc Lowndes, and scores of others. A list of Aleck's friends and acquaintances could only be made by consulting the *International Who's Who* which was first published that year (and in which he was prominently mentioned).

Aleck had finished with the apartment in the Beekman Campanile (he sold it to Noel Coward), and he looked around for a house. He found one that was involved in an estate at Sneden's Landing in Nyack, near Charles MacArthur and Helen Hayes, but his offer was refused, and that autumn he moved into a very expensive apartment house at 10 Gracie Square, in uptown Manhattan on the East River, again.

He wrote to Lilly Bonner that fall, however, explaining his new mode of life: he had sublet an apartment for three winters, a part of his new program, which included the purchase of half of Neshobe Island for his own use and the conversion of his stone shack to a nine-room, year-around house "from which I expect, in due time, to be buried." He was not in attendance very much of the year, for he seemed always to be off somewhere, as visiting Samuel Hopkins Adams in California, plus all his scores of other friends in the Hollywood region, summering at Lake Bomoseen, and, this year, visiting Washington often.

Aleck's newly awakened interest in political affairs led him to make a speech at a Democratic party gathering in Fair Haven, Vermont, on October 14. He went to the old red brick high school that night and was immensely amused to be introduced by Park H. Pollard of Proctorsville—who was Calvin Coolidge's first cousin, even if he was chairman of the Democratic State Committee.

He told Alice Duer Miller at about the time of the election that he might possibly run for the United States Senate from Vermont, on the Democratic ticket, and he removed his official residence from New York City to Castleton, Vermont, just in case.

This year Aleck and Harold Ross opened negotiations again for Aleck to resume a regular page in the *New Yorker*. Aleck asked for $400 a page for "Shouts and Murmurs." Ross agreed if Aleck would guarantee at least forty pages a year. Ross realized that "the value of having you continuously, or more or less so, is the important thing" and the letter to Aleck was a very friendly and very agreeable one. Aleck wanted to go back to the *New Yorker,* too, but a problem developed in the shape of a profile of Aleck written by Wolcott Gibbs.

Aleck and Ross had agreed that the profile be written. It was conceived as the story of Big Nemo—renaming Aleck after a comic strip of earlier years which featured a small boy who had wondrous, but always pleasant, dreams. Gibbs came to see Aleck at his apartment. Aleck answered questions genially enough, then asked Gibbs to get any additional information from Jo Hennessey. So the research was completed. Aleck was shown the profile after it was written, and he approved it. He did not like all of it, but he was not seriously disturbed by the articles, except in one respect. During his war years (and Ross's) on *Stars and Stripes* one of their friends had been Sergeant Seth Bailey who wrote a signed humorous column for the newspaper called Letters from Henry's Pal to Henry. Bailey had been a reporter on the Portland *Oregonian* before the war; he was one of those professionals who automatically mixed well with the original *Stars and Stripes* gang—but with one exception, he had a bad habit of extending checks and otherwise using pieces of paper to obtain capital when he needed it. After the war, Seth Bailey made his way home with the others but soon he disappeared into the far west, and the next thing Aleck knew of him he was incarcerated in San Quentin prison for forgery. (Aleck rather enjoyed writing to David Lamson in California and reminding him that when Lamson was in Death Row he had been taken out for his airings by Seth Bailey.)

After his sentence was served, Bailey came East, borrowed from Aleck and Ross and others, and began a succession of newspaper jobs. He never seemed quite able to stay on the straight and narrow for very long—not committing any crimes, but managing to remain in trouble in ways that others might avoid easily enough, such as by using a careless picture to accompany an article in a true crimes magazine, and subjecting the magazine to a serious lawsuit.

Yet no matter what Bailey's misdemeanors against society might be, Aleck was determined to help him and protect him as much as he could against the slings of an unkind world. Time and again he invited Bailey to New York to be his guest and paid his way. Time and again he bailed Bailey out of financial difficulties.

In the *New Yorker* profile, Gibbs disguised Bailey's identity by calling him Sergeant Quirk, and Aleck seemed to accept this attitude. Then, when the profiles were run, Aleck took umbrage at them. Many of his friends were angry and told him that he had been done in by Ross. He was worried lest Bailey lose his job or be hurt by the mention of his name. So Aleck broke with Ross, it was said, and refused to return to the *New Yorker* after the profiles had run. This letter was quoted:

> To me you are no longer a faithless friend. To me you are dead. Hoping and believing I will soon be the same, I remain
>
> Your quondam crony,
>
> A. Woollcott

In his biography of Woollcott, Samuel Hopkins Adams indicated that the breach with Ross then was irreparable and that Aleck flounced away, refusing ever again to have anything to do with him. Jo Hennessey, Aleck's right hand of those years, had quite a different idea about the difficulties—if there were any difficulties. True, Hennessey said, Aleck was annoyed by the articles because the changes he wished were not made. But he was not that annoyed. In later years when he and Ross encountered each other in some New York restaurant, they would sit together at the same table and spend hours talking.

Aleck did not like the second Mrs. Ross, Hennessey said, and this accounted for much of the apparent coolness between the men. They just did not see each other any more socially, particularly since Ross moved to Stamford, Connecticut, and Aleck remained in the city with his life centered on upstate New York and Vermont. But as for a "feud," Hennessey said it did not exist—and, of course, Aleck's letter hoping both would be dead meant absolutely nothing, it was a letter he might have written to his best friend of the moment.

Certainly an important reason that Aleck did not go back to the *New Yorker* that year was a much more reasonable one: he went back to radio broadcasting instead. He did several broadcasts during the early autumn, including one for his favorite charity, the Seeing Eye, which provided guide dogs for the blind. Aleck had written widely about the Seeing Eye organization, and had broadcast in its favor several times during recent years. Each broadcast or article could be counted on to bring several thousand dollars in contributions to the charity, too.

Aleck's second effort concerned the political campaign. Having decided that he was for Franklin D. Roosevelt he set out to do something about it. In the fall he began a series of broadcasts, telling the nation why he was going to vote for Roosevelt. He made one such broadcast on October 20 and another on October 27. He also began negotiations with CBS and the Granger Pipe Tobacco Company to sponsor the Town Crier beginning in January, 1937. He was to have $3,000 a week for broadcasting every Tuesday and Thursday evening at 7:30.

He could not wait until January to begin again and was easily inveigled into another Town Crier broadcast in November, regarding John Gielgud's Hamlet.

> ANNOUNCER (With Bell): Hear Ye! Hear Ye! Hear Ye! Alexander Woollcott, the Town Crier.
>
> This is Woollcott speaking. Here's the Town Crier, sworn to silence but busting on to the air again after less than a fortnight. It was only a week ago last Tuesday that I urged on all within reach of this old larynx that they vote for—what was the name?—Oh, yes, that they vote for Franklin Delano Roosevelt. Well, my friends, you saw the result. And by the way, I'm now the richer by a hundred bucks.

The lovely Alice Longworth was so incautious as to make an election bet with me. Her check has just arrived with a suggestion that I give it to my favorite charity. I shall. It may console her to know that the entire sum will be devoted to providing food, clothing, shelter and medical attention for a poor broken-down old newspaperman named Alexander Woollcott.

Well, drunk with success, I now venture to make another recommendation. Once in a blue moon when I read a book—such a book, let us say, as *Goodbye, Mr. Chips* by James Hilton, I'm discontented until I've been up and down our street telling all the neighbors they're crazy if they don't get it at once. Now, for the first time in many a long day I'm that way—as Walter Winchell says—I'm just that way about a play. Here in New York at the Empire Theatre, I've seen a great play so beautifully acted that my impulse is to ring the church bells, declare a public holiday and suggest to His Honor, the Mayor, that he arrange with the police for dancing in the streets.

I can't pretend that this play is my discovery. Indeed it was a four-star success before ever the first white men disturbed the peace of the James River in Virginia, and it will still hold humanity enthralled long after all the giants engaged in the recent election are themselves forgotten men, will still be played, I think, when this continent is as spent as Europe and the center of civilization has shifted elsewhere—south perhaps—south to the now sleeping valley of the Plata. The shouting and the tumult dies. The captains and the kings depart. Still stands the play called *Hamlet—Hamlet, Prince of Denmark.*

I suppose there *are* people to whom *Hamlet* says little. Like Polonius, *they're* for a jig or a tale of bawdry or they sleep. Indeed, I once knew two young farmhands who came to town to see a musical show and went to *Hamlet* by mistake. During the first intermission, in a saloon across the street, they sounded pretty bitter about it. One was for beating it then and there, while his more cautious friend wanted to try one more act. "But," he said, "if that nut in black comes on again, I'm going home."

To most of us, however, *Hamlet* is, and ever will be,

the play of plays. It so happens that I've seen all the notable New York performances of that nut in black during the past forty years. There've been three good ones—Forbes Robertson, John Barrymore and now this young Englishman, John Gielgud. But never before have I seen the entire play so completely brought to glowing life as it is by them all now at the Empire by Lillian Gish as Ophelia, by Judith Anderson as the Queen, by George Nash as the First Grave-digger, by Arthur Byron as Polonius and by John Gielgud as Hamlet. I've been twice. I shall go again. I covet every opportunity to see it, for I feel that, by the law of chances, it is scarcely probable that I, or perhaps anyone now living, will ever again be *able* to see *Hamlet* so completely realized as it is now by young Gielgud and the rest in this, the 11th month of 1936, at the Empire in New York. I have no time to say more. I have no right to say less. All's Well (Bell) All's Well (Bell) All's Well (Bell) All's Well.

This broadcast contained all the elements of a Woollcott Town Crier program, a little name-dropping, an easy familiarity with his audience, an unrestrained enthusiasm, and a solid, meaty critique of a work of art or a positive addition to the American scene. Woollcott's detractors usually failed to give him credit for that—they so detested his style that they could not see the substance.

Usually, too, Aleck's reportage was all there and was all correct. Certainly this was to be more true after the spring of 1935 than it had been before.

When Aleck was broadcasting for Cream of Wheat, he received a pathetic little message from a lady who signed herself Susan, who said she lived somewhere north of Troy, in an upper floor room in an old tenement on the bank of a deserted canal. She lived with her eighty-six-year-old sister, Minnie. They had no fuel except what they found in refuse piles and along the railroad right of way. They brought their water up from the canal and boiled it for drinking. They had no electric light, except, she said, the public street light was near their window and lighted their dingy room. They earned their meager living by sewing on piecework for the local shirt factory. One would sew while the other recited passages from the Bible.

They told how they loved to listen to Aleck. "I prop Minnie up in bed," Susan wrote, "and, oh, Mr. Woollcott, I wish you could see her face when she hears your voice. You see, you make it seem as though one of our own had come back to us through the long-ago years. . . "

The letter asked for nothing. The ladies did not even sign their last names or give their accurate address. Rather the letter did ask for something, but for a favor that was easy and pleasurable for Aleck to grant. The ladies wanted him to read the Twenty-Third Psalm to them over the air. Minnie, the sister who was eighty-six, particularly wished it.

Aleck went on the air. "There is something I must read because I have been asked to do so by one whom no one could refuse. The next two minutes of this program are addressed solely to her. I do not know her name or where she lives and would not tell you if I knew. She is eighty-six years old and will not again see the childhood home toward which all her thoughts run on these long, cold, winter nights. . . . Man and boy, I have worked ever since I was a kid and have, in my time, been given many and varied jobs to do, but none —I think you cannot doubt this—none in all my life I have been more earnestly anxious to do well. I can only try. I will try now."

He was superb. He read the Twenty-Third Psalm and thousands of listeners wrote in to tell him that they had never heard it read so well before.

A month later came a second letter from Susan. Minnie was dead, she said, from old age, and privation. Aleck had made her last days happy. "Dear Mr. Woollcott, you brought a little bit of heaven to us that winter night. . . "

Susan now told something of their story. The father was a ship captain, lost in a storm with two of their brothers. A third brother had "gone wrong." Grief had killed their mother. Their old and valued house on the hill above Penobscot Bay had been sold to meet debts. The family silver and all their jewels had gone. They had drifted into New York state and had found the shirt factory. They had never again left its bleak side because here was the only security and independence they had known since their father's death. They would not accept charity.

For weeks Aleck carried these letters about with him, and he instituted a search for Susan. He sent Jo Hennessey north, and Hennessey combed the records of Belfast, Maine, where Susan said the family had come from. He found nothing. Aleck broadcast, appealing to Susan to reveal herself, only to him. He would protect her secret, he said, and help her only as a younger brother might. There came nothing, no response, until several months later, when Nurse O'Brien wrote to Aleck, stating that Susan, too, was dead. She had died while actually listening to Aleck, said Nurse O'Brien.

"When it got time for you to talk she asked me to raise her up in bed," the nurse wrote, "and put her sister's Bible in her hand. I turned the dial and Mother of God pretty soon if you didn't begin to talk to her. I wish you could have seen her little wasted face, when you called her your sister. It looked like a light had been lit and was shining through her eyes and skin. She stretched out both her arms like she was taking hold of your hands. . . . "

There was an enclosure, an old-fashioned gold locket enclosing a strand of hair that had come from the head of Susan's mother.

Aleck now redoubled the search. He sent Jo Hennessey to Troy, which was the general area of the postmarks of the letters. One was Watervliet, and two were from Albany, but the area specified was the Troy area. It abounded with shirt factories and disused stretches of canal. Hennessey searched for weeks. He walked up and down the old canal, and he investigated every tenement he could find. He had a name—Susan Lovice Staples, for Susan had so signed the last letter. He had descriptions. He had Nurse O'Brien's name. But he could not find Nurse O'Brien registered in the district. He could not find a Father O'Reily, who had been mentioned in the letter from the nurse. He could not find a shirt factory that might identify two aged spinsters from New England.

He could find no death records. He could not find anything at all.

Hennessey suggested that Aleck had been victimized by a practical joker. Aleck refused to believe it. Still no person was ever found who could identify anything about these two old ladies.

Hoax?

Perhaps, yes. In the view of Hennessey and of Samuel Hopkins Adams, most certainly a hoax. Adams cited the fact that all deaths in New York state must be reported. He cited the requirement that all nurses must be registered. But the fact is that all deaths in New York state have never been reported, and many women, midwives and practical nurses, who call themselves by the title of nurse are registered nowhere. The one stumbling block to belief is the mention of Father O'Reily, and even if it was O'Reilly or O'Riley, he was never found by Jo Hennessey.

Hoax, yes or no?

No one ever discovered the truth about Minnie and Susan.

In time Aleck came to accept the view that he had been victimized and he once accused a Hamilton acquaintance, saying this man, a professor at another college, was the only person in the Albany area who had the background and the opportunity to hoax him thus. The professor denied it in a way that Aleck could not but believe. If he were to play a practical joke on Aleck, he said, it would not be at the expense of his kindliness and humanitarianism. No, if it was a hoax, it came from someone in the brittle crowd that surrounded Aleck in the later years of his life. It might have come from Charles MacArthur—but Charlie MacArthur was not regarded as a practical joker who would sustain a trick for months. MacArthur liked to have strange bits and pieces about him: he once bought a part of a moribund rail line so that on the back of his stationery he might print a railroad map of all the eastern United States, with the large claim that this was the route of his railroad, and then in faintly discernible type the legend "and connecting lines." But he was not cruel.

It might have been Harpo or Charles Lederer, who loved

Aleck enough to do anything to him, but if it was hoax, whoever perpetrated it became worried by the lengths to which Aleck took the search. If there was a Nurse O'Brien she never came forward, and so the secret of the two old sisters remained.

Following the decision to sign a new contract for radio, and following the re-election of FDR, Aleck broadened his sphere of interest and activity to include politics and government in a way that he had not done before. He made new friends among the foremost political reporters of the land. He had known Arthur Krock of the New York *Times* for many years, now he cultivated that old friendship. He had known Walter Lippmann since the days of the *World*. He refined that acquaintance. He carried on a friendly correspondence with Ida Tarbell, the muckraker and biographer. He became a close friend to Dorothy Thompson, and one day she wrote: "Lots of people write and praise by column, but most of them don't matter, while you—well, you do." On another occasion, Miss Thompson wrote that she sometimes wished she had married Aleck instead of her own husbands (including Sinclair Lewis), whom she termed "unmarriageable."

Most of all, however, Aleck cultivated the bright young reporters of Washington, including the Alsop brothers, Joseph and Stewart. He knew Joe best, and they carried on a spirited correspondence. When he went to Washington he made it a point to spend an evening, or part of one, with Alsop. Yes, by 1937 he had broadened his activities to include Washington, and as the date for the inauguration approached he was writing Presidential Press Secretary Stephen Early (Dear Steve) about arrangements. (Aleck had known Steve Early since *Stars and Stripes* days in France.) Aleck was now preparing to come into his most influential and effective period, which would be as a broadcaster.

XXVIII

Christmas, 1936, was a merry and exciting season for Aleck, his friends, some of his erstwhile friends, and his business acquaintances. For this was the year that might be characterized as the Christmas of the Big Seagram's Fracas.

Aleck could see no particular difference between broadcast sponsorship in which he was associated with either a mush or a pipe tobacco, using neither product, or in outright testimonial for another product. The line has always been a fine one because advertisers always like it to be believed that the "talent" they employ or pay to perform returns the favor by using the product, and in radio in the 1930's some far-fetched efforts were made to associate Aleck and other radio personalities with the products they advertised. Aleck accepted this system as a part of the capitalist way of doing things, and long before he had taken full advantage of the system. In the 1920's, he who never smoked cigars, except perhaps in euphoria at college banquets, endorsed Muriel Cigars for a substantial fee. In 1934 he endorsed the Chrysler Airflow automobile, after traveling to Detroit on what he called "a faintly discreditable business prospect of my own." He did, at least, acquire a Chrysler in one way or another in that transaction.

In the autumn of 1936 the Seagram Distilling Company approached Aleck for an endorsement of Seagram's Pedigree Whiskey. Aleck very seldom drank whiskey. Not for nothing was he credited by Bartlett with the quotation "out of these wet clothes and into a dry martini." This endorsement was to take the form of a letter written by Aleck, lauding the whiskey, and accompanied by a photograph of him. It was to be sent to a large mailing list of corporate executives and others who might send whiskey as a gift, and Aleck supplied part of the list.

So, well before Christmas came this letter to thousands and thousands of people:

> If you are planning to give me a present this Christmas, I beg of you NOT to make it something indestructible, which would only add to the litter of my life. The safest bet is whiskey, and you could hardly do better than Seagram's Pedigree, that rare, 8-year-old Imported Bonded whiskey of which Seagram's, and with good reason, are so proud.
>
> But why, as they say in the drama, am I telling this to you?
>
> Well, it's because the Seagram people have seduced, bribed, and corrupted me into doing it. Besides, it happens to be true.
>
> Here's hoping.
>
> A. Woollcott

Coming from another this endorsement might not have aroused any particular emotion. Coming from Aleck it aroused emotion of many kinds. Eustace Tilly, the phantom of the *New Yorker,* in the person of E. B. White, wrote a public answer in Talk of the Town, advising Aleck that he would not get whiskey from Tilly, but a tippet lined with hand-picked burrs, and accusing Aleck of turning, apparently single-handedly, Christmas into a season "pervaded with the faint, exquisite perfume of well-rotted holly berries."

Herbert Bayard Swope, who had been itching for reprisal since Aleck blackballed the Hertzes from the Campanile apartment, sat down and dictated an angry letter to Seagram's.

> Gentlemen:
>
> I had placed an order for your Pedigreed Bonded Whiskey, for personal use and for Christmas gifts, when Mr. Woollcott's "letter" reached me. As he never drinks whiskey, and, therefore, is unable to judge its value—an inability that is not confined to whiskey—it follows that his letter

must be regarded as deliberately misleading—a failing of which he is frequently guilty.

In these circumstances I have cancelled my order for your product, and I shall advise my friends to follow the same course.

If Aleck's endorsement of the whiskey was not quite what it should be in terms of pristine literary integrity, Swope's letter was also questionable, as biographer E. J. Kahn, Jr., noted. It was hard to see why Swope would have placed an order for a Seagram product since he was a consultant to Schenley, the major Seagram rival. And, of course, despite any pious belief of any magazine editorial staff that the publication of advertising does not indicate an endorsement of the product, the public has always had quite the opposite idea. So what was the arguing all about? It could have been nothing but spleen venting by Swope, and a joking retort, with a slightly venomous air to it, from the *New Yorker* direction.

Outcry came also from the daughters of brother William in Baltimore. Aleck received a Valentine, with the following couplet attached:

Buy stocks on the margin if you must,
But don't trail the family name in the dust.

This was more by way of being a joke than a chiding remark, for in Baltimore brother William was gestating a family of literary figures himself, and one of them, Barbara Woollcott, would go on to write a book of her own about the family.

No one criticized Aleck when he went on the air under sponsorship of Granger Pipe Tobacco and openly espoused the cause of a tobacco he never smoked.

Some of Aleck's friends chided him and he responded, with Howard Dietz, for example, by flying into one of his celebrated rages. For some reason Aleck's friends expected a standard of honesty from him that they did not set for themselves. It was flattering, perhaps, but it was scarcely comforting to him.

Aleck's feeling about endorsements was indicated by his actions in the next few months. He endorsed a tennis racket and he endorsed Pullman travel. He was well paid for both, and he turned the money over to charity, at least in the case of the Pullman Company, where his charity was the American Civil Liberties Union.

Aleck answered the *New Yorker* criticism in a letter in which he called attention to the liquor advertising in the magazine. But that did not disturb the editors, who rested serene in their belief that they were above mammon, not in the midst of it.

Still Katherine and E. B. White were distressed when they learned that Aleck took the chiding personally and believed that someone at the *New Yorker* was nursing a grudge against him. (People there were nursing grudges, although E. B. White did not happen to be one of them.)

So White sent Aleck a placatory Christmas card, which indicated the problem of the writer in a commercial society as well as anything ever written:

> Dear Woollcott:
>
> Serving the *New Yorker* in my capacity as jackanapes of all trades, I sometimes discover myself in the act of muddying up my friends and acquaintances—as in the case of you and the Seagram letter. I always throw myself into these discourtesies with a will, dreamily hoping to achieve heavenly grace through earthly impartiality. My wife tells me you are convinced that we maintain a Dept. of Animus; but my true belief is we have as little animus as is consistent with good publishing. In your case, my own animus, if any, was against the frantic society to which we all fall victim, in varying measure, & to which you lured my attention at this white season by your open affair with La Seagram. After all, a man's personal excesses are his own business. Privately, I may wish you joy of the lady, but publicly I must give so lewd an alliance a jab, mustn't I?
>
> With best wishes,
>
> E.B. White

Aleck went to Washington just after the first of the year to attend the inauguration of the man he had helped to elect. He stayed at the Carlton Hotel and called at the White House. It was the first move in what would become a very close association with Mrs. Roosevelt, and an amicable, but more distant one with the President.

In this year Aleck's rise to fame was complete in the sense that for the first time he was parodied as a writer. It came in the *Saturday Review of Literature* in an article by Timothy Fuller. It was "The Story of Jack and Jill—as it might be told by William Faulkner, P. G. Wodehouse, and Alexander Woollcott." The parody of Aleck's work was excellent, in that it did follow his unusual and definite style.

"There has come to me recently," wrote Aleck's parodist, "through various and sundry channels, a little gem of a story, which, if your slightly hoarse Town Crier is not amiss, should warm the cockles of even the most petrified hearts, a story albeit that simply screams to be retold over and over again, by cozy firesides, in hidebound club rooms, everywhere from transcontinental airplanes to Sunday school picnics."

Aleck's broadcasts in 1937 certainly indicated his wide range of enthusiasms and since it was as broadcaster rather than as stylist of the printed page that Aleck left his greatest impact on America, the range is worth examining. On March 11, Aleck told the story of Verdun Belle, and never told it better. This constant retelling of tales irritated his friends. John Winterich remarked on Verdun Belle: "Ever since the late spring of 1918 Verdun Belle has been supporting Alexander Woollcott," he wrote. Of course he did not mean it, but he was awed by Aleck's ability to rehash the tale so many times—perhaps not fully considering the different audience at which Aleck aimed. This last audience for the story, the radio audience, was the largest of all, and for any duplication of the old, there were a thousand who had never heard or read the story before.

On March 16, Aleck did the Lizzie Borden story again, repeating and amplifying what he had written for print earlier.

"I shall always be sorry I never met Lizzie. After all there was only one Lizzie Borden. Of course that was plenty."

But there was far more to Aleck than such twice-told tales, and he kept his audience because he managed to dish up varied fare. Two days after dealing with Lizzie Borden, Aleck was discussing literary usages in a manner set to appeal to a wide audience:

. . . Tonight's broadcast will deal—and deal sternly—with the care and use of that instrument of communication . . . which from force of habit we still call the English language. I can give the keynote in a single anecdote—something that befell me nearly twenty-eight years ago. If it's still fresh in my memory, it's because it happened at the start of my apprenticeship. My first night in the newspaper business. . . . My first assignment was an obituary of a woman who'd expired that afternoon. A woman of no importance but she'd given up the ghost in a fashionable neighborhood and, since all newspapers are snobs, this made her passing worth at least a paragraph. With anxious care as to street number, date of birth, spelling of name, etc., I wrote that paragraph and turned it in to the night city editor, Frederick T. Birchall, who's since become famous as a foreign correspondent. In those days Boss Birchall had a red beard and a roving eye and the curious habit of addressing everyone from the police commissioner to the office boy as either Sweetheart or Dearie. I stood by while he inspected my first effort. Neatly typewritten, it began with the sad news that Mary Van Rensallear Whoozis had just died of heart failure. When he got that far, the boss gave a low moan and began plucking hairs from his auburn beard. Next he seized his pencil, struck out the word "failure" and in its place wrote the word "disease." Then, turning as if to rend me limb from limb, he noticed for the first time that I was a newcomer, and straightway took the trouble to give me my first lesson in journalism. "Not heart *failure,* Dearie," he said, "we all die of that."

In ten seconds he'd taught me more than I'd learned in all my courses in composition at school or college. Impressed on me forever that in speaking and writing, the first and only important consideration is to employ those words which will exactly convey one's meaning. All the rest—though parents and pedagogues often seem unaware of the fact—all the rest is so much frill and folderol. As frill and folderol I classify most of what is taught in school under the head of grammar and all of what is generally meant by correct pronunciation. In the matter of pronunciation, the canons of good usage are vague at best—changing from year to year and never the same all over the country. Any person would do well to observe them who attaches importance to social advancement. They'll be useful to him. Just as he'll do better not to wear a sweater to the opera or eat peas with his knife or think that at a dance *these* days he can get by with the turkey-trot or the bunny-hug. In short, they're edicts of fashion and local edicts at that. No less, but no more. They've nothing to do with the eternal verities. When you're careless about "who" and "whom" or split your infinitives—which is often a good thing to do—or, when, like me, you wind up an occasional sentence with a preposition, you're being unfashionable, perhaps, but that's all. No worse, I assure you. And don't let anyone tell you different.

It's comic to watch the frenzy of parents and school marms in their well-meant efforts to police the wild, unkempt speech of the young. In this they behave like the hen who hatches some ducks and tries to keep them off the millpond. Too often their regulations are as artificial as the self-imposed rule of the little girl who vows she'll walk all the way home from school without once stepping on a crack in the sidewalk. When dear teacher tries to prevent her charges from saying "he ain't" instead of "he isn't" or "it's me" instead of "it's I" or "go slow" instead of "go slowly," she's courting defeat because there's no real sense to her prohibitions.

While I do indict the teachers, it's worth noting that the higher you go the fewer. Why, here's a Princeton professor coming out in defense of "ain't" as a sturdy contraction with an honorable tradition. And I'm delighted with a story James Hilton told me the other day about a history exam at Oxford. In answer to the question "What do you know about the Lombard League?", one of the students correctly wrote down just the word "Nothing." For that, the examiners were about to give him a zero when they had the grace to realize that the real error lay in the sloppiness of the question. So they gave him full credit.

I was delighted by that story because in matters of

speech, it's not elegance that interests me but exactness. Precision. Surgical precision. I suggest that those of us whose trade is in words, whether put down on paper or tossed onto the patient air-waves and all those whose job it is to teach that trade might better concentrate on the really grievous injury done our medium every day by those who so ignore the primal eldest meaning of a word that eventually it loses its sharp edge as an instrument, its exact value as currency. Let me give a few illustrations—all in the pattern of the old story about Noah Webster, the man who wrote the dictionary. Of him it used to be told that his wife once caught him in the pantry in the act of kissing the cook. "Why, Mr. Webster," she said, "I'm surprised." "No, my dear," he replied, "I'm surprised; you're amazed." My own interest in such distinctions began in high school. I caught it from my teacher of physics. Like all his successors in that field, he never managed to teach me anything about physics, but as a side-line he did impress me with the importance of trying to say what I meant. His pet aversion was the man who would say "transpire" when he meant "happen." Against such sloppiness he preached so passionately that to this day I wince when I hear that particular blunder. Exactly used, "transpire" means "leak out." If, when you merely mean "happen," you keep saying "transpire," that useful word will soon cease to convey its original meaning. Now, mark you, this is worse than merely using a niblick for a mashie shot. No permanent harm's done then. But the man who says "transpire" when he means "happen" is a little brother to the nitwit bride who uses her husband's razor to sharpen pencils with. After she's done that a few times, the razor may still be good for sharpening pencils, but her wretched husband will have to grow a beard.

In the same way I find that many of our newspapers no longer seem able to distinguish between "prone" and "supine." Your vocabulary is impoverished every time you forget that a man is prone when he lies face down, supine when he lies on his back. A few weeks ago in one of our better New York dailies I read a description of a well-

> dressed woman lying prone on her back on Fifth Avenue. I'd like to have seen that. Must have been quite a sight. . . .

In June he told the story of the death of Mary White, the daughter of William Allen White. He had told that story before. White had written it originally in the editorial pages of the *Emporia Gazette* in 1921. Aleck had even *broadcast* this tale before, but by request he repeated the sad story of the lithe young girl whose head strikes a tree branch as she is galloping through a park on her horse, and who falls, seems to recover, and then dies from concussion.

During the springtime, Margaret Mitchell, author of *Gone with the Wind,* had exchanged a number of legends with Aleck, and one of these he now used on the air, but in his inimitable style, with his own fillip:

> Let me begin by passing on to you an account of something which happened one morning two weeks ago in a department store in Chicago. My informant has supplied names and addresses but for reasons which should be clear as I go along, it will be better if I leave them out. This report was the end of a story that began in a house in Mississippi late last December. A young woman—a college girl home for the Christmas holidays—was startled one night, long after the household had gone to sleep, to hear on the gravel drive outside, the long unfamiliar sound of hoof beats and carriage wheels. The vehicle, whatever it was, stopped short on the old-style *porte cochere*—came to a halt under her window, which was open wide. She got out of bed and went to see what this midnight visitation could mean.
>
> It was a clear night and the moon was at the full—a white landscape with sharp black shadows. Underneath her window stood a hearse. The driver had wrapped the reins around the whip socket and got down from his seat. A lanky fellow in an old-style frock coat and stovepipe hat. At the sight of her peering down from her window, he took off his hat and looked up at her. His face was white as a mask and across one cheek ran a jagged scar. Even as she noticed these things—she was destined never

to forget them—the driver spoke to her in a clipped metallic voice. What he said was: "Room for one more." At that she fainted and found herself lying on her bed, her heart going like a trip-hammer. It took all the gumption she had to get up and look out of the window just to assure herself there was nothing really there—that she had been dreaming.

Now this same dream came to her on three successive nights, which tended to diminish the gayety of her Christmas holidays. Always the details were the same. The old-style plumed hearse. The restive horses—pawing the gravel. The driver with his scarred face the color of a fish's belly. Always he stood hat in hand and looked up at her and said, "Room for one more." But the days went by and she herself forgot about it. Then, two weeks ago this sequel came.

She was visiting friends in Chicago and had set forth one morning on a shopping tour. The department she sought was on the eighth floor and she drifted with the crowd of shoppers toward an elevator that was filling up. It was one of those marginal cases where she might or might not have to wait for the next one. She was just hesitating when she heard that voice again. "Room for one more." The clipped metallic voice she had heard under her window in the moonlight months before. This time it was the elevator man speaking—trim in his smart uniform and visored cap. But it was the same face. Dead white with the scar on the cheek. "Room for one more." All this happened in less time than it takes to tell it. Began and ended in the space that a breath is held. Her reaction was instinctive. She just stepped back. Before she realized why, the gate had clanged to and the car started up without her. A minute later the elevator fell to the bottom of the shaft and everyone in it was killed.

Well, that's the story as it came in on Saturday, arriving in a lather by air mail from some faithful listener who knows and shares my interest in the uncanny. It was sent to me for my comment. Well, this is my comment. I don't believe a word of it. Now, mind you, I look upon the

> White Queen as a piker. If you, too, were brought up on Alice's adventure through the looking-glass, you will remember that the White Queen, when she was a young girl and had her strength, was able to believe six impossible things, every day before breakfast. Why, that's nothing. I can do that much with one hand tied behind me. But in this instance, I didn't even bother to wire out to Chicago and inquire if any of the stores there had been having elevator trouble. I was able to dismiss the yarn at once because I happen to know from personal experience that that elevator has been crashing regularly at the rate of about once a week for the past fifty years—crashing in pretty much all the territory from San Francisco eastward to Warsaw. In fact, the legend has always been particularly active in Poland, where the driver of the hearse, instead of being marked by a scarred and livid face is always identified by a great shock of brick-red hair. In France the hearse is usually heard rattling over the cobblestones beneath the window of an inn in Dijon and the elevator crash occurs, after a suitable interval, in a hotel in Paris. In England the warning first comes not from a hearse driver but from a man carrying a coffin on his back. In this country the vision usually appears somewhere in the South. The story is always bobbing up as having just happened to an undergraduate at Randolph Macon at Lynchburg in Virginia, and the spectral hearse halts under a dormitory window. And the story is a hardy annual around Atlanta, according to Margaret Mitchell. Like myself, the woman who wrote *Gone with the Wind* is a collector of such grisly anecdotes. It was she who suggested that I tell this one in a broadcast this year. I said I would if it bobbed up again and sure enough it did. . . .

Two days later Aleck offered something entirely different, including political commentary. Taking his listeners back five years he said: "In Chicago next week the Republicans will helplessly nominate Herbert Hoover," then launched into a tale further afield.

"In Munich an agitator named Adolph Hitler made a scene in court yesterday. He was being examined by a Jewish lawyer and naturally refused to answer. The court fined Adolph a thousand marks. Times will change."

A few days later Aleck was talking about Seeing Eye dogs, then about Harpo Marx, then about that dog who went off with the burglars from the Long Island house.

Aleck had gained a reputation as a drum beater. This spring, his attention to the works of John Steinbeck shows why.

On March 18, he dropped a mention of Steinbeck's *Of Mice and Men.*

> In the new novel by John Steinbeck called *Of Mice and Men*—an unforgettably beautiful and compassionate story, by the way—one of the characters is a huge, benevolent idiot with the muscles of a chimpanzee and the mind of a six-year-old child. This amiable giant so adores every puppy he sees that he can't keep his enormous hands off it. And he's so clumsy that he soon fondles it to death. Must we sit back helpless while we watch such brethren fondling the life out of a valuable word like "flair"? These destructive people may have hearts of gold but they damage our language. They should all be shot at sunrise.

On Thursday, April 15, he told the story of the Pirate of Monterey from *Tortilla Flat,* a Steinbeck book published two years earlier. When he had finished:

> So endeth the tale of the Pirate of Monterey and his buried treasure and what he bought with it. Why have I told it tonight? Well, isn't this the week set aside in the calendar for celebrating the brotherhood of man and beast? Why have I told it at all. Partly for its own sweet sake, of course. I *like* it and I'm free to say so. You see it's not *my* story. To be sure I've just told it largely in my own words, but what's good in it is the work of a better man. A young Californian named Steinbeck. You will find it scattered prodigally through a golden book of his called *Tortilla Flat.* What I've done here is gather up his pieces and put them together. When *Tortilla Flat* was published nearly two years ago it caused no great stir. But today all America is making mighty mirations over the

> same author's new work—the one called *Of Mice and Men.* Like its predecessor, this, too, is a tale at once bawdy and tender. It's full of lust and blood-letting. Indeed, I'm under obligation to report here that much of it will outrage the squeamish. But it's full, too, of something for which the fittest descriptive word has somehow gone out of fashion. We don't hear it much anymore. That word is "loving-kindness." I look upon *Of Mice and Men* as a masterpiece. But of its great success I'm a little jealous. Jealous in behalf of the elder brother that no one paid much attention to. This broadcast is my way of saying that *Tortilla Flat* was a pretty good book, too. And still is.

On June 29, Aleck was again praising *Of Mice and Men*:

> Another notable book of this very year, John Steinbeck's *Of Mice and Men,* was also an involuntary second draft. The first had been laboriously written in an old ledger. After six months of work it was finished and Steinbeck put it aside to cool. Then it happened one day that he deeply offended his setter dog, Toby. Went off somewhere and left him locked up in the house. Thus basely deserted, Toby got even by attacking that ledger in which all summer his master had been so absurdly interested that he wouldn't take a walk or stop to play. By working at it good and hard, Toby reduced the manuscript to confetti. All the king's horses and all the king's men could never have put it together again. The book, since written afresh, has been far and away Steinbeck's greatest success. Now he is wondering whether he might not have done well to try the earlier ones on the dog. At the very least, the publishers should carry an endorsement from Toby on the jacket. Something like this. "I never enjoyed any book so much as *Of Mice and Men.* I fairly ate it up." In a recent paragraph on this episode I carelessly alluded to Toby as a setter with a heart of gold but no pedigree to speak of. This comment elicited this furious telegram. "Outraged, STOP. Pedigree as long as history. STOP. My mother field trial winner. STOP. Can you say as much?" The telegram was signed Toby Steinbeck. I told you all dogs were snobs.

His manner was joking, but his repeated mentions of Steinbeck and his works were most helpful to that young author. It might not be correct to say that Aleck *made* any author. Perhaps James Hilton's *Goodbye, Mr. Chips!* would have been discovered by an American publisher in the pages of the *Atlantic Monthly* and brought forth as a book without Aleck's help. Perhaps Steinbeck would have risen as far, if not as rapidly. But he did rise more rapidly because of Aleck, for Aleck, enthusiasm once aroused, continued without rewinding.

Pathos, humor, folksiness, drama, tragedy, heroism—Aleck mixed his tales with the care and skill of a master painter. The Aleck of Verdun Belle might be the source of scoffing by his erudite friends, but the Aleck who also spoke of men and peace could not be scorned.

> We all know what happened at Versailles. The men who made the war made the peace. Only Mr. Wilson preached the brotherhood of man and his voice was drowned out. At that barren outcome we are entitled to all the emotions except one—we are not entitled to surprise. War is born of greed and vanity and fear. It is nourished by hate and its end result is bitterness. We cannot glorify force and set men to killing each other and then by ordering the guns to cease firing—by merely blowing a whistle—expect them suddenly to act with sweet reasonableness. That did not happen the last time: it will not happen the next.
>
> On this point in recent years a vast amount of nonsense has been written. It has been a favorite topic with many silly people, but the ones who seem to me dangerously silly are those who lightly assume that Mr. Wilson might easily have taken another course and who airily imply that under similar circumstances—do you see their shadow already across our path?—under like circumstances we, the people, would act quite differently. I do not believe that. Why? Well, as far as I have been able to observe even the people of this tumultuous democracy are seldom governed by that creed of conduct which was set forth in the

> Sermon on the Mount. A sermon preached nearly 2,000 years ago. We memorize it when we are children and many of us listen to it with approval when we dress up on Sunday and go to church. At times, with our lips, we repeat it. But never with our hearts. In our hearts we don't believe it. . . .

In 1937 and thereafter as long as he broadcast, Aleck's power became immense. Shortly after the war, at a Hamilton Commencement, Aleck had met Colonel Theodore Roosevelt, Jr., and his wife the former Alice Longworth. The acquaintance had ripened into friendship, and although strained by political arguments in the days of "the other Roosevelt" the friendship had continued. One day in 1937 Aleck broadcast an appeal to the public in behalf of the colonel. He was then an editor at Doubleday Page and Company in Long Island, and he was putting together an anthology of favorite poetry. After Aleck's mention of this, and his request that his listeners pick out the favorite poem they had tucked away, Roosevelt was deluged. He received 40,000 poems from Americans.

"Last time I was in America I listened with joy to your Sunday evening performance. It must be very wonderful to have that enormous audience in the hollow of your hand." These were the words of Somerset Maugham, in a letter written Aleck that summer of 1937. Wonderful, yes, but sobering. And sometimes Aleck was a very sober fellow, in spite of his playful ways.

One day in 1937 Arthur Hopkins and Aleck's other friends of the theater gave a testimonial dinner for him at the Lotos Club. Many celebrities were there, including John Gielgud, Maurice Evans, Helen Hayes, David Warfield, Lillian Gish, Sidney Howard, Judith Anderson, Henry Hull, Philip Merivale. They ate fruit cup and green turtle soup, fish and squab chicken, and strawberry mousse, and Aleck made a wise and witty little speech, dedicated to those who said the theater was decaying. "The theater has been in a state of decay, according to its critics, for the past 3,000 years. At that rate it should be pretty well gone by now. Yet I have seen a vital revival of Richard II. And I have seen a WPA revival of Dr. Faustus that is worth seeing." It was not the theater that had decayed but the critics, said Alexander Woollcott.

In this year, whatever Aleck did became worthy of note. One day in the spring he was called upon to speak to a club stag gathering and he adjusted his repertoire of stories accordingly. No one bothered to tell him that the microphone before him was hooked to the airwaves of a local radio station instead of just to the loudspeaker system, and then, the radio people were aghast and cut him off the air when some purple language was emitted. The incident was duly reported among the doings of the famous by *Literary Digest,* and added another crooked stick to the Woollcott legend.

Aleck's reputation grew, even among the tarnishing stories. Ezra Pound, an old Hamiltonian then resident in Rome, wrote Aleck to ask him to expose the "enormous swindle of governments."

"Why me?" Aleck asked.

"Because you are not merely a funny man," Pound responded, "but the most influential broadcaster and critic in America, and the logical man to tell Americans that a nation need not pay rent for its own credit or submit to the dehumanization of mankind."

"The damnedest collection of friends in the world," was the way one acquaintance characterized Aleck's social life. It was true. The prototype of Metz the mad naturalist who invaded that simple Ohio town of *The Man Who Came to Dinner* with his thousands of cockroaches was Dr. Gustav Eckstein. Aleck had met him in 1936 after he became interested in a little book of Eckstein's about canaries, and in 1937, when Aleck went to Washington and supped at the White House he also made a pilgrimage with Neysa McMein and Eckstein to the National Zoological Park in Washington. Presto—Aleck had a new interest, birds and beasts.

This constant extension of interests was one of the vital factors in Aleck's life, it made him eternally young, but it also sapped his energy. This year, besides broadcasting and traveling to zoos, Aleck spent parts of several months at the island, visited Booth Tarkington at Indianapolis *and* in Maine, and again became an actor. At the end of the year, Aleck was offered, and accepted, a part in a new play by S. N. Behrman, called *Wine of Choice,* in which he played a part that critic Lloyd Lewis called "cosmopolite Pygmalion who nurses the artistic careers of young women and acts as sort of a male Elsa Maxwell to Long Island society." Aleck had turned down the role, but later accepted it.

How little the busy world of New York knew about Aleck was indicated by Burns Mantle, who went back many years with Woollcott to the old New York *Times* days, in his study of *Wine of Choice*:

> No one seems to have the least idea why Alexander Woollcott wants to act. The Old Town Crier is one of the most successful of radio commentators. His books have an amazing sale. He has saved his money and bought himself an island where he can get away from practically everything, including it all.
>
> Yet, here he is treading the creaking boards of the Guild Theater in Behrman's *Wine of Choice,* preceded from point to point by a torso that cries out for club sofas and deep arm chairs.
>
> I can understand why the Theatre Guild should want Mr. Woollcott to act. His is a name to conjure with. . . .
>
> But I still am at a loss to understand why Mr. Woollcott should want to do it. It cannot be vanity. Not entirely. The Old Town Crier is too smart not to know he never will endanger any professional actor's job, or add anything of salable value to his own reputation. He knows he can never be anything more than a superamateur.
>
> Perhaps it is just a lark. A break in the Woollcott routine. A change from the monotony of reading, writing and figuring income taxes. Whatever it is, I wish him joy of it. . . .

Anyone who knew Aleck knew why he loved to tread the boards, but not so very many of the celebrities of America knew Aleck. Wreathed in this air of mystery, Aleck went on the road for three months with the play.

XXIX

THE MORE PROMINENT ALECK BECAME, it seemed, the less sure of himself he was, the easier it was to offend him, and the more arguments he busied himself in arousing. When *Wine of Choice* opened at the Guild Theater in New York in February, 1938, Lucius Beebe, the man about town of the New York *Herald Tribune,* suggested that he would like to interview Aleck. Somehow Beebe's tone or manner irritated Aleck and he refused the interview whereupon Beebe attacked him in his widely read column. Aleck then gave interviews to Ward Morehouse, drama critic of the New York *Sun,* and H. Allen Smith of the *World-Telegram.*

Confronted by various newspaper men, Aleck played it for all it was worth. He said that interviews were dull and that he got about 75 requests a day for them. He also indicated that he had never heard of Lucius Beebe. Did they not mean William Beebe, the oceanographer?

"Beebe?" he asked. "I thought he was on the bottom of the ocean."

This, of course, kept the controversy very much alive, which was just what the public Woollcott wanted.

He had developed a heady, sometimes galling, openhandedness of criticism. When Mrs. Eleanor Roosevelt went to Thornton Wilder's *Our Town* and said it depressed her, he rose quickly in its defense and chided the first lady of the land.

> And now, as your senior and better in dramatic criticism, let me make a word of comment on your progress as a play-goer. The late Charles Frohman used to say that sometimes it wasn't the play that failed, but the public. I gather from your diary that when you went to see *Our Town*

> you were not at your best. I am afraid you didn't give what I could conscientiously call a good performance. If, at that gentle masterpiece, you were "depressed beyond words," it must have been on some evening when you would not have been spiritually equal to reading, let us say, Gray's *Elegy*.
>
> So now this is what you must do. You must eat some lettuce, read a little Charles Lamb, take a nap and go to see *Our Town* again. After that, kindly report to me at once and oblige.

Now the character who was to be parodied in *The Man Who Came to Dinner* was truly emerging—the Aleck of short temper, of exaggerated remark and insult. This became painfully apparent to Aleck himself when Paul Bonner encouraged some people from the British Broadcasting Company to seek Aleck out. They called him by long distance telephone. He was sound asleep when the call came in and he was annoyed and suspicious that it might be a practical joke so he was insufferably rude to the caller. He wrote Bonner in explanation, if an explanation was possible. And it seemed to be, for later that year Aleck did do some broadcasts under the title "Letter from America."

His attitude that year was to seek semi-retirement to Vermont, as much as such was possible for him. He ran for the library board in Castleton, Vermont, and was elected. He served faithfully on that board for the remainder of his life.

However, he continued to add to the circle of his acquaintances, making friends with Justice Felix Frankfurter (whom he called Binkie), among many other government officials in Washington. He wrote now for the *Reader's Digest*, telling his twice-told tales, and when there was a hiatus, DeWitt Wallace wrote Aleck saying the *Digest's* subscribers were fretting. He continued to give away his time and money. He made a speech to the Nieman Journalism Fellows at Harvard University, and he spoke to the students of tiny Castleton State College in Vermont. He gave more Myers lectures at Hamilton. He did much more. He gave the college library a stream of books, he made the college choir famous by persuading CBS to broadcast the choir with himself as master of ceremonies and with such guest stars as Orson Welles. He quarreled with many, but his quarrels never seemed to be final, except with a few. With the *New Yorker* they were *not.* Even while quarreling with Ross after the Gibbs profile Aleck was sending suggestions to E. B. White and others for profiles—as with a profile of Dorothy Thompson. He continued to make gestures of the greatest generosity and good will to dozens, scores, hundreds of those around him. A youngster named Cecil Eagan came to work at Neshobe Island one summer. With little more recommendation than that, Aleck sent the boy through college and medical school. Dorothy Parker wrote an article—"Soldiers of the Republic"—about the Spanish Loyalists, which appeared in the *New Yorker.* Aleck caused it to be published as a pamphlet. Highly paid as he was for commercial writing, he contributed without charge to the text of the Hamilton College prospectus for potential students.

Through Aleck's close association with many intelligent and influential persons in England he had a much sharper view of the state of the world in 1938 and 1939 than most Americans. After Munich, Rebecca West wrote him feelingly that she had the most awful feeling that her government had just sold the British people down the river. Aleck read and heeded. By the spring of 1939 he was making broadcasts with a frankly political flavor to them, as on March 7 when he told the story of a shipwreck, of those in the lifeboats beating others off "so that their despairing hands let go and they sank back into the sea. That is what happens at time of shipwreck. Time of shipwreck. For great multitudes, what else, my friends, is this? Beating the drowning off our raft. Isn't that just what we, the luckier nations of the world, are doing every day to the refugees in flight from the despotism of Middle Europe. Barring the road to the most pitiful migration since the world began?"

He concerned himself very much with the affairs of Hamilton College. He tried to persuade Robert M. Hutchins, chancellor of the University of Chicago, to leave Chicago and come to Hamilton as President. He attended trustee meetings faithfully. He secured honorary degrees for Helen Hayes and Paul Robeson—whom he persuaded to accept them—degrees which honored Hamilton as much as the recipients.

When war actually came to Europe in the summer of 1939, Aleck was much distressed; more, he hoped that he might get into it. He wrote William Paley at CBS asking that he be given a job as a reporter in England for the network during the war. Paley turned him away gently. He wanted reporters, not pundits in England then, and besides, Aleck was then in his fifties.

So Aleck set out on a round of even busier times to try to forget that he was being relegated to the sidelines. It was during this period, in 1939, that *The Man Who Came to Dinner* was being conceived and hatched. It began after a weekend spent by Aleck at Moss Hart's country house in Bucks County, Pennsylvania, but of course there was nothing new about the idea of writing a play in which a part was made for Aleck to play Aleck. S. N. Behrman had already done it twice. What was new was that this play was written around Aleck as the central figure.

In the beginning there was some thought of Aleck taking the lead in the Broadway production, but the idea was abandoned because no one wanted to take the chance that the play might be hurt by unfavorable reviews which would review Aleck instead of the play. Aleck did have a hand in the choosing of Monty Woolley for the part, and he did agree to play the part himself for a time in one of two road companies that were being formed.

Aleck went west on a speaking tour, and then on March 6 he opened in the part of Sheridan Whiteside at the Pasadena Civic Auditorium, and immediately the speculation began as to whether he was as good an Alexander Woollcott as Woolley. Quite probably he was not, because Aleck had himself to play, and Woolley was simply portraying a preposterous character.

In April Aleck was playing the role in San Francisco, when he suffered a heart attack and had to cancel his performance. It was serious enough to hospitalize him.

Aleck did his best to keep the secret, but it would not be kept. He hated personal publicity of this kind, he hated being helpless and a subject of pity by his friends.

When they learned that he had fallen ill, hundreds of them wrote, telegraphed and telephoned to discover the truth of the matter. Seldom was a man so loved as to receive so much attention. Sinclair Lewis, whose house in Woodstock Aleck had visited many times, wrote:

> Dear Alec. . . . On hearing, so soon after a happy lunch with you that you had been taken ill, I had a special pang of regret and sympathy. But you and I are indestructible—we must at least be cousins—both of us native Vermonters by achievement instead of mere accident, both great comedians, both pretty competent writers of advertising (for and against) when we have to be, and I have a warm faith that you will come out blooming, as I have after every debacle. . . .

Aleck was taken to Syracuse, where Al Getman practiced medicine, and Getman undertook his care. After a few weeks, he was well enough to travel to Neshobe Island, and was ordered to stay there, in bed at first, and then island-bound, while the doctors waited to see just how much activity he might undertake in the future.

He was really now a cardiac cripple, although he refused to accept it. Had he opted to remain quiet most of the time, cut his schedule almost to nothing, and spent many hours in bed each day Aleck might have prolonged his life for a number of years. He did not even consider such a course. He had lived his life the way he wanted to live it. He would continue to do so.

While island-bound Aleck continued to carry on his correspondence. He was somewhat chastened by his experience, somewhat sadder, and filled with self-hate.

In the autumn Aleck was able to get back into the swing of life, which he did with gusto. Roger Baldwin, director of the American Civil Liberties Union, asked him to serve on a committee to protect the rights of all minority groups—including Nazis. Aleck demurred. He had, he said, an old prejudice against serving only nominally on any committee. More, he had doubts "as to the course the Union will take and should take in the times that lie just ahead. There must be some satisfactory formula for withholding civil liberties from those who use them to serve a dictatorship which holds all such liberties in professional contempt." Aleck agreed to meet Baldwin and discuss the matter, and announced himself ready to be convinced to the contrary, but Baldwin seemed to realize that Aleck's sympathies had turned most warlike.

And they had. In every respect. Aleck was particularly determined to support Franklin D. Roosevelt for a third term, for he felt that Roosevelt was needed in office at this time; his determination showed itself as belligerence. In September, when the New York *Times* came out for Wendell Willkie, Aleck wrote to Arthur Hays Sulzberger saying Willkie was a bumptious, common, flighty mountebank. "The fact that the man who wrote the '*Times* for Willkie' editorial really thought so too probably accounts for the tortured quality of the most laborious piece of praise the *Times* ever published."

Sulzberger remonstrated with Aleck for his belligerence. A few days later Aleck replied:

> Your letter of September 25th, so much more temperate than mine, winds up with this question: "Where is the excellent, objective drama critic I used to know?" To answer you explicitly he is on an island in a lake in Vermont and his guests at the moment—Samuel Hopkins Adams, Ethel Barrymore, and Thornton Wilder—all happen to be vehemently pro-Roosevelt and it would be impossible for him to get up an argument around here.
>
> In your letter you say that you made no secret of the fact that Willkie has disappointed you just as he has me. It was my point that you did make a secret of this on the editorial page. I was of the opinion that this constituted a breach of trust. I am still of that opinion. I think too that there must be uncomfortable hours when you wonder if I am not right. . . .

Just before election day Aleck appeared on a Democratic Party radio show, made a sharp attack on Sulzberger and the *Times* for supporting Willkie. From Chattanooga came a swift and slashing attack by an old friend—interesting and revealing not because it shows a side of Aleck, but because it shows the climate of emotion in which Aleck and his friends lived in this parlous political season of 1940. The attacker was Aleck's friend—or now former friend—Adolph S. Ochs, Jr.,

Sulzberger's brother-in-law, and publisher of the Chattanooga *Times*:

> I don't know how this election will turn out, but I do know that last night, at the Democratic vaudeville show, Alexander Woollcott, sandwiched between a clog dancer and a jazz band, made a sorry contribution to national dignity and did not enhance his reputation as the leading man of American letters.
>
> Your crack at Arthur Sulzberger was cheap and unworthy of you.
>
> I hereby submit my resignation as your faithful leftenant. You might take on Elliott Roosevelt.
>
> Please give my regards to Coca-Cola—or whatever your dog's name is. He is not such a brilliant stylist, but he has better manners than his master.

Following the election, Aleck pursued his argument with Arthur Sulzberger from the point of view of public interest, and in it he indicated a shrewd awareness of the problems of newspaper publishing in the middle of the twentieth century.

> Perhaps you realize that I am incurably romantic about the newspaper business and feel for the *Times* something of the sentiment which any grateful person feels for the school at which he was happy. Being romantic I am always thrown for a loop when I come upon disconcerting reminders that a great newspaper is not only a public institution, like the Rockefeller Institute or Harvard University, but also a piece of private property in somebody's pocket.
>
> Incidentally, I saw the late Joseph Pulitzer, in testamentary mood, attempt to guard the *World* as a public institution by creating a trust and noted the chicanery in the surrogate's office by which the purpose of the will was defeated and the trust put in the control of three heirs by whose futility and greed the *World* was first milked and then murdered. The failure to tell that story when it was fresh was a disservice to the profession. When, by inheritance or any other process, a newspaper like the *Herald-Tribune* can be under the control of a person with the mentality, if any, of Ogden Reid and when a paper

with the circulation of the Chicago *Tribune* can be directed by a Bertie McCormick, it is small wonder that the press of America has fallen low in the public esteem and become politically impotent. Such men make your own job harder. . . .

I have long given you credit for the fact that the *Times* is, all told, a better paper than it was in my day, more expertly produced and more interesting. I even think the dramatic department is better, which is saying a good deal.

From all I hear you are so constituted that you would never want to be the hero of the piece but you will have to be the villain whenever the *Times* stoops to partisanship. I can never quarrel with the *Times* for criticizing Roosevelt's procedure and opposing his re-election. I can and did quarrel with the *Times* for being less candid about Mr. Willkie and I further think its editing of the campaign news was less impartial than in the storms of the 1912 campaign, when the editorial page was against Teddy Roosevelt but the news department gave him the best break he got anywhere in the country. What do you yourself think of keeping the Gallup Poll well hidden except when it would be a comfort to the Willkie-ites? And what do you think of the *Times* when it honors as front page news the basely exploited episode of Steve Early and the Negro policeman, with Master Dewey threatening to investigate and all that discreditable nonsense?

It seems to me that when the *Times* becomes partisan, then its responsible head becomes a fair target. Or it did so seem to me when I spoke at Carnegie Hall on Monday night. Whether, after a year's reflection, my judgment will still approve the course I then took I cannot tell. I wonder if you yourself, a year from now, will think that the *Times* did well in the past election. If after that interval you are willing to tell me, I shall regard the communication as confidential. In the meantime, I should like to say that I envy you your job and think that for the most part you have done it magnificently. I have been watching with a greater interest than you would have any reason to suspect. . . .

This was Aleck the combatant. Aleck the radio personality

was combatant, too. He appeared on DuPont's "Cavalcade of America" in a program which featured the "Battle Hymn of the Republic," and Aleck as master of ceremonies, and he directed the program into a salute to militant patriotism. "It was absolutely beautiful," wired Robert Sherwood. He broadcast on a Canadian Broadcasting Company program, and urged sending "ships and destroyers and planes and pilots" to Great Britain to fight against the fascists, "but no more words."

Aleck was certain that he was dying, he called himself a "dying newspaperman," but he was preparing to go out, in defiance to T. S. Eliot's poem, with a bang rather than a whimper.

XXX

ALECK WAS DETERMINED to get into the war, somehow. He was too old for service in any official capacity and his heart attack ruled him out. Yet he wanted to go to England and to help the war effort in which he believed.

At first it seemed there was no way to get there. So Aleck bided his time. He joined E. B. White and others in fighting against what he considered to be the cancerous America First Committee, and he attacked Charles A. Lindbergh, who was making speeches against American involvement in the European war. His was no half-hearted attack, nor any exhibition of personal spleen, but a statement of conviction, given in the strongest radio broadcast he ever made, on May 25, 1941, six months before the United States was forced into the war:

> All over this country there is a great murmur of voices. Confabs from countless cracker-barrels. Talk under many an evening lamp. Men and women, old and young, rich and poor, wise and foolish, all talking freely about the war. How long will it last? How will it turn out? Are we in it now? Can we stay out of it? Listen and you will hear something as unmistakable as the footfalls of fate. The historic sound of the American people making up its mind.
>
> To that discussion I feel I must add my two cents worth. . . . It is my guess that most people in this country have it quite clear in their minds what this war is about. The people of Germany, always strong in their conviction that they are a master race and now in the grip of an armed gang, headed by an able and murderous adventurer named Adolf Hitler, have set out to take command of the world. The war is being fought to decide whether or not

they will get away with it. Leading in the fight to stop Hitler in his tracks are the people of the British Commonwealth of Nations. To them, when he took command, Winston Churchill offered blood and tears and toil and sweat. He brought them one thing more. Self respect! That is an imponderable by-product but it strikes me as important and enviable. Enviable? Well, if you want to know just where you *do* stand in this whole matter, ask yourself one question. Which would you rather be right now—an Englishman in England or a Frenchman in France?

From the outbreak of this war the sympathies of America were immediate and almost unanimous. There was never any question about that. The people of this country had got Hitler's number right at the start. From the first, by an overwhelming majority and as evidence of their natural inclination toward fundamental decency, they were against him. I suppose that the history of this nightmare year will someday be written by an American who at this moment is lying in a cradle pensively sucking his thumb. Unless in his prime all expression in this country is dictated, there is no reason why his work should not be honest and, if so, I hope he makes it quite clear that the immediate opposition to Hitler which developed in this country was not achieved by British propaganda. It was achieved by German propaganda. We knew all about Hitler but our sources were original. Our notion that a world dominated by him would be unfit to live in comes from his own words, his own declared intentions, his own acts as reported to us in accounts O.K.'ed by his own censors. From the first, we knew he was an enemy and if we are not at war with him right now, it is not because of any obstruction put in the way by the isolationist senators, nor because we Americans are—as we are so often inaccurately described—a peace-loving people. If we are not officially at war with Hitler today it is for one reason. It is because, as things stand right now but may not stand for long—he cannot get at us.

Yes, we the people were immediately and properly partisan in this war. And when, in the slow processes of democracy that judgment found political expression, we guaranteed the beleaguered English our full material support. By the pledges of both candidates in the last election, by the testimony of every poll yet taken by Dr. Gallup, by the action of our representatives in Congress and of the President himself, we pledged full aid to England. Ex-Colonel Charles A. Lindbergh now urges that this assistance be withdrawn. He wants us to break our promise in the matter, to run out on the British and, so curious is his mentality, he thinks to encourage us in such base desertion by assuring us that England is going to be defeated. On this point he may be right. I would not know about that. Neither would he. If the words of our retired eagle ever reach as far as England, Mr. Churchill must derive some comfort from his knowledge that all fighters in a tight place have heard such talk since the world began. Among Washington's discomforts during the long winter at Valley Forge was the repeated prediction from the Lindberghs of his day that he didn't have a chance. Yes, Lindbergh keeps announcing the doom of England and always his statement is received with cheers and bursts of applause. This gives you a rough idea of what kind of people bulk large in his mass-meetings.

For here is a fact which Lindbergh and his colleagues of the America First Committee, must face. Whether they admit it or not, whether they like it or not, whether, indeed, that is any part of their purpose, they are working for Hitler. Have you any doubt—any doubt at *all*—that Hitler would have been glad to pay Lindbergh an immense amount—millions—for the work he has done in the past year?

Indeed, if Lindbergh shares the opinion of Hitler held by the rest of us—on this point, to be sure, he has thus far been ominously silent—his heart must skip a beat when, in the still watches of the night, he realizes that if he *had* returned to this country as Hitler's paid and trusted agent, his public activity would have been in every particular just what it has been to date.

Now, don't get me wrong about this. I doubt that Lindbergh has taken or would take German money. It so happens that we do not know, and, thanks to the reticence of General Wood, have been unable to find out just who *has* put up all the money for the costly goings-on of the America First Committee. But I should be greatly surprised to learn that any considerable part of that money came directly or indirectly from Hitler. That does not alter the fact that they are all working for him. For they, like all the rest of us, are trapped in a tragic irony. In this world today there is no such thing as neutrality. You are either for Hitler or against him. You either fight him or you help him.

All of which is important but not fundamental. Even though the America First Committee is being cheered on and helped by some of the most vicious people in this country, even though much of what has been said by its principal speakers strikes *me* as fraudulent and poisonous nonsense, its fundamental argument can be and has been advanced by some honorable men and women—the argument that in the long run the prospect of the good life in America will best be served if we try to make this continent a fortress and retire inside it. To make sense, they must assume that even with Hitler in command of the Atlantic and in cahoots with Japan, we'll be left unmolested to build that fortress. If they really think that, they do not live in America at all. They are already in Paradise—a fool's paradise.

But even if the America First Committee can fairly be described as a Fifth Column, the really dangerous one is the Fifth Column that is in your heart and mine—the Fifth Column that is in all part-time citizens, in each of us who would so like to go our pleasant ways and pretend all this is no affair of ours. Why should we be bothered? Business as usual. Pleasure as usual. Look into your heart and see.

Preoccupied as he was with the war, Aleck still took time out to do something he had long wanted to do: play the part of the chorus in *Yellow Jacket,* that play he had so enjoyed when it came to Broadway in his youthful days as critic. He wore a mandarin gown and a skullcap, and he read and addressed the audience telling them the action, while Harpo Marx cavorted about the stage as the prop man. They played at

Marblehead, Massachusetts, that summer to capacity audiences.

Aleck was occupied with his usual run of work, criticizing books and plays in magazines. He devised a President's Crime Shelf of detective stories for Mr. Roosevelt. He helped Friend John T. Winterich when he wanted a job with the Library of Congress, since Friend Archibald MacLeish was librarian.

He was friendly with Kenneth Roberts, but when Roberts wrote *Oliver Wiswell,* a novel about the Tory side of the American revolution, Aleck took exception to some of the promotional efforts of Doubleday Page and Co. in a letter to Nelson Doubleday:

> There has been sticking in my crop for several days the notion that I, presumably one of many, should send you a word of protest about an advertisement of *Oliver Wiswell* which I saw in the *Times,* on the daily book-page, a week or so ago. I refer to the one in which that curious piece of fiction was blandly presented by your publishing house as the long suppressed historical truth which had been "banned" from our text books. Of course you and I know that this is—if I may reach for the *mot juste*—horse-shit.
>
> Kenneth's new and retroactive Toryism is an interesting psychiatric case. His own state of mind enabled him to write, with passionate conviction, a good story of the American Revolution from the Tory point of view. It is about as faithful a *history* of the Revolution as would be an account of the last eight years in the White House written by Alice Longworth. You were right and lucky to publish *Oliver Wiswell* but for your firm to adopt and endorse the viewpoint of its protagonist in your effort to sell copies of the book strikes me as nothing short of degrading and shameful.
>
> Trusting that you have long since crapped all over the dimwit responsible, I beg to remain. . . .

In the summer Aleck began negotiating with the British

Broadcasting Company and the British Ministry of Information to do a series of broadcasts *in* England about American affairs. In the autumn, plans completed, he boarded the British destroyer, *HMS Resolution*, at Philadelphia, laden with lipsticks, canned bacon, silk stockings, razor blades, soap and other items of which his English friends were in short supply after two years of battle. After twenty-one days at sea they reached England, and he went to the Dorchester Hotel in London. He visited many friends. He spent one evening with Rebecca West and her husband, and their mad cook who tried to get the house blitzed by leaving all the blackout curtains undone.

In England Aleck made half a dozen radio talks, on Julia Ward Howe, on Oliver Wendell Holmes, the younger, on Benedict Arnold and on Stephen Foster. Brendan Bracken, British Minister of Information, wired him praise. He received hundreds of letters from his British friends and from plain people who had enjoyed his words and who were inspired by them and by the feeling that America would come to help Britain in her hour of need. He saw Winston Churchill for a few moments, which, for Aleck, made his trip worthwhile. Bernard Shaw, an aging but ageless Shaw, met with Aleck, an ageless but aging Woollcott. He came home by way of Lisbon (air) and then New York (American Export Lines). The journey had been exhausting but Aleck never felt better about any effort he had made. He had not earned a penny while doing it. This was one of his efforts for the cause he believed to be mutual between Americans and Britons, months before others came to that same conclusion.

Home again, Aleck turned his hand to earning a living, to keep up his charities and good works. Dr. Al Getman, his physician, had died; Aleck arranged to send the doctor's son to prep school. But this took money and he agreed with DeWitt Wallace to write what he openly called Twice Told Tales—resurrections of old stories and legends done in pure Woollcottian prose. These tales were extremely successful, even more successful than a series in 1940 called "Lessons in English," in which Aleck called attention to common errors in writing, both professional and private. DeWitt Wallace said the tales were "classic," and he wrote enthusiastically, enclosing checks for $2,000, enough to warm any writer's heart. That year, 1942, Aleck became a roving editor of the *Digest,* with a guarantee of $24,000 a year for an article a month.

He was toying with the idea of another Woollcott Reader. The second reader, much like the popular first one, had been brought out in 1937, and, like the first, it had represented Aleck's enthusiasms; from Dorothy Parker to Gustav Eckstein. Yet Aleck, as astute a self-critic as ever existed, felt that the second reader was something short of the first in quality, and he hesitated to do a third. In the last few months of his life he did make plans to edit a new anthology, for which he would receive no royalties, to be entitled *As You Were*—addressed to the American serviceman. In this connection he sent letters to hundreds of friends, calling on them to nominate selections for the table of contents. Then, by the process of selection, aided by his own prejudices, he would complete the job.

Aleck was also involved this year with Clifton Fadiman, Sinclair Lewis, and Carl Van Doren as a judge or leading figure in the Reader's Club. This board selected books of classic interest to be published in cheap editions.

Aleck did not realize how much strain the trip to Europe had put on his heart, and he tried to return to his old level of activity, writing, reading, seeing people by the day and by the hour. He had, for several years, made the Gotham Hotel his headquarters, and his suite there was always filled with people—even now when he had been cautioned against overdoing.

The overdoing was his undoing. In February he was talking to officials of the Blue Network about returning to the air as the Town Crier. He had agreed to do a Dickens broadcast for Christmas time, reading *A Christmas Carol* over the air. In March he was again flat on his back in the Good Shepherd Hospital in Syracuse, with another heart attack. This time even Aleck was convinced that he must take it easier, and when he came out of the hospital he cut down on his activities. He canceled his plans for a radio series. He gave up the idea of war work. Lucy Drage came from Kansas City to help nurse him; she and Dorothy Parker spent much time with him, amusing him, playing word games and card games and putting up with his bad disposition.

Aleck's will to live was sadly worn. He was bitter and dispirited and he so indicated to others. He told Sam Adams that he did not think life was worth the effort.

He resigned from the board of trustees of Hamilton College—a certain indication of his own feelings of inadequacy and a personal recognition of his perilous state of health.

By late spring, 1942, Aleck was better, but then his gallbladder began to trouble him, and he went to Peter Bent Brigham Hospital in Boston for its removal. He was not at all sure he would live; he was petulant about the operation, checked into the hospital and then left again, appearing at Jo Hennessey's Boston hotel late in the evening and demanding that his assistant find a suite of rooms for him. It was impossible; Aleck had to content himself with a room; and he did. The reason for his leaving the hospital was not pique—he insisted on seeing Charlie Chaplin's latest film, *The Gold Rush,* because out of gratitude for all Aleck had done to further his career over the years, the film was dedicated by Chaplin to Woollcott. Aleck was touched.

Messages for Aleck clotted the hospital switchboard and flowers and presents filled the halls. Letters came in for him by the dozens. Seldom, it seemed, was there a man so beloved—was there ever one of such sharp tongue so beloved in history? Aleck was annoyed by all the attention: he did not like to have his friends peering at his incision, so to speak, and he blamed Frode Jensen for letting people know where he was and what had happened to him. He was partly right, but only partly; Jensen could not resist the pressure brought on him by Aleck's friends.

By the end of June Aleck was sufficiently improved in health and disposition that he looked upon the world with more of his old zeal for life. "There is a real chance," he wrote Clifton Fadiman on June 30, "that I shall not only be up and about again in the fall but in considerably better health than I have known in several years."

The doctors did not agree. Aleck let them have their say, and then he compromised with them: He said that he would spend the summer quietly at the island, recovering his strength. Then (he said privately), he was going to go back to his old pace of life, quite confident that it would probably kill him. But he would not live out his string of years as a semi-invalid. Having made that vital choice, Aleck did improve rapidly, both in spirit and in health.

Much of Aleck's world was passing away. Neysa McMein had fallen one night while arising to get a glass of water and had broken her back. She had recovered. (Aleck had gone to New York earlier in the year and spent some of his recuperative time in the Baragwanath apartment, where he and Neysa ran a salon, one day receiving twenty-seven callers.) Neysa came to the island, and the two invalids spent many happy hours together, until one day Aleck insisted on going on a long drive to see the fall greenery. Neysa's back gave out on the trip, they quarreled, and she left the island, telling him they must not be together for some time. Aleck, recognizing one of the symptoms of his disease (irritability) was contrite and sorry, but it was too late: neither had long to live, they would never again set eyes on one another.

Alice Duer Miller had been ill for some months, and in August, she wrote Aleck that she was dying, swearing him to secrecy. Aleck told no one except Harpo Marx. He felt that Harpo had a right to know, telegraphed him, and Harpo went to see Alice Miller, to spend one last comforting day with her in the hospital.

So Aleck's world was slipping away. Just as buildings came down in New York City, just as the old Round Table had gone from the Algonquin, as the Thanatopsis and Inside Straight Club had died out, so Aleck's world was vanishing. There *was* still a spark. He decided he would have a rickshaw to cart him around the island, to save his heart and breath in a grandiose way. So Jo Hennessey was set to search for one, advertising in Chicago and elsewhere. Finally, after a nationwide hunt one rickshaw was found—in a Vermont barn. It was brought to Neshobe, where it proved to be too heavy for use, except as a conversation piece.

Aleck had not been much of a family man, but now he took his brother's family to his bosom. He kept in touch with Barbara, Nancy and Joan Woollcott, and sent frequent checks, to support their college educations or to help with their young marriages.

His old friend Edward Sheldon, the playwright, sent Aleck a number of carrier pigeons bearing the unlikely names of Ham, Eggs, Snooky, Juliet, Jack and Jill, with instructions on breeding and care. Aleck took up the hobby with some interest but only for a time.

In the spring, when Aleck seemed likely to die, or so he believed, he decided to put all his affairs in order. One thing he wished to do was end the bickering with Ross, and he wrote to him on April 18:

> Dear Ross:
>
> I've tried by tender and conscientious nursing to keep my grudge against you alive, but I find it has died on me. In the matter of that chuckle-headed pathetically unsuccessful lawbreaker, Sergeant Bailey, I still think that you were incredibly cruel in intention and a liar after the event; but it dawns on me a little late that, like most people I know, I, too, have been both cruel and dishonest at one time or another in my life. Anyway, what of it?
>
> Perhaps in this somewhat abusive letter of reconciliation I ought also to tell you, in case our paths should ever cross again, that the next time you get drunk and start pawing me in public or in private, I shall again reach for the nearest available weapon—a glass of vitriol perhaps—in an effort to induce you not to continue a practice I find enraging.
>
> I was actually sorry to hear you've been sick. Give my love to Frances. . . .
>
> Your former companion-in-arms.

Ross replied:

> Dear Alec:
>
> I am late in writing this because I have been in Washington for three days where I not only had no typewriter or other writing facilities but barely more than half a room. They are now putting two in a room down there, to speed up the war, and I saved myself from a roommate only by registering "and wife," although my wife is in California. In the event that your alert mind instantly turns this into

a blackmail opportunity, I will report that I have already advised the lady, and while I may not be believed entirely, further notification would be anticlimactic. I went down to see my daughter but also saw a number of people I craved to see, including Winterich and Giegengach, who I would report are unchanged as far as I can see and are great men. Winterich is working hard in his academic way, seriously, but amused at it. Giegie is public printer, having the largest patronage roll in Washington. This was undoubtedly to be expected. He has doubled the government printing office space and equipment and replaced all the old equipment, employs 8,000 people, and has six automobiles at his personal disposal. He was able to transport me around town as of old. Winterich travels by street car and, in fact, Frank Murphy, of the Supreme Court, does too, but not Giegie or his friends. Giegie spent an evening telling me the fun he has with congressmen and MacLeish, who wants things immediately because the President wants it printed. The printing office uses twenty tons of paper a day, printing mostly crap.

As I said in a telegram which I assume you have received, I'd rather have got that letter from you than anything else I can think of, except possibly full restitution by the Guaranty Trust Company, which recently allowed me to be forged out of all my worldly cash and securities [by an employee]. I have Lloyd Stryker on that case but will probably get nowhere. I don't give a damn, really, and, as a matter of fact, am able to get a big laugh out of the new tax proposals of Roosevelt, which will cut everybody in the world down to about my size. I chuckle when I think of Fleischmann, Jane Grant, etc. As to the Bailey business, to change the subject in the middle of a paragraph, I want to say just a few words and then never any more. I was brought into consultation when he got that job in Chicago, by an old employer of mine who knew much about Bailey through having been involved in the efforts to spring him from San Quentin. Gibbs and I thought that Bailey had been completely protected in his piece (which turned out to be the case) but as a precaution I called my old employer and asked him what would happen if Bailey should be suspected as the hero of Gibbs's piece. The o.e. was amazed that I'd called him. "Nothing would happen," he said, "What is one more ex-convict on the Chicago *American.*" In just those words. I'm always getting blamed for things I certainly didn't write and didn't have much to do with. Gibbs is almost as jealous of his pieces as you are, and either of you would tear an editor to pieces and not think about it twice. That Bailey story got to be a classic and I'd heard it dozens of times from the raconteurs: it was in the public domain if anything ever was.

I should like to visit you if you want me to. I am having dinner tonight with Silberberg, who says he has a letter from you inviting him up. I could go up with him sometime, or otherwise. My ulcers raised hell but are quiescent at the moment. I made Washington and back without complications, and probably could travel more. I haven't had a drink in 16 months, although I smoke, which is worse, theoretically. If you're in a position to be called on, let me know—and in a mood. One anecdote and I will close. I always told Aunt Fon an anecdote in conclusion. Time, the magazine, called up the other day to ask about the *Stars and Stripes* and I (who probably should never cast a stone) said that a piece they'd had on the S&S the week before had mistakes in it. The lady researcher (who was doing the telephoning) jumped me for details. I said Adams and Rice weren't privates, etc., and where did Time get the dope that Harpo Marx was on the staff? She said Harpo had told Time he was on the staff and that Who's Who said so. By God, Harpo has got it in there, evidently. I meant to look it up but forgot. If so, his gag is ruined so far as Time is concerned. There is much talk of a new S&S. I am going to a dinner to mark the appearance of the new one, or of "Yank" I think they are going to call it. They are going to print in New York and distribute it all over the world. This would take two Waldoes, and I don't think God ever made more than one.

Much good will and many good wishes. . . .

By this time, wasted by his disease (he was down to 160 pounds), Aleck's temper was so uncertain that he took offense where none was meant:

Dear Ross:

I got your telegram and the letter which slowly followed it and they open up a chance to say something forgetfully omitted from what I had thought, not without good reason, might be my last communication with you. That is about the *New Yorker*. It is, it seems to me, the best editorial accomplishment that had taken place in this country in my lifetime. It does err, I suppose, from that form of monotony which you yourself foresaw and predicted as long ago as when we were both in West 47th Street. I seldom miss a copy and I read it from cover to cover more nearly than I do any other publication. I always thought that you contributed more than any other single person to the success and flavor of the *Stars and Stripes* and I don't see how the credit for the *New Yorker* can go to anyone else. It was one of the more comical sequels of that Profile you did of me that the Lunts have never bought a copy since. When you have printed an especially good piece, I cut it out and send it to them.

In your letter to me you say "I should like to visit you if you want me to." My answer has to be that I don't. This is because of an earlier sentence of yours "As to the Bailey business, I want to say just a few words and then never any more." Only the Hitlers of this world can issue their own statements on a controversial matter and then order the subject closed. There are, I suspect, a good many things about the story of that particular Profile which I do not know. I am absolutely sure that there are certain things about it which you don't know, in the course of which there was considerable lying, treachery, and cruelty. For how much of this you were responsible and how much Gibbs I am not sure, but, as long as I live, I could never talk across a dinner table with you or even play a game of cribbage without wondering.

I have, as you probably know, a reason for wanting to put my house in order. I obeyed the impulse to let you know that all the warmth had gone out of the grudge I held against you and that there was no reason why we should ever meet without an exchange of friendly greeting. We once had a friendship which was in many ways unique in my life and which I both cherished and enjoyed. Perhaps the rupture of such a relationship can never be healed, but certainly it could not be attempted in our case until after the whole issue between us had been thrashed out to its last detail. I should not enjoy such a parley any more than you would, but it is a necessary operation. So never come here without bringing a copy of that first instalment with you together with any correspondence you think of as supporting your side of the argument. Your loving friends used to send me letters you wrote on the subject and in one of them I remember your giving it out that I was really wounded by the whole Profile and merely hung my displeasure on the Bailey incident. As far as I know, that was untrue. Certainly I can recall no complaint against the second instalment and I never read the third.

Having named the terms on which I would be glad to have you visit me, I don't expect you to come at all, but, in case I have underrated your desire to see me, I suggest that you wire when the time comes and find out if I am here. The doctors are even now (please tell this to no one, even Winchell) in consultation on a matter which might remove me from this refuge for a considerable time.

You may recall that you bade Gibbs speed up his work on this contribution because I was due back on the staff in about three months and you couldn't print Profiles about members of the staff. For the first time I have a twinge of regret that he succeeded in his intentions. I have never lost the account of his war adventures which Giegengack dictated to a *Stars and Stripes* stenographer. I have just been re-reading it and it would make a honey of a Profile for the *New Yorker*. I trust you will not be rat enough to order a Profile of Giegengack done at once.

It was a touching letter, filled with love and recrimination; a true specimen of Aleck's soul. He could not bear to say he was wrong or sorry, yet he heaped praise on Ross's head for his professional accomplishments. Ross recognized this, obviously:

Dear Alec:

I didn't mean my remarks in the Bailey matter to read that way. The implication was probably due to hastiness. I have been so God damned rushed lately that I haven't had time to do things carefully or even spare myself as is expected of one with ulcers. I hesitated to mention Bailey in the letter at all, under the circumstances, but I had wanted for years to put in that brief explanation. I intended a tone of apology for doing so but apparently failed in this subtlety.

I am willing to answer any questions you should want to ask about Bailey or any other person or subject in the first part of the profile, or any of the rest of the parts, for that matter. In fact, I'd rather like to state my case. Much time has passed, of course, and my magnificent memory isn't what it was, but I stand ready to do what I can. The fact is I regarded myself as having very little to do with the project, and I didn't have. As I recall it, I deplored the whole undertaking when Gibbs first proposed it and I know that when it got under way my viewpoint was that it was an undertaking between you and Gibbs.

I will write you further later, being swamped at the moment. I should like very much to see you, and am willing to answer any questions that might remove from your mind the points you wonder about. One thing: I can recall no imposition of secrecy that I am under regarding any element of the piece. I am willing to explain anything I know about, and I can deny knowledge of things I don't know about with a clear eye and a clear conscience.

Sincerely yours,
H.W. Ross

Alec:—As to Giegengack, I won't do anything to interfere with your plans for a piece, and I am unselfish enough to hope you do it, whoever it is for, I have always thought you ought to write it.

R.

So it was arranged that Ross would come to the island to see Aleck.

> Dear Alec:
>
> I have your letter and will take steps to come up as soon as I can get in the clear. I am up to my nipples in hot water, what with half of the staff going off to war, a limitation of fifty-seven gallons of gasoline for six weeks, the Holy Name demanding that we stop printing "son-of-a-bitch," and so on. This war is much harder on me than the last one. I don't know how to get to Vermont, or to the Lake after I get there, but will take this matter up later. I am very anxious to see you.
>
> Sincerely,
> H.W. Ross
>
> Have a note from Alice M. up there. I will try to make it, but I don't see how I can.
>
> R.

Then came Aleck's second illness of the year, followed by Ross's own illness, and slow recuperation. Once Ross started for Bomoseen, but got only as far as Saratoga. It was arranged that the old friends would meet again in New York during the winter to resolve their differences. Resolve them? They were already resolved in the correspondence that continued all summer. The two sick ones would simply get together and comfort one another with reminiscences. And the last of this correspondence, in October, left it that way.

Much of the last few months of Aleck's life was spent in the mending of fences and the strengthening of old ties. He was not able to do too much, but he did what he could for the war effort in which he believed. In November he came to New York to make a broadcast for the Stage Door Canteen. Lucy Drage wrote of him at this time:

> . . . Aleck loved me and had exaggerated ideas of my qualities. In those last days when I was with him at Lake Bomoseen, Dorothy Parker and Jo Hennessey came every day from their homes on the mainland. We played anagrams and after bearing with me for some time Aleck would say, "Why Lucy, you are so stupid, anybody could guess your

thoughts." Everybody would laugh and I would retire to my needlepoint.

That was one Aleck, the friend. There was another Aleck, the one about whom Bennet Cerf was to write later:

> He fought with no holds barred for the things he believed in, although he could become as much aroused in a defense of Minnie Maddern Fiske as for an all-out campaign against fascism. He truly loved the theatre and his unbounded enthusiasm helped some really good plays to catch on with the public. He turned several books into best-sellers single-handed, although a summary of the titles reveals all too clearly a taste that was most erratic, if not downright over-sentimental and second-rate. (A few of his more violent enthusiasms: *Beside the Bonnie Briar Bush, The Chicken Wagon Family, Lost Horizon, Goodbye, Mr. Chips.*)
>
> One of the prerequisites for his idea of a masterpiece was its discovery by himself. A new play or book that was recommended by somebody else was usually doomed in advance. When he raved about something and the whole world did not echo his sentiment, Woollcott became truly convinced he had discovered a classic and embarked upon a crusade that stopped at nothing. . . .
>
> Woollcott's manners, atrocious to begin with, became progressively worse when he discovered how much people were willing to take from a great celebrity. *The Man Who Came to Dinner* crystallized and enhanced the Woollcott myth a hundred fold; it turned his insults into high comedy, and undoubtedly prevented his being socked in the jaw at least twice a week. His closest friends forgave him his rudeness, his bad sportsmanship, his failure to understand the very fundamentals of fair play. True, Harpo Marx dubbed him "just a big dreamer with a remarkable sense of double-entry bookkeeping." Noel Coward addressed him as "Little Nell of Old Dreary." Robert Benchley called him "Louisa M. Woollcott." To George Jean Nathan he was the "Seidlitz Powder of Times Square." Charlie Brackett swore that he wouldn't even talk to a man who wouldn't make a good magazine article; Heywood Broun added that

an exception might be made for sycophantic souls who would play ghost to his Hamlet—and *never* step out of character. Edna Ferber averred that he was just "a New Jersey Nero who mistook his pinafore for a toga."

* * *

One evening I brought to a dinner party a lovely young lady whose aunt and uncle are both well-known California novelists. Woollcott was playing cribbage with Alice Duer Miller, and couldn't be bothered with rising from his seat. He inspected her coolly, however, and deigned to remark, "I know your aunt and uncle, of course. Your aunt is a splendid woman. Your uncle is an obscenity." (I borrow here a Hemingway device to indicate a four letter word that is not used in family magazines.) The young lady won my heart by replying, "My definition of that word, Mr. Woollcott, is a man who uses it to a lady he is meeting for the first time!" I'll say for Woollcott that he threw back his head and roared with approving laughter.

An observer and acquaintance with the prescience of a philosopher, Edmund Wilson, was the only one among Aleck's many friends and acquaintances who ever seemed to put the two Aleck Woollcotts together in the same room. Wilson and Aleck went back a very long way, and because of it Wilson understood Aleck, with all his warts, better than any of Aleck's close friends. He was to write this:

I knew Woollcott only slightly, but my relations with him were based on an aspect of him which may not have been very well known. He was born at the North American Phalanx near Red Bank. The North American Phalanx was one of the longest-lived of the socialist communities that flourished in the middle of the last century, and Woollcott's grandfather was for many years the head of it. My family knew all his family, and my grandfather, who was a doctor at Eatontown, brought Woollcott into the world.

When I first came to New York and met Woollcott, I did not connect him with the Woollcotts of Red Bank or the curious old Fourierist building, half barracks and half hotel, to which I had been taken to call as a child. At that time, when I had just started working in the office of *Vanity Fair,* to which he was a distinguished contributor, I saw his more crinaceous side. I provoked him to ferocity one day by asking him who the Father Duffy was to whom he was in the habit of referring as if he were the Apostle Paul. I had spent a year and a half in France during the war but had never happened to hear of Father Duffy; and I had not grasped the fact that Woollcott had created for himself a calendar of saints whose glory must not be questioned.

But one day at the Algonquin he asked me whether I was the son of lawyer Wilson of Red Bank, and we talked about the Phalanx.

One day I met him in the West Forties somewhere between Fifth Avenue and Broadway. He was going very fast, but stopped a second and said brusquely, "I'm having a play produced!" I asked him what it was called. "*The Crime in the Whistler Room,*" he snapped and passed on. *The Crime in the Whistler Room* had been the title of my play at the Provincetown. Later on, when I published a study of Kipling, he wrote me several long letters on the subject, about which he had some sober and shrewd ideas. I had also, however, been writing about Dickens and praising his gloomy later novels; and this elicited from Alec a sulky "I do not care to discuss Dickens with you." He did, nevertheless, indicate his preferences; and I could see him as a child in the phalanstery lying in the hammock on a summer day with *Pickwick* or *David Copperfield.* His point of view was perfectly infantile. It turned out that he did not like *Bleak House* simply because it was the only one he had not read as a child.

In the meantime, however, in the years of the depression, I had had with him a curious interview. I had been traveling around the country doing articles on labor and economic conditions, and he wrote me that he had been reading these articles and said he would like to talk to me. I invited him to dinner with us, but he replied that he was a much older man than I and that I ought to come to him. So I called on him at Sutton Place, where he occupied a splendid apartment that looked out on the East River. As soon as I entered the room, he cried out, without any other greeting: "You've gotten very fat!" It was his way of disarming, I thought, any horror I might have felt at his own pudding-like rotundity, which had trebled since I had seen him last. He did not rise and was wearing a dressing-gown, so I inquired whether he had been ill. He answered shortly, no; and wanted to know whether I thought he was ill because he was wearing a dressing-gown. There were other guests, and they kept coming and going. Drinks were brought—by a butler: Woollcott never stirred from his chair; and there was a backgammon board, at which people were playing. A secretary in a room beyond was typing an article for him; and he would rap out from time to time peremptory orders to the butler, who was feeding a phonograph in a neighboring room with Gilbert and Sullivan records.

He made no attempt to talk to me, and I wondered why he had wanted to see me. At last there came a moment, however, when all the guests had gone and there was nobody but him and me. His demeanor changed entirely. He began to speak naturally and frankly: a note of uncertainty came into his voice, and a look of distressful anxiety tightened his brows above his spectacles. He asked me about the Communist movement in America. I told him a little, and he went on to talk about the North American Phalanx—on which he had been collecting material and about which he meant some day to write. He said that he had always known that labor was going to be the great force in the modern world; and he told me about the Labor Day rites at the Phalanx over which his grandfather had presided. He said that the kind of thing I had been doing was the kind of thing he should like to do: he should like to go around the country and see what was going on—he had friends in the West and the South whom it would be easy for him to visit; and the only thing that had prevented him from doing so was the fact that, reduced as his income was, he had difficulty in finding a chauffeur who could also do dictation and typing.

Then another batch of guests came in, and Woollcott resumed his role in the theatrical-journalistic New York world in which he was both a "personality" of print and a "star" in an eccentric part. I wasn't sure that anybody but me could recognize in his anagrams and croquet, his Dickens and Gilbert and Sullivan, his idealization of stage reputations like the Barrymores and Mrs. Fiske, and his general wide-eyed excitement of the semi-suburban Jerseyman over all that was going on in New York—could recognize in this the persistence of the atmosphere and the habits of an old-fashioned country life with which I was familiar from my childhood, but which seemed quite exotic, almost perverse, in the modern New York of the thirties.

Both Alecks came to New York that winter to stay. Early in January Aleck agreed to appear on a round table discussion of the tenth year of Hitlerism in Germany over the CBS network. On January 23, the day of the program, he lunched with Mr. and Mrs. DeWitt Wallace, and later in the day made sure that a large bouquet of flowers was sent to Mrs. Wallace. Late in the afternoon he left the Gotham. Jo Hennessey, who had accompanied him down from the island went out to dinner, for it was understood that Aleck would not need him that night, since he was going to dine at the CBS executive dining rooms and then appear on the program.

Aleck went to the CBS building at 485 Madison, and in the dining room joined Harry D. Gideonse, president of Brooklyn College, Marcia Davenport, the novelist, Rex Stout, the mystery writer who was chairman of the Writers War Board, and Dr. George N. Shuster, president of Hunter College. After drinks and dinner, they adjourned to the studios and the program began.

There Aleck exhibited what the *New Yorker* called "his famous ability to coil and strike." Germany, he said, deserved Hitler just as much as Chicago deserved the Chicago *Tribune*. He chose that simile because the *Tribune* had been so inimical to his hero, Franklin Roosevelt, and his friend, Mrs. Roosevelt, and had fought the entrance of the United States into the war in which Aleck believed.

That was nearly his last statement. Fifteen minutes after the broadcast began Aleck scribbled on a piece of paper a message, and passed it to Gideonse. "I'm feeling sick," it said. Then he slumped before the microphone. Gideonse helped him out into the hall, and to a sofa, where he lay down. Dr. Edmund Devol, his old friend Eddie from the days of Base Hospital No. 8, was called and came.

"I am dying," Aleck said. And although he was taken to a hospital and treated with all the science of medicine, Aleck's last words brooked no argument. Within a few hours he was dead.

NOTES

CHAPTER I

The references to the reception of the play *The Man Who Came to Dinner* come from the files of the New York *Times* and the New York *Herald Tribune* in the autumn of 1939. References to the thoughts of Edward Sheldon and others come from the correspondence in Harvard's Houghton Library.

CHAPTER II

The Frode Jensen story comes from conversations with Joseph Hennessey, for many years Alexander Woollcott's manager and companion, and from Jensen's correspondence with Woollcott, as preserved at Houghton Library. Parts of it also come from correspondence with Dr. Al Getman, Mrs. Eleanor Roosevelt, and others. The report of the memorial service after Woollcott's death comes from the files of the New York *Times;* the tale of the burial of his remains from Professor Robert Rudd of Hamilton College. The story of Fourierism comes from the Stewart Holbrook book *Dreamers of the American Dream,* from the *Encyclopaedia Britannica,* from the writing of Edmund Wilson in the *New Yorker* and the *Nation* after Woollcott's death, and from the Samuel Hopkins Adams biography of Alexander Woollcott. Certain portions are also fully detailed in several of Aleck's letters to friends, especially to Laura Richards. Some recollections of his early life are from a letter from Lucy Drage, girlhood friend of Aleck's sister Julie, others in various letters written much later in life.

CHAPTERS III, IV, V

The study of Aleck's college years comes from several sources. Samuel Hopkins Adams knew Aleck then. Adams was a recent and successful graduate of Hamilton who had made a name for himself as first newspaper and then magazine reporter. When Aleck was in school Adams was involved in the muckraking of the early years of the twentieth century, and Aleck looked up to him, and also admired him from afar.

Part of the information about Aleck's school days is from a conversation with Robert Rudd, part from a letter from C. Mossman McLean, an upstate New York businessman in the 1960's. Other parts are contained in letters, either in the possession of Harvard University, or those lent to Joseph Hennessey and Beatrice Kaufman for their collection of Woollcott's letters, which was published by Viking Press. The note about Woollcott's education, college course by course, comes from the records of Hamilton College. The files of the Hamilton literary magazine, "The Lit," contain a large number of contributions from Aleck. The tales of the Charlatans come largely from Aleck's own later reminiscences in letters and in articles, and from Robert Rudd.

CHAPTER VI

Sources for the tales of Aleck's college peccadilloes were C. Mossman McLean, Robert Rudd, and the Adams biography, the Hamilton College records, the files of the Hamilton *Literary Monthly*, and Aleck's own later reminiscences.

CHAPTER VII

Aleck's problems with the mumps were described thoroughly by Samuel Hopkins Adams and were alluded to from time to time by Aleck in correspondence with relatives and friends. The tale of his tribulations as a police reporter comes from a magazine article Aleck later wrote about some of his more harrowing moments. The story of his adventures in Coatesville, Pennsylvania, comes from the files of the *Times*, and from a letter written to him years later by Walter Davenport, later editor of *Collier's*.

CHAPTER VIII

The story of Aleck's rise to fame, if not fortune, as drama critic of the New York *Times*, is from the Adams biography, from Aleck's own correspondence, gleaned here and there, and from the pages of the *Times.* The struggle with the Shuberts was delineated in the *Times* for all to see. The incident concerning William Winter was recounted in a letter from Winter to Aleck. For some reason Aleck saved this letter, and it remained among the very few pieces of his memorabilia that date from the period before World War I. He followed Winter's advice in future years.

CHAPTER IX

The story of Aleck's first book is from the book itself, *Mrs. Fiske,* and from the many letters Mrs. Fiske wrote to him during their collaboration. The tales of his experiences are drawn from many sources, largely from Aleck's own later writings and particularly his broadcasts as the Town Crier.

CHAPTER X

Heywood Broun told the story of finding Aleck in his cubicle at Base Hospital No. 8. Aleck told the stories of his meanderings in the fields of Brittany and of his adventures in the *buvettes.* The account of his Christmas with the Brouns comes from his correspondence.

CHAPTER XI

Many times in the years after World War I, Aleck was to reminisce in print about his adventures as a reporter and editor of *Stars and Stripes.* Part of this study of his record comes from his writings over the years, part of it comes from James Humphreys, then a typist in the poetry section of the newspaper and later a master at Kent School in Connecticut. John T. Winterich, Harold Ross, Aleck, and Abian Wallgren were to keep in touch, more or less, in the years that followed. Since the articles in *Stars and Stripes* were generally anonymous, and nearly all of Aleck's work was unsigned, it might have been difficult to pick out his war reportage, since Ross and others had a hand in reporting from the front, too. At the end of the war, however, Aleck's dispatches were culled and from them was assembled the book *The Command is Forward,* published by the Century Company in 1919. This book was the basic source for the study of Aleck's war reporting, plus conversation with James Humphreys.

CHAPTERS XII, XIII

Aleck told the tale of "The Sacred Grove" and his encounter with Damon Runyon in Coblenz in magazines and on radio, and eventually it appeared as an essay in his collection *While Rome Burns.* The tales of Paris are almost exclusively from Aleck's own writings over the years and from broadcasts. The anecdotes regarding Edna Ferber come from the Ferber-Woollcott correspondence.

CHAPTER XIV

The tales of the Algonquin Round Table are taken from many sources: from Aleck's own writings, from the Adams biography, from correspondence with various members, from Harpo Marx in conversation and in his book *Harpo Speaks.* The tale of the manner in which Aleck came to write *Mr. Dickens Goes to the Play* comes from the author's introduction to that book.

CHAPTER XV

Most of the information about the conduct of the New York *Times* drama pages in this period is the result of study of the pages themselves, with a number of assists from Aleck. Correspondence with Edna Ferber and others in this period gives a feeling for the activity of the Woollcott group. The complete program of the Round Table's adventure into drama—*No Sirree*—was saved by Aleck in his papers. The sources for the tales of the Round Table and the Young Men's Upper West Side Thanatopsis and Inside Straight Club were Aleck's reminiscences, Harpo Marx and his book, and E. J. Kahn, Jr.'s *The World of Swope*, published by Simon and Schuster in 1965.

CHAPTER XVI

The tales of the establishment on West 47th Street were contributed by Dame Rebecca West, Harpo Marx, and Joseph P. Hennessey. Aleck's relationship with Neysa McMein was the subject of conversations between the author and several sources, including Dr. Josephine Evarts of Lakeville, Connecticut, whose sister shared an apartment with Miss McMein during this period.

CHAPTERS XVII, XVIII, XIX

The basic source for the story of the gradual envelopment of Neshobe Island by Aleck and his friends was Joseph Hennessey, who eventually took charge of the island for Aleck, and finally inherited it and lived on it for some time. Most of the sources for other tales in these chapters are noted in the text. The Swope relationship was explored by E. J. Kahn, Jr., in his biography of Swope, to some extent by Adams in the Woollcott biography, and it appears in much of Aleck's varied correspondence of this period. Harpo Marx, in book and person, is responsible for the material about his relationships with Aleck.

CHAPTER XX

Principal witness as to Aleck's way of life in the apartment on 52nd Street was Joseph Hennessey, although there were others, including drama critic Ward Morehouse, and Harpo. The breach with Swope's *World* comes from Aleck's correspondence of the period. Although he saved little else from the period, he did save one of Swope's famous memoranda.

CHAPTER XXI

The tale of Emil Stehli's suspicions of Aleck and Lilly Bonner was reported to Aleck many years later in a letter. The tale of Aleck's summer at Cap d'Antibes comes from Harpo's book and from various tidbits in Aleck's letters of the period. Stories of Aleck and his family and of her own special relationship with him come from Lucy Drage of Kansas City. Harpo told the author the tale of his birthday present, the story of the raid on the bawdy house in the New York *Times*. Aleck and Frank Lloyd Wright carried on a brisk and entertaining correspondence for many years, including much material which delineated both characters very strongly. Robert Rudd is the source for the tale of his special relationship with Aleck. The friendship with Henry Ke-an Yuan is unfolded in the correspondence of this period between Aleck and the younger man.

CHAPTER XXII

Source for much of the material about Aleck's early days in radio is the Adams biography. Christopher Rand, a graduate of Groton, told the author the story of Aleck's unhappy visit with the Reverend Endicott Peabody and his boys. The tale of Arnold Gingrich's encounter with Aleck is from a letter written to the author by Mr. Gingrich. I chose the story of the rise of *The Lives of a Bengal Lancer* to best-sellerdom, to show Aleck's power over the reading public, for here was a book without particular significance or even very polished style that he managed to turn into a public rage, almost single-handedly. The incident did not show Aleck at his best, intellectually, and that is another reason I chose it. There was nothing seriously wrong with the book, it was an adventure story about India; it was the kind of story that appealed to Aleck very much, almost as much as the sentimental tales that showed men doing good to one another.

CHAPTER XXIII

The reports of Aleck's trip to the Far East in 1931 come from his correspondence and from various articles written for such American magazines as *Cosmopolitan* and *Collier's.* The Faulkner critique, typical of Aleck at his best, appeared in *McCall's* magazine. The Swope feud story is told by Kahn in the Swope biography and by Adams in his book on Aleck, and by Aleck in various letters written at about this time.

CHAPTER XXIV

Danton Walker described his encounter with Aleck at Wit's End in a column in the New York *Mirror.* Aleck the political commentator was not to be found very often, but he did crop up from time to time in the Woollcott articles in any publication, and most frequently when Aleck appeared on radio. The clue to one side of Aleck is surely given in his letter to Laura Richards in the autumn of 1931, when he revealed to her the books that had influenced him as a child. They were books that he attempted to tout to readers of another time in the belief, perhaps mistaken, that they ought to be read by every literate person. It was this adherence to the past, yes, even in the case of Charles Dickens, which brought on Aleck much contumely from contemporaries who concerned themselves only with the living now. But Aleck was not Mr. Treacle. He had read Hemingway's *A Farewell To Arms* no less than five times by 1932, by his own statement. Aleck's pithy commentary on *Death in the Afternoon* was a minority report in its day, but his remark about Hemingway's "sedulous virility" certainly was repeated in essence by critics of a later time, some of them apparently believing they had discovered the thought. Aleck's reports on the Russians are remarkable for their open-mindedness and great good humor in a time when few Americans were willing to see anything but evil in the Soviet experiment. His considered opinion, then, about the Russian theater should have packed more weight in America than it did. Of course this was simply another manifestation of the burden of Alexander Woollcott all his life, serious people—the intellectuals—seldom took him seriously, except to lament his force as an American tastemaker. Yet few of the intellectuals concerned with universities and criticism stopped long enough to compile a list of good books on Russia for the average American, as Aleck did on his return from Russia. Aleck's review of Herbert Agar's book *The People's Choice* is notable for being Aleck at his most pungent, and also at his intellectual best: he cannot resist a scatological pun on Agar's name ("Ah, Agar, Agar, we need the sheer roughage. . . .") but he gives a book with which he completely disagrees much more of a chance than modern reviewers find time to do.

CHAPTER XXV

Robert Rudd is the source for the origin of the language that Aleck used most of his life, and with as much gusto at the end as he had during his college days. My contention that Aleck had many of the elements of greatness agrees in part, at least, with the feelings of Edmund Wilson, the critic and man of letters. Reviewing Aleck's letters in the *New Yorker* after his death, Wilson remarked that they showed a side of Aleck that he had never known, and that he liked them better than anything of Aleck's he had ever seen. Noting that such statement might not mean much, because he had not particularly been a fan of Aleck's, Wilson also said that he really did like Aleck's presentations in his letters. The comments of Bennett Cerf about his feud with Aleck come from Mr. Cerf, and indicate that unfortunately Mr. Cerf saw only the public Aleck. He was one of the few Americans willing to stand up and be counted forever after on the grounds of his own opinion.

CHAPTER XXVI

The account of Aleck's activities in 1934 comes from Jo Hennessey and from Aleck's correspondence. His struggles with his own reviewers comes from the *Nation*, December 18, 1935, wherein he was reviewed by Mr. Louis Kronenberger, and the Omaha *World Herald*, which also attacked him that winter. Aleck literally saved David Lamson's life by taking an interest in the Lamson murder case.

CHAPTER XXVII

The *Yale Review* in the spring issue of 1936 reviewed *While Rome Burns* and *The Woollcott Reader* under the title "The Art of Story Telling." The tale of Minnie and Susan was told to the author by Jo Hennessey, who did all the legwork in trying to track down those totally elusive ladies.

CHAPTER XXVIII

The story of the Great Seagram's Fracas comes from several sources: Kahn's biography of Herbert Bayard Swope, the Adams book, and Aleck's correspondence. If much space seems to be devoted to Aleck's broadcasts in this period, the direction is quite intentional. Aleck's broadcasts tended to disappear into the ether, and it is only through the kindness of Jo Hennessey, who saved many of them, and a few which were preserved in the papers given to Harvard University, that they are available outside the musty files in some far-off CBS warehouse in New Jersey, where they could scarcely be uncovered save for use in a major lawsuit. Aleck's broadcasts indicate the catholicity of his interests, and between 1934 and 1937 he became the most powerful of critics.

CHAPTERS XXIX, XXX

Aleck's attack on Lindbergh and the America First supporters came on May 25, 1941, in a broadcast from Boston which he entitled "Fight For Freedom." His final correspondence with Harold Ross is contained in the Harvard University papers. Bennett Cerf's critique of Aleck appeared in the August, 1944, issue of the *American Mercury*. Edmund Wilson's kind words and his discussion of Aleck's Fourierism appeared in the *Nation* on February 6, 1943. The anecdote about Mrs. Dewitt Wallace and the flowers was told to the author by Dewitt Wallace.

INDEX